W9-ARP-456

COMMON CORE CODE X™

STUDENT EDITION

[COURSE II]

Further credits and acknowledgments appear on pages 324–326, which constitute an extension of this copyright page.

Published by Scholastic Inc. Printed in the U.S.A.

ISBN-13: 978-0-545-62352-0

ISBN-10: 0-545-62352-9

(meets NASTA specifications)

1 2 3 4 5 6 7 8 9 10   123   22 21 20 19 18 17 16 15 14 13

Text pages printed on 20% PCW recycled paper.

[Welcome!]

Dear Reader,

Do you ever ask yourself big questions like, "What does it mean to be an American?" or "What simple steps can people take to make a difference for those in need?" These are some questions you will explore together as you read Code X.

Ancient Romans created the first codex, or bound book, almost 2,000 years ago by stacking sheets of paper on top of each other and binding them. The codex quickly replaced long scrolls of written text, forever changing the way people wrote and read.

In the same way that ancient Romans built up sheets of paper to form the codex, we have created our Code X to allow you to build on what you know. The more you learn, the deeper you can dig into the texts you read. The Common Core Code X gives you a whole new way to access texts. You'll ask questions to analyze and understand different kinds of texts from *The New Yorker*, *Science World*, and other books, magazines, poems, and plays. You will write about how authors view democracy, and about what happens when natural disasters strike.

There's a lot to learn and investigate in Code X, so it's time to get started. Let us know what you think! Email us at CodeX@scholastic.com.

Sincerely,

The Editors

The Editors

COURSE II | Table of Contents

UNIT 1

WRITING PERFORMANCE TASK

Write the story of an important event or decision; it can be real or imagined. What understanding or insight did this experience reveal?

CONTENT AREAS

TEXT 1 TEXT 2

TEXT 3

UNIT 2

WRITING PERFORMANCE TASK

"Sports performance has just as much to do with mental strength and agility as with physical prowess." Develop or refute this claim in an argumentative essay.

CONTENT AREAS

TEXT 1 TEXT 2
TEXT 3 TEXT 4

UNIT 3

WRITING PERFORMANCE TASK

Compare and contrast two writers' perspectives on democracy. Analyze the strategies they use to convey their perspectives.

CONTENT AREAS

TEXT 1 TEXT 2
TEXT 3 TEXT 4

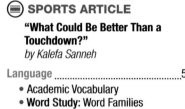

UNIT 4

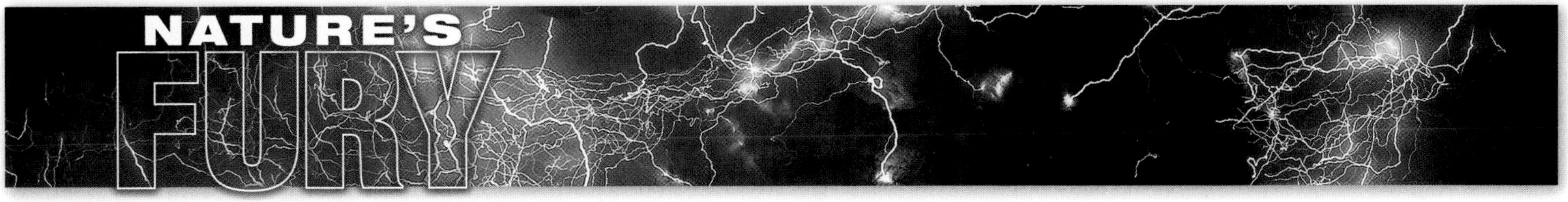
NATURE'S
FURY

UNIT 5

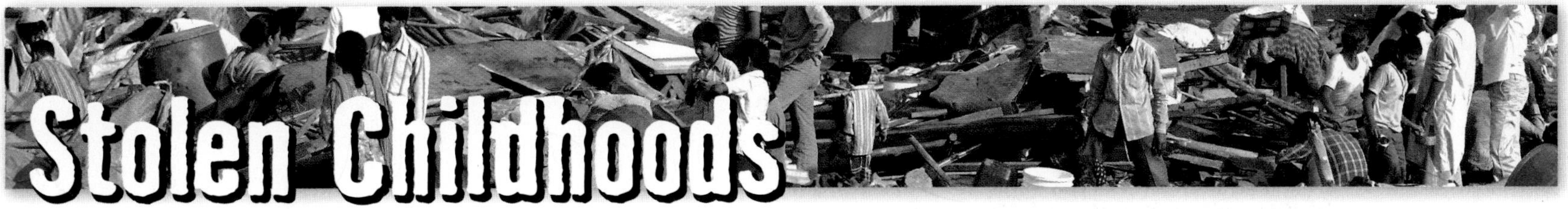
Stolen Childhoods

UNIT 6

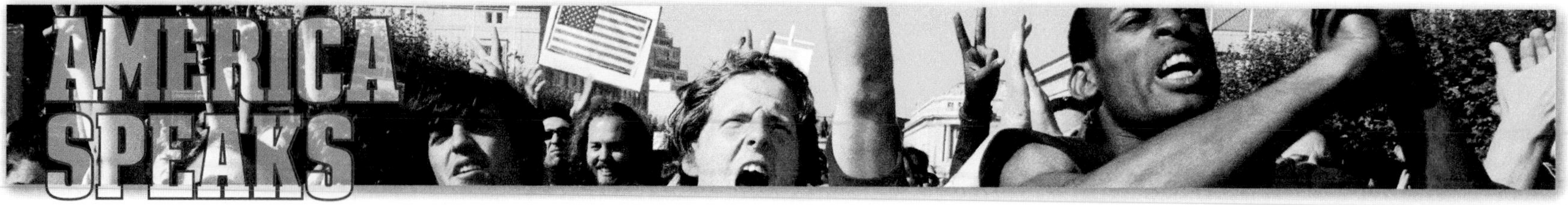

WRITING PERFORMANCE TASK

These writers claim a specific vision of what it means to be an American. Compare and contrast their perspectives, referencing their literary devices and figurative language.

CONTENT AREAS

TEXT 1 TEXT 2 TEXT 3

UNIT 7

WRITING PERFORMANCE TASK

Trace the authors' lines of arguments regarding effective ways to fight poverty. Evaluate the specific claims, distinguishing which claims are supported by reasons, facts, and evidence, and which are not.

CONTENT AREAS

TEXT 1 TEXT 2 TEXT 3

NOVEL STUDIES

Throughout the course of the year you will read two novels. You will read some sections with your teacher and peers and some sections on your own.

- ***Inkheart*** by Cornelia Funke is a fantasy novel about a fictional character who comes to life.
- In ***Monster***, Walter Dean Myers tells the story of a sixteen-year-old boy's involvement in a fatal shooting.

Inkheart
by Cornelia Funke

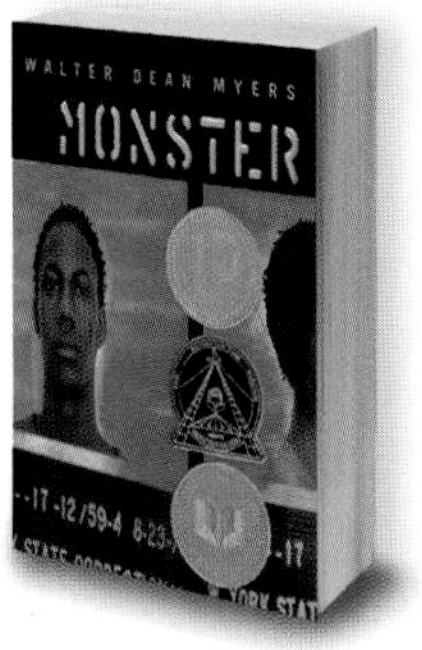

Monster
by Walter Dean Myers

CONTENT AREA ICON KEY

As you read the texts, you will learn about science, economics, history and the arts. The more you read the more you learn about the world around you.

US History

Economics

Civics and Government

Science

Math and Statistics

Technology

Individual and Society

Fine Art

Environment

World History and Geography

Earth and Weather

Literature

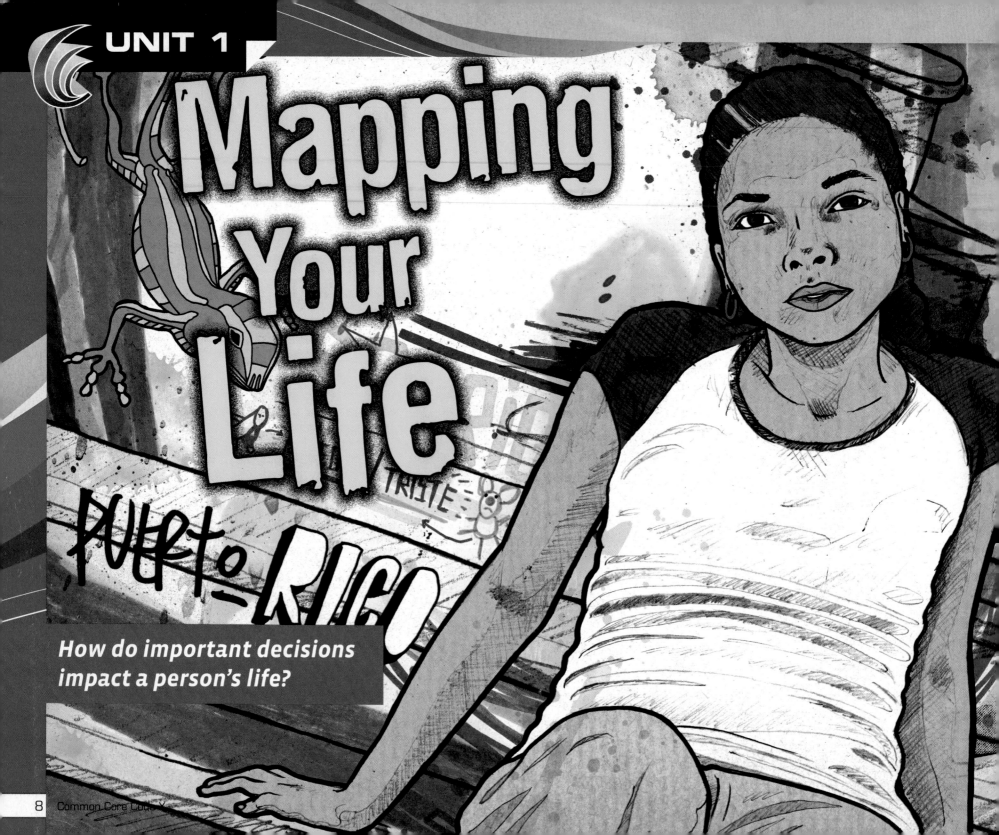

Mapping Your Life

How do important decisions impact a person's life?

Unit Introduction

In a novel excerpt and a poem, discover how important decisions are made and understand the insight that goes into making important decisions.

In the excerpt from *Call Me María,* Judith Ortiz Cofer tells the story of a girl who is coming to terms with how her life has changed and the important decision she will have to make about where she is going to live.

Robert Frost, in the poem "The Road Not Taken," writes about the narrator's choice between traveling two different roads and the impact that decision has on the narrator's life.

WRITING PERFORMANCE TASK

Write the story of an important event or decision; it can be real or imagined. What understanding or insight did this experience reveal?

NOVEL EXCERPT/POEM

from ***Call Me María***
by Judith Ortiz Cofer

Language
- Academic Vocabulary
- Word Study: Roots and Prefixes

Reading Narrative Text
- Identify Evidence
- Key Ideas and Details
- Craft and Structure

"The Road Not Taken"
by Robert Frost

Language
- Academic Vocabulary
- Word Study: Reference Materials

Reading Poetry
- Identify Evidence
- Key Ideas and Details
- Craft and Structure

SPEAKING AND LISTENING

Debate Opposing Arguments
- Collaborate and Present

Rubric: Debate
- Scoring Guide

WRITING

Writing: Narrative
- Student Model
- Analyze the Model
- Generate Ideas
- Organize Ideas
- Language Study: Narrate Events with Variety
- Conventions Study: Use Phrases and Clauses
- Revise, Edit, and Publish
- Performance Task Rubric

EXTENDED READINGS

Autobiography
from ***My Beloved World***
by Sonia Sotomayor

Academic Vocabulary

From *Call Me María* by Judith Ortiz Cofer

Rate your understanding of each word. Then read its meaning and write a sample sentence.

Word	Meaning	Example
flawless (*adj.*) p. 14 ① ② ③ ④	without any mistakes or weaknesses	The flawless diamond was worth millions of dollars.
humble (*v.*) p. 16 ① ② ③ ④	to lower in dignity or importance	
endure (*v.*) p. 16 ① ② ③ ④	to be in a difficult situation without complaining	
resolve (*v.*) p. 17 ① ② ③ ④	to find a satisfactory solution to a problem	
dramatic (*adj.*) p. 17 ① ② ③ ④	sudden and striking	
transform (*v.*) p. 20 ① ② ③ ④	to change something so it appears very different	

Rating Scale | ① I don't know the word. ② I've seen it or heard it. ③ I know its meaning. ④ I know it and use it.

Word Study

Roots and Prefixes

A **root word** is a word that comes from another language and is used to build English words.

A **prefix** is a word part at the beginning of a word that changes its meaning. You can use word parts to determine the meaning of a word.

- *form* is a Latin root that means "shape" or "appearance"
- *trans-* is a Latin prefix that means "across" or "change"

Use the root *form* and the prefix *trans-* as clues to determine the meaning of each word below. Then answer question 3.

1. *form* means _____.
2. *transform* means _____.
3. How can snow transform a regular city street?

from *Call Me María*

by Judith Ortiz Cofer

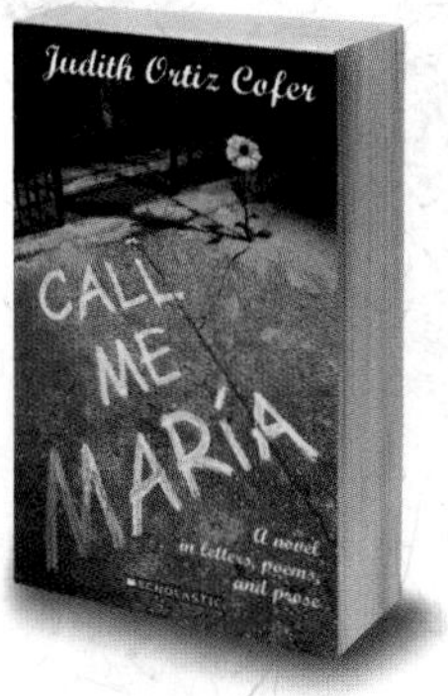

It is a warm day, and even in this barrio
the autumn sun feels like a kiss, *un besito*,
on my head. Today I feel
like an iguana seeking a warm rock
in the sun. I am sitting
on the top step of the cement stairwell
leading into our basement apartment
in a city just waking
from a deep and dark winter sleep.
The sun has warmed the concrete,
rays falling on me like a warm shower.
It is a beautiful day
even in this barrio, and today
I am almost not unhappy.
I am a different María,
no longer the María *Alegre*
who was born on a tropical island,
and who lived with two parents
in a house near the sea
until a few months ago,
nor like the María *Triste*, the lonely
barrio girl of my new American life.
I am fifteen years old.
Call me María.

Words to Know

barrio: *(n.)* a Spanish-speaking neighborhood

Close Reading

Writing

1. What point of view does the author use? Find words in the text to support your answer. What is the effect of using this point of view?

Because the author uses the pronouns ___, ___, and ___, I can tell that she is writing in the ___ person. The effect of using this point of view is ___.

Point of View

Point of view is the perspective from which a story is told.

In **first-person point of view** the narrator is part of the story *(I, me, my, we, us, ours).*
In **second-person point of view** the narrator gives information or addresses someone *(you, yours).*
In **third-person point of view** the narrator tells another person's story *(he, she, her, they, them).*

Literary Analysis

2. Find details in **lines 12–24** that describe María *Alegre* and María *Triste*. Why does the author include these descriptions? Which "María" does the narrator associate with her "new American life"?

Close Reading

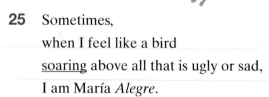

Literary Analysis

3. What is the effect of comparing Maria *Alegre* to a "bird" and a "dove" and comparing Maria *Triste* to an "underground creature" and a "mouse"? Provide examples from the text.

Writing

4. How do similes and metaphors in the poem help the reader better understand María?

The similes express ___.
The metaphors express ___.
They help the reader because ___.

Simile and Metaphor

A **simile** is a comparison of two unlike things using the words *like* or *as.*

- *The soccer player is like a tiger on the field.*

A **metaphor** compares two unlike things by stating that one *is* the other.

- *The soccer player is a tiger on the field.*

Sometimes,
when I feel like a bird
soaring above all that is ugly or sad,
I am María *Alegre*.
Other times,
when I am like a small,
underground creature,
when I feel like I will never
see the sun again,
I am María *Triste*.
My mother used to call me
her *paloma*, her dove,
when I was *alegre*,
and her *ratoncita*,
her little mouse,
on the days when I was *triste*.
Today I am neither.
You can just call me María.

My Mother, the Rain. *El Fin*

¶**1** It is April of the first year of my American life when my mother finally comes to visit us.

I sit on the top step as the hour of Mami's arrival approaches. It is a warm evening and the sidewalk is crowded with people sitting on folding chairs, mainly women and

Words to Know

soaring: *(v.)* flying like a bird

children. The noise level rises steadily as radios are brought out and people adjust the volume of their voices to compete with the music. I like to listen to the old women talking about their previous incarnations as island *puertorriqueñas*. Some of them talk only about how much better life was en *La Isla*: the people were kinder, the weather perfect, the *arroz y habichuelas, plátanos, pollo frito, café con leche, maví*—talking about the food as cooked by their mamás makes some of them stand up on the top step like poets inspired to recite verses to their native land. *¡Ay, ay, ay, bendito!* But someone always points out that beautiful scenery did not fill empty stomachs. "*¡Hay que comer, hijas!*" One has to eat. No one disagrees with this opinion.

¶**3** I listen, but do not speak. I know that even though I am in their circle, I am not really a part of the powerful barrio women's society yet. They all know that a different kind of hunger brought my father and me to this island in the city, but one more difficult to satisfy than food hunger or money hunger. My father missed the barrio of his younger days; he had to come home, and I wanted an American education. The barrio women, Pura, Isabel, Clara, Cordelia, Concepción, and their new American children, Lynette Gómez, Janice García, Joey Flores, and all the ones that would come after them, were new here like me—and the new barrio dwellers would have to take on new colors to survive. I know this from having studied island chameleons as a child, the talented little lizards always come back to their original colors when they feel safe in their environment. I can see the women in front of this building in our American city are not that different from the women in their porch rockers on the Island.

In the late afternoons and sometimes even at night, I sit on our building's front stoop to enjoy their Spanglish poetry slam and gossip sessions. As I wait for Papi's car to drive up, with my mother in the passenger seat, I dream that Mami will now join me on these old steps. Here I will teach her about my new American life, and she will decide to stay with us.

Words to Know

incarnations: *(n.)* former or future lives

chameleons: *(n.)* lizards that change color to match their environment

Close Reading

Text Structure

5. How does the structure of the text change in **paragraph 1**? What type of information does the author provide? How is the information different from the information provided in the free verse poem?

Words and Phrases in Context

6. The author compares the old women to "poets inspired to recite verses to their native land." What does this comparison tell you about how the women feel about their homeland? Find details in **paragraph 2** that explain why the women left.

Writing

7. Compare María's actions to the actions of the island women. How are they similar? How are they different? What is the "different kind of hunger" that brought María and her father to New York City?

María and the island women are all from ____, but they came to New York for different reasons. The women came because ____, and María came because ____. In the barrio, the women ____. María acts different from/similar to them when she ____.

Close Reading

Words and Phrases in Context

8. What is the meaning of *strutting* in **paragraph 5**? Find the context clues that help you determine the meaning.

Context Clues

Context clues are words in a text that help you figure out the meaning of an unfamiliar word. Sometimes words are defined in the text or their meaning is suggested.

Text Structure

9. Look at the sentence in **paragraph 5** that begins, "He is trying hard to be a gentleman . . ." What idea is set off by dashes in the middle of the sentence? How does this idea relate to the rest of the sentence?

Literary Analysis

10. Find details in the text that the author uses to describe Mami's appearance. What tone does the author create with the details she gives about Mami?

Tone

Tone is the author's attitude toward the topic. Authors express tone through word choice, imagery, and details.

¶**5** Papi pulls up in front of our building in his sleek parrot-green Thunderbird. There are wolf whistles and wild clapping from some of the women. The car has barely stopped moving when several children wearing only underwear or shorts climb on its shiny hood. Papi is wearing a new red shirt and black pants and his hair and mustache are blue-black from the *Nice 'n Easy* hair color I put in it. He is not the same man as he is in his blue workman's uniform. He is not strutting as usual, and I can tell something is wrong. He is trying hard to be a gentleman, but after he opens the passenger door for Mami—she swings her tanned legs out of the car with the grace of a dancer; her movements are a ballet—he slams it hard. He pulls away too fast, wheels squealing. Something has happened between them. But I do not want to think about problems just then, I just want to run into my mother's arms.

It has been a whole year since I have seen her! I notice that Mami's face is as perfectly made up as that of a model in a glossy magazine. Her **flawless** complexion and athletic body are the result of a lot of hard work. She always said to me: *María, you do not need to be rich to be healthy and look good; money buys you dermatologists, orthodontists, and hair stylists, but exercise is free, and a person who takes care of her looks tells the world that she respects herself.* I had put on my happy mouth today, just for her—Berry Berry Red, a new shade, and I had curled my hair. *Alegre, Alegre.* Call me María *Alegre*!

¶**7** Mami gives me a big, big smile and opens her arms for me to come to her. I feel like I am in a play. I feel the eyes of the barrio women behind me. They are watching me to see who I really am. Am I an Island woman or a barrio woman? Can I be both?

I see Mami's eyes sweep over the scene on the stoop leading to our building. I know she disapproves of this society, definitely not the kind of club that she wants

---

Words to Know

complexion: *(n.)* color and appearance of skin on the face

dermatologists: *(n.)* skin doctors

orthodontists: *(n.)* dentists who help teeth to grow straight

me to join. I know what she sees: the old women with legs spread wide to cool themselves blatantly staring at us, the sweaty children running up and "tagging" Papi's car, leaving dirty handprints on its gemstone finish, while he is trying to maneuver into a tight spot. The same things that normally make up my front-yard world, one I thought I was finally beginning to understand, now embarrass me. I imagine seeing the crude scene through Mami's eyes. Her eyes that open every morning to the turquoise sea, *un cielo azul*, to her ears that hear Spanish spoken in a completely different way than the way we use the mother tongue here.

¶**9** I run to hug her, to protect her.

I will get her past the evil tongues, *las malas lenguas*. And once we are safely inside our little basement apartment that I have scrubbed and cleaned for her visit, she will see that I have made a true *casa* for Papi and me in the middle of this foreign place, this cold city.

¶**11** There are murmurs and giggles from some of the barrio women as they watch the elegantly dressed Mami and me walk down into our apartment, our arms around each other. She is wearing an ivory suit of some soft material, perhaps silk, and big, dark, and matching soft brown leather shoulder bag and pumps. Very island Puerto Rican dressy. And very unusual attire on our block, where men walk around in their T-shirts and cut-off shorts at this time of year and women wear as little as they can. It is a matter of surviving the heat in the city.

"*Mira*, the fancy *pájara* is about to inspect her golden cage," Clara points her nose at my mother, speaking loudly enough for us to hear. Some of the children take up the chant, "*Pájara, pájara*. Pretty bird, pretty bird."

Words to Know

blatantly: *(adv.)* impolitely and obviously

attire: *(n.)* style of dress

Close Reading

Writing

11. In **paragraph 8**, the author describes how Mami sees the barrio women. In **paragraph 11**, she describes how the barrio women see Mami. How do their different perspectives affect María? Find details in the story that illustrate María's reaction to each perspective.

When Mami notices ___ about the barrio women, María feels ___.

When the women notice ___ about Mami, María feels ___.

Being aware of both perspectives creates a conflict because ___.

Words and Phrases in Context

12. In **paragraphs 9 and 10**, why does María want to protect Mami and show her that she and Papi have "a true *casa*" in the barrio?

Perspective

Perspective is a personal opinion or attitude about something.

Close Reading

Text Structure

13. The author chooses to present María's conversation with her mother without dialogue. What techniques does the author use to let the reader understand Mami's perspective, even though María is telling the story?

Literary Analysis

14. Analyze how the setting outside María's home affects her actions. How does María respond to living in the barrio with its active street life?

Literary Analysis

15. The story grows more complex as María and her mother interact. Which events in **paragraphs 16 and 17** add to the rising action of this story?

Story Elements

Rising action is a problem or series of conflicts that builds in intensity.

The climax is the most exciting or important part of a story or experience, which usually comes near the end.

Falling action is the events that lead to the solution of the problem or conflict.

¶**13** There is unabashed laughter in the circle. I am ready to defend my mother against their rudeness, though I know I would also be condemning myself to their persecution. They are enjoying *el gufeo*, goofing off, Spanglish style. The catcalls and verbal abuse inflicted on the ones who act snobbish around the gate keepers, as Whoopee calls the old women who sit, watch, and comment on everything that happens on our street, are a familiar part of daily life here. Everyone gets **humbled** by the *viejas*. They teach the game to the younger ones. But *el gufeo* is not what I wanted Mami to **endure** on her first minutes in the barrio. At the risk of my own future, I start to tell them to shut up. But Mami squeezes my hand. I look at her calm face, the cool smile that says, *Do not worry*.

They cannot touch me. She leads me slowly past them, bearing with grace their laughter and sarcastic gazes. Some of the younger women clap and whistle as if we were putting on a show for them. The old ones look at us in solemn silence. They were once Island women themselves. They know. Sometimes you are born to be one or the other. Sometimes you can cross over.

¶**15** I *know* the *viejas* respect my mother's self-control. I lead Mami by the hand down the steps and into #35½ Market Street, our apartment under the ground. We sit close together on the sofa, not saying anything for a few moments. She had asked Papi for a few hours alone with me. She looks around and then leans over to switch on a lamp. I had forgotten that she couldn't stand dim rooms.

We talk about everything for a while. I can tell that she has something on her mind. But I already know she will not stay. It is obvious that this is a visit. It is only when I offer to show her the little white painted room where *Abuela* had stayed—I had painted it yellow for Mami—she begins to cry.

¶**17** She admits that she will not be moving in with us. She has fallen in love with another man, a fellow teacher. Did I remember him? Julio? He teaches history at her

Words to Know

unabashed: *(adj.)* not ashamed or embarrassed

persecution: *(n.)* bad treatment due to differences in beliefs

catcalls: *(n.)* loud cries of disapproval

school. They are in love. She is asking Papi for a divorce. He had been furious when she told him on the way here.

"María, I thought that he would have gotten used to the idea of our separation by now. I believed we could present this to you like civilized people. *Pero tu papi no cambia.* He is the same *papi-lindo* I met in high school. He expects to be loved unconditionally by everyone—at least by all the women. It has always been this way with him."

¶**19** I just shake my head. Both my parents are wrong about each other. It is breaking my heart to hear her speak about my father this way. I decide it is better for me to be silent for now. I had learned long ago that fights between my parents could not be **resolved** by me. If I defend him, she will be hurt, and vice versa.

She asks me to return to the Island and live with her and Julio. She says this is not the place she had imagined for me.

¶**21** My head hurts. My chest hurts. I smell her familiar perfume, I listen to her voice until she says all she has come to say. Then I show her my little, cave-like bedroom. I show her how I can feel the giant boiler, the Dragon, in the winter by putting my ear to the wall.

When we come back to the living room, she is calmer. I let her sit at my desk under the street-level window where I watch legs go by when I do my homework, when I write to her. I read her some of my Instant Histories. I tell her about Uma, *Papi-lindo*, about *Doña* Segura, and about my best friend, Whoopee Dominguez, who had interested me even before she stuck her face at my window because of her combat boots and her powerful voice. Mami holds my poetry notebook in her hands a long time and then she presses it to her heart in a very **dramatic**, Puerto Rican–*telenovela* sort of way. "*Eres una poeta, María,*" she said.

Close Reading

Academic Vocabulary

16. What does *resolved* mean? Why doesn't María try to resolve her parents' conflict?

Literary Analysis

17. The author uses sensory details in **paragraphs 21 and 22** to convey María's response to Mami's request that she return to the "Island." Find details in the text that describe the senses. What effect does the author achieve by including these details?

Writing

18. The action of the story builds to a climax on this page: María makes an important decision. What is the decision? Infer from details on the page what she decides to do.

María must decide ____. After she listens to her mother, María tells Mami about ____. These details indicate that María has decided that she will ____.

Close Reading

Words and Phrases in Context

19. What does the statement that "There are many ways to be a foreigner" in **paragraph 29** mean? What are some ways that María and her parents are foreigners?

Literary Analysis

20. In the poem at the beginning of this selection, María remembers her mother calling her a *paloma* (dove) when she was *alegre* (happy), and a *ratoncita* (mouse) when she was *triste* (sad). Now, María says that a small black bird—*el pájaro triste*—wants to be set free. Why does the author present María's *triste*, or sad side, as a bird, rather than as a mouse, at this point in the story?

¶**23** "In three languages, Mami. I am a trilingual poet."

"Three languages? English, Spanish . . ."

¶**25** "And Spanglish." I read her my instant history of Whoopee.

Mami laughs at my third language. "You are good at Spanglish, María. You know it's what your father spoke when he was growing up."

¶**27** "And what he speaks again now, Mami."

Then she began to cry again. "It is like we are from two different countries, *hija*. Both Puerto Ricans, but we have never spoken the same language."

¶**29** I know what that feels like. There are many ways to be a foreigner. I spend the evening comforting my mother.

Mami will not stay. The man she loves now, Julio the historian, who takes her to museums, was due to pick her up here, in front of our building. They are going to spend a day or two in New York, going to museums of course, and then they will return to the Island. Listening to her plans makes me feel as if a small black bird called *el párajo triste* has just awakened inside my chest. It wants to be set free, to come out through my eyes as tears, through my mouth as angry words, black feathers that would shock and frighten my soft-spoken, well-dressed island mother. But I keep *la tristeza* inside me.

¶**31** I let her talk. She keeps looking at her watch. She asks me again if I am *completamente segura*, certain without any doubt that I want to stay in *this* place. I just nod. How can I explain to her that what she called *this place* with so much disdain is now *mi isla, mi casa*. Also, I have responsibilities: I have to make sure the tenants of our building get their leaks fixed, their apartments painted, their favorite

Words to Know

trilingual: *(adj.)* able to understand and speak in three languages

foreigner: *(n.)* a person from a different country

tenants: *(n.)* people who rent homes

songs sung by Papi. *El Súper* needs his assistant. Maybe, *quizás*, I say when she asks me if I will meet her and Julio at the Museo del Barrio. I do not tell her that I am not ready for outings with her and her future husband yet. *Sí, claro,* I will call her *mañana*.

I say good-bye to Mami in the street, *adiós, Mami, adiós.* The front stoop is now populated by the quieter night people. The old gate keepers who had worn themselves out during the day are now fanning themselves quietly, watching over the tired-to-the-bone single mothers holding sleepy babies on their laps.

¶**33** She says in her most tender Mami-voice, her *azúcar*-coated voice, "Write, María. Mi María *Alegre*, call if you need me."

Close Reading

Writing

21. Analyze how María's building and New York have become *"mi isla, mi casa"* ("my island, my home"). Explain how setting details help the reader understand María's decision.

María's statements that ___ and ___ illustrate that ___.

Literary Analysis

22. How does the tone shift in **paragraph 31**?

Words and Phrases in Context

23. What is the meaning of *disdain* in **paragraph 31**? Find the context clues that helped you determine its meaning.

Words and Phrases in Context

24. María says, "Maybe, *quizás*," when her mother asks if María will spend time with her and Julio. Why do you think María responds this way? Which details in the text help you determine her reasons?

Close Reading

Literary Analysis

25. The events on this page are part of the falling action of the story. Describe the events in your own words.

Writing

26. What is the significance of the phrase "her eyes were looking past me, looking for her future" in **paragraph 34**? How does this sentence indicate what María's relationship with her mother will be like in the future?

The author uses this expression figuratively to express the idea that ____.

Academic Vocabulary

27. Earlier in the story, the street was crowded, hot, and dry. Use context clues to define what *transformed* means in **paragraph 35**. What else has been transformed in this story?

Words and Phrases in Context

28. Why does the author end **paragraph 35** with the words "We are home"? What does this sentence reveal?

I say, "Yes, yes. Sí, Mami," in my little María voice. Neither *triste* nor *alegre*. Call me María. Just María. I kiss her cheek and she holds me close for a moment. But I knew her eyes were looking past me, looking for her future to drive up. Julio. *El amor.* Spanish is so beautiful. A perfect language for love. *El amor.* A few raindrops fall on us.

¶**35** A black car pulls up. Mami waves to me as she hurries to a big Eldorado, a rental, already bearing the evidence of dirty little hands all over it. It is starting to sprinkle. The old women are folding their <u>aluminum</u> chairs and hurrying inside. I hear windows being raised, voices calling out "*¡Que lluvia!*" It is not a complaint. The smell of rain is a promise of a cooler night for my neighbors and for me. The rain, la lluvia, is a blessing on the long hot nights of this barrio. Tonight, I will wait until the street is wet, shiny, and **transformed** before going in to begin writing the letter to my mother, the one I want her to find waiting for her when she returns to the Island. I will tell her I am glad that she is happy. I will tell her not to worry about Papi and me. We are home.

Words to Know

<u>aluminum</u>: *(n.)* a lightweight metal

¶36 Spanish Words and Phrases

el Fín – The End

un besito – a kiss

alegre – happy

triste – sad

paloma – dove

ratoncita – a little mouse

puertorriqueñas – Puerto Rican women

La Isla – The Island

arroz y habichuelas – rice and beans

plátanos – bananas

pollo frito – fried chicken

café con leche – coffee with milk

maví – a Puerto Rican beverage

¡Ay, ay, ay bendito! – Oh my goodness!

¡Hay que comer, hijas! – We need to eat, daughters!

un cielo azul – a blue sky

las malas lenguas – the evil tongues

casa – house

mira – look

pájara – bird

el gufeo – goof

viejas – elderly women

Abuela – Grandmother

Pero tu papi no cambia. – But your Daddy doesn't change.

papi-lindo – pretty boy

Doña – Mrs.

telenovela – soap opera

eres una poeta – you are a poet

hija – daughter

el pájaro triste – the sad bird

la tristeza – the sadness

completamente segura – completely sure

mi isla, mi casa – my island, my home

El Súper – The Superintendent

quizás – perhaps

sí, claro – yes, of course

mañana – tomorrow

adiós – good-bye

azúcar – sugar

el amor – love

¡Que lluvia! – What rain!

Close Reading

Text Structure

29. What effect on the story does the inclusion of Spanish words and phrases have? How does the use of Spanish help the reader understand how María combines her past and her present? Provide examples from the story to explain.

Words and Phrases in Context

30. Find the Spanish words and phrases that describe food. Then locate those words and phrases in the text on **page 13**. Why does the author include those details in Spanish?

Identify Evidence | Analyze Individuals, Events, and Ideas

Reread the excerpt from ***Call Me María,*** highlighting details that show how the setting of the story affects the narrator's feelings and actions. How does the author introduce, illustrate, and elaborate on individuals, events, and ideas that show how setting affects character?

- As you read, use the Setting Evidence column to record examples from the text that show how setting affects character.
- In the Explanation column, explain how the evidence introduces, illustrates, or elaborates individuals, events, and ideas. Also, note any techniques the author uses in the example, such as simile, metaphor, descriptive language, and sensory details.

Setting Evidence	Page	Characters	Explanation
1. "It is a beautiful day even in this barrio, and today I am almost not unhappy."	11	María, the narrator	Because of the weather, María feels fairly well, even though she lives in the barrio instead of the island where she grew up. (descriptive language)
2. "The noise level rises steadily as radios are brought out and people adjust the volume of their voices to compete with the music."	13		
3. "Papi pulls up in front of our building in his sleek parrot-green Thunderbird. There are wolf whistles and wild clapping from some of the women. The car has barely stopped moving when several children wearing only underwear or shorts climb on its shiny hood."	14		
4. "I imagine seeing the crude scene through Mami's eyes. Her eyes that open every morning to the turquoise sea, *un cielo azul*, to her ears that hear Spanish spoken in a completely different way than the way we use the mother tongue here."	15		

Setting Evidence	Page	Characters	Explanation
5.			
6.			
7.			

Key Ideas and Details

Determining the Central Idea

1. Summarize the key idea of the excerpt from Ortiz Cofer's *Call Me María*. What is the central idea of the text? Use evidence.

2. List three key setting details that Ortiz Cofer introduces in this excerpt. Explain why each detail is important to the central idea.

Setting Detail	Significance

3. List two literary forms that are included in this excerpt. Explain how the author uses each one to develop the central idea of the story.

Form	Significance

Craft and Structure

Structure of the Story Excerpt

1. How does including the literary form of poetry at the beginning of the excerpt from *Call Me María* add meaning to this text?

2. How does including the literary form of the narrative text in most of the excerpt of *Call Me María* add meaning to this text?

Narrator's Perspective and Purpose

3. Describe the different perspectives in **paragraph 15**.

4. What are the advantages and disadvantages of first-person point of view?

5. Why might the author have chosen the first-person point of view? Use examples from the text to support your opinion.

Free Verse Poem

A **poem** is a form of creative writing that uses sounds, rhythms, and the emotional power of language to express ideas. A **free verse poem** does not rhyme.

Poems often use **imagery**—descriptive words and phrases that create pictures in the reader's mind—to express thoughts and ideas.

Narrative Text

Narrative text describes experiences and events from the point of view of a narrator. Narrative text is often written in the first-person point of view.

Narrative Perspective

Narrative perspective is the voice a narrator uses to describe what he or she sees or feels. Authors use descriptions and anecdotes to communicate perspective.

Academic Vocabulary

"The Road Not Taken" by Robert Frost

Rate your understanding of each word. Then read its meaning and write a sample sentence.

Word	Meaning	Example
diverge *(v.)* p. 27 ① ② ③ ④	to separate and go in different directions	The runners will diverge when they reach the lake, each taking a different path.
wear *(n.)* p. 27 ① ② ③ ④	use of something that damages it or makes it less perfect	
tread *(v.)* p. 28 ① ② ③ ④	to step on while you are walking	
hence *(adv.)* p. 28 ① ② ③ ④	in the future; after a period of time	

Rating Scale | ① I don't know the word. ② I've seen it or heard it. ③ I know its meaning. ④ I know it and use it.

Word Study

Thesaurus

A thesaurus is a book that contains lists of synonyms. Some thesauruses also include antonyms.

Read the thesaurus entry for *look*. Then read the sentence below and answer the questions.

look
(v.) examine visually
(syn.) admire, behold, consider, contemplate, eye, gape, gawk, gaze, glance, glower, inspect, notice, observe, peer, regard, scan, see, stare, study, view, watch

I look down the road.

1. How does the meaning of the sentence change if you use the verb *glance*?

2. How does the meaning of the sentence change if you use the verb *stare*?

The Road Not Taken

by Robert Frost

Two roads **diverged** in a yellow wood,
And sorry I could not travel both
And be one traveler, long I stood
And looked down one as far as I could
To where it bent in the undergrowth;

Then took the other, as just as fair,
And having perhaps the better claim,
Because it was grassy and wanted **wear**;
Though as for that the passing there
Had worn them really about the same,

Words to Know

fair: *(adj.)* pleasing, beautiful

Close Reading

Text Structure

1. Which words rhyme in the poem? What is the effect of using rhyme?

Rhyme

Rhyme is the use of words that end with the same sounds.
Example: *He put his hand in the sand.*

Reading a poem aloud makes it easier to identify rhymes.

Writing

2. What decision does the narrator need to make? How can you tell this decision is difficult for the narrator? Find the phrase in the second stanza that lets you know the narrator has made a decision and acted upon it.

The narrator must decide ____.
You can tell the decision is difficult because ____.
The phrase ____ indicates that the narrator made a choice.

Words and Phrases in Context

3. According to the narrator, why does the road taken have "perhaps the better claim"? How is it the same or different from the other road?

Close Reading

Academic Vocabulary

4. What does *trodden* mean? What might be the color of the leaves that had not been "trodden black"? Support your response with text evidence, and use the word *trodden* in your response.

Words and Phrases in Context

5. Reread **lines 14 and 15**. Why does the narrator "doubt if I should ever come back"?

Academic Vocabulary

6. The author imagines telling the story of his decision "ages and ages hence." What does this tell you about the importance of the decision?

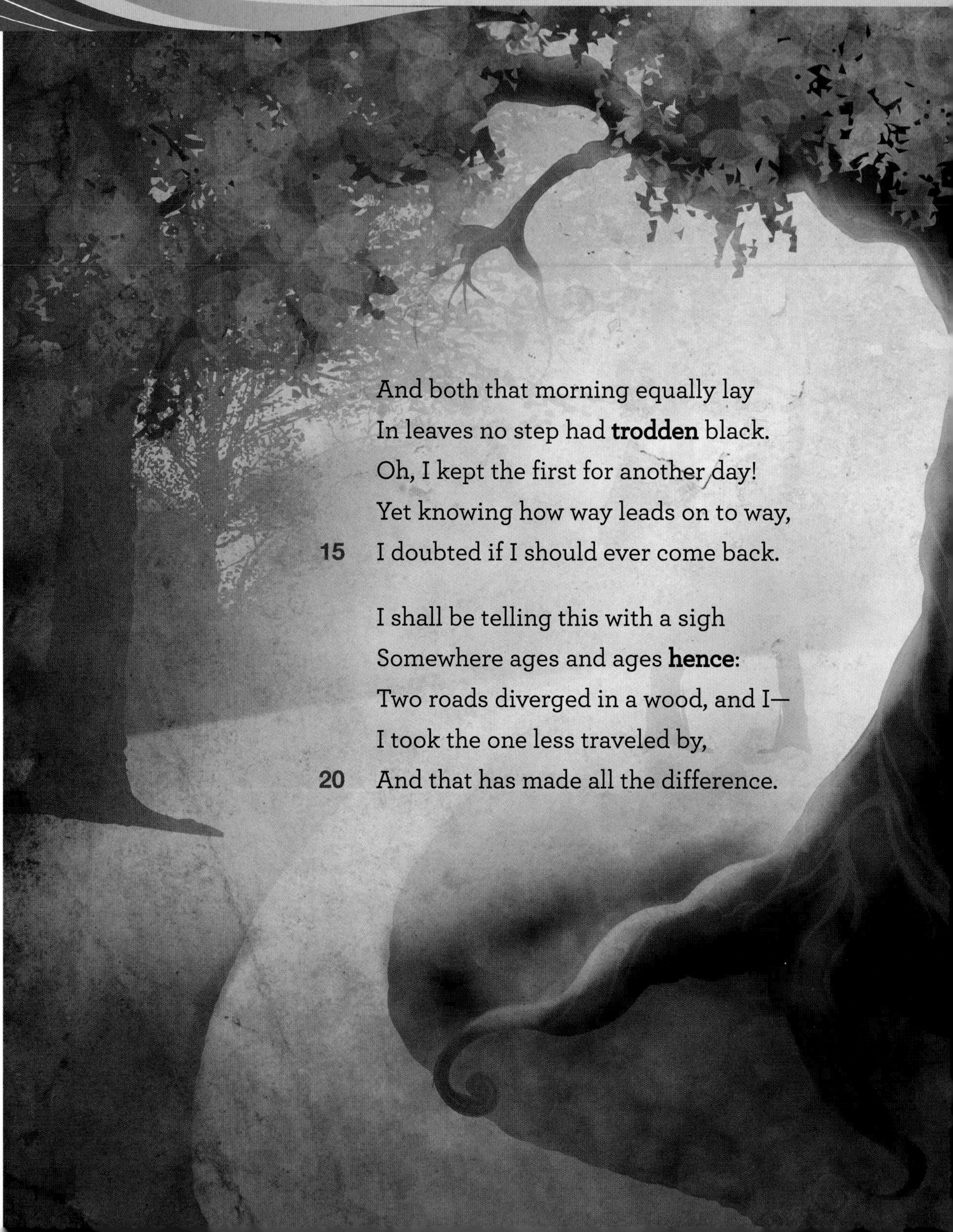

And both that morning equally lay
In leaves no step had **trodden** black.
Oh, I kept the first for another day!
Yet knowing how way leads on to way,
I doubted if I should ever come back.

I shall be telling this with a sigh
Somewhere ages and ages **hence**:
Two roads diverged in a wood, and I—
I took the one less traveled by,
And that has made all the difference.

Close Reading

Words and Phrases in Context

7. Why does the narrator state that taking the road less traveled "has made all the difference"?

Writing

8. Why does the poet name this poem "The Road Not Taken" rather than "The Road Less Traveled" or just "Two Roads"? What idea does the poet convey by focusing on "the road not taken"?

By using this title the author emphasizes ____.

Literary Analysis

9. This poem can be read literally (as a narrative), or it can be interpreted figuratively (as a metaphor for all of life's decisions). What is the main message that applies to both interpretations?

Identify Evidence | Analyze Individuals, Events, and Ideas

Reread **"The Road Not Taken,"** highlighting details that show how the decision of the two wooded paths affect the narrator's thoughts and actions. How does the author introduce, illustrate, and elaborate individuals, events, and ideas?

- As you read, use the Evidence column to record examples from the text that show how the decision the narrator faces affects him or her.
- In the Explanation column, explain how the evidence introduces, illustrates, or elaborates on individuals, events and ideas.

Evidence	Page	Explanation
1. "Sorry I could not travel both . . ."	27	The narrator's main conflict is that he or she would like to travel down both roads but cannot.
2. "long I stood . . ."		
3. "looked down one as far as I could . . ."		
4. "Though as for that the passing there / Had worn them both about the same,"		

Evidence	Page	Explanation
5.		
6.		
7.		

Key Ideas and Details

Determining the Central Idea

1. Summarize the key idea of Frost's "The Road Not Taken." What is the central idea of the poem? Use evidence.

2. List three key setting details that Frost introduces in the poem. Explain why each detail is important to the central idea.

Setting Detail	Significance

3. List two aspects of the poetic structure of "The Road Not Taken" and what each one adds to the central idea of the story.

Element of Poetic Structure	Significance

Craft and Structure

Structure of the Poem

1. How does the structure of the stanzas in this poem help tell the story?

2. How do the rhyming lines and rhythm affect the way the poem is told?

3. Compare and contrast the structure of the excerpt from *Call Me María* and the structure of "The Road Not Taken."

Author's Purpose

4. What purpose did Frost have in writing the poem "The Road Not Taken"?

5. What purpose did Ortiz Cofer have in writing the selection from *Call Me María*?

Poetic Structure

A **stanza** is a group of lines that relates to one idea. Many poems are organized in stanzas.

In some poems, lines in each stanza rhyme. A poem's **rhyme scheme** is the pattern of rhyming lines in each stanza.

Author's Purpose

Author's purpose is the reason an author writes a story or poem. Authors write to inform, to entertain, or to persuade.

Collaborate and Present

Present a Claim and Debate

Assignment: The narrator in the poem "The Road Not Taken" must choose between two paths. Work in groups to debate which path was the right choice, the road taken or the road not taken. Present your claim using reasons, and support your reasons with evidence from the poem.

Analyze the Content

1. Consider the following questions:
   - Which setting details indicate that the road taken/not taken is better?
   - How does the narrator choose? Which details support the idea that the narrator thinks the road taken/not taken was the right choice?
2. Choose one example of a detail in the poem that indicates which road is the right road. Explain why you think this example is particularly effective.

Example	Effect

Present Your Argument

3. Use the talking points above to write your statement and present it to your group. Other group members should also present their arguments.

Acknowledge and Respond to New Ideas

4. Evaluate another speaker's argument and claims. Are the ideas sound? Is the evidence relevant and sufficient? Write a brief response critiquing the argument.

Report

5. Report to the class about your group debate.

Seeking Clarification

- So your argument is . . .
- In other words, you claim . . .
- If I understand you correctly, you are arguing . . .

Evaluating Arguments

- _____ claimed that
- _____ gave evidence that
- _____'s claim was/was not valid because

Presentation

- Be still and have good posture.
- Speak loudly and clearly.
- Listen carefully to opposing claims and respond to them.

Debate Checklist

Use the checklist below to evaluate your collaboration skills, reasoning, and final presentation. Think carefully about your work. If you know you completed an item thoroughly, give yourself a check (✓).

COLLABORATE AND PRESENT CHECKLIST		
Comprehension & Collaboration	**Evidence & Reasoning**	**Presentation of Knowledge & Ideas**
☐ Come to discussions prepared, having read and studied material. ☐ Refer to evidence to reflect on and contribute to the discussion. ☐ Follow rules for discussions and lead others by example. ☐ Pose/respond to specific questions. ☐ Make comments that contribute to the topic under discussion and bring discussion back on topic as needed. ☐ Delineate others' arguments and claims, and evaluate reasoning and evidence. ☐ Present claims, emphasize key points with relevant details, in a focused way.	☐ Present the purpose of the debate and the question to be debated. ☐ Clearly present my claim. ☐ Present reasons and exact words and phrases from the poem to support my claim. ☐ Listen to others' claims and accurately describe them. ☐ Evaluate others' claims using relevant details from the poem.	☐ Adapt language to a variety of contexts and tasks to demonstrate knowledge of formal English. ☐ Include multimedia components (e.g., graphics, images, music, sound) and visual displays. ☐ Use appropriate volume/tone (clear, not too fast, too slow, or too loud) and avoid using "like" or "ummm." ☐ Have strong posture, a confident stance, and make frequent eye contact. ☐ Occasionally move from one spot to another without fidgeting. ☐ Smile and appear to be relaxed.
Number of ✓s in this category: ___	**Number of ✓s in this category: ___**	**Number of ✓s in this category: ___**
Total # of ✓s: ___		

Add up the total number of checks (✓) in each category. Then use the scoring guide below to calculate your final score.

Scoring Guide			
16 to 18 ✓s	**13 to 15 ✓s**	**11 to 12 ✓s**	**10 or less ✓s**
④ Exemplary	**③ Meets Standards**	**② Needs Work**	**① Does Not Meet Standards**

Read the Model

Writers of narratives use many techniques to craft stories about real or imagined experiences or events. The writer of this narrative uses the first-person point of view and a sequence of events to tell about an important realization that the narrator made. Read and discuss the model narrative below.

Narrative

A **narrative** describes experiences and uses a series of events in time as its text structure.

The introduction engages the reader by establishing the setting and introducing the narrator and/or characters.

- Find the clues that describe the narrator's point of view.

The body uses description, figurative language, and transition words and phrases to develop characters and events.

- Find the clues that describe the challenge the narrator faces.
- Find the transition words.

The conclusion follows from narrated events and contains the resolution.

- Describe the resolution and what the narrator learned.

Learning to Learn

Based on an excerpt from *My Beloved World* by Sonia Sotomayor

I was smart. I worked hard and loved to read. I was not afraid to try new things. While growing up in the Bronx, I also kept in mind what our mother taught us: Education is the key to success in life. It's the way to get ahead. Mother did everything she could to make sure that we had a good education.

In the fifth grade, I learned another important lesson. Mrs. Reilly, our teacher, would give us a gold star each time we did something really well. I was very competitive, and those stars were like irresistible cookies. I wanted as many as I could get. Once I started making As, I wanted more. I vowed to have at least one more A on every report card than I had on the last one. I had to figure out how to do that.

I noticed that some students always got good grades, so one day I approached one of the smartest girls in class. I asked her how to study. She was very happy to help me. She explained that while she was reading, she underlined important facts and took notes. Before a test, she reread the relevant chapters.

After getting all this information, I tried her technique. It worked like a charm, and soon I was making excellent grades. I even got to move to a seat near the window where all the really good students sat.

You'd think anyone would know those techniques, but we weren't taught study skills, and it would have taken a long time for me to learn them on my own. This experience taught me to use any willing person as a teacher. It taught me to seek out mentors, to ask for guidance, and to learn whatever a friend could teach me.

Analyze the Model

A narrative includes a narrator or characters, setting, plot events, a problem or conflict that a character faces, a climax, and the resolution to the problem.

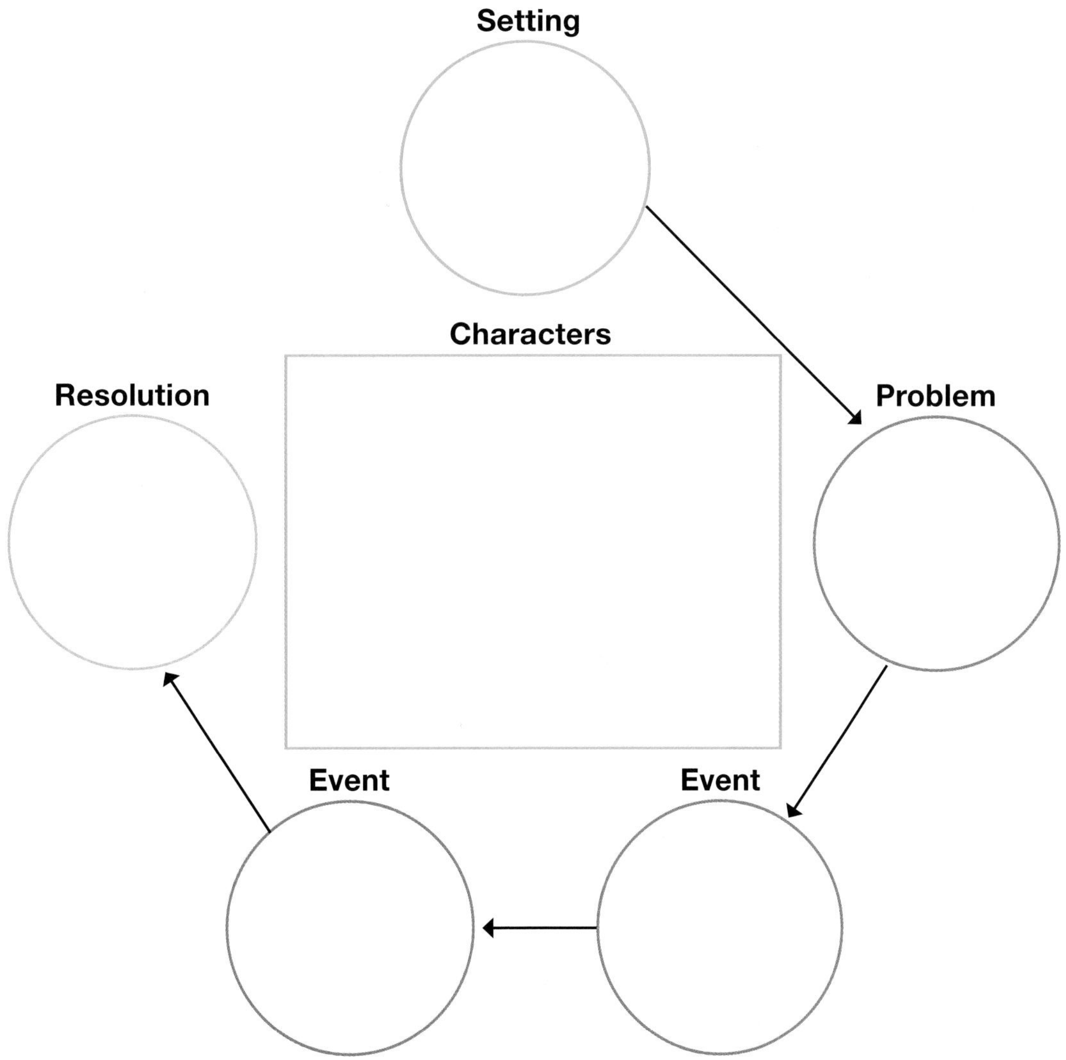

Character Development

Writers describe characters by showing what they think, say, and do, and by showing how characters react to people, places, and settings over the course of the story.

Writers also use the following techniques to help readers picture characters:

- descriptive details
- simile and metaphor
- sensory language

Step 1 | Generate Ideas

[Write the story of an important event or decision; it can be real or imagined. What understanding or insight did this experience reveal?]

What You Need to Know | Examine the evidence you have collected from *Call Me María* about an important decision and the events that led to it. (see pages 22–23)

What You Need to Write | Select techniques used in the text to incorporate into your narrative.

Call Me María

Character and Setting
Text Example:

Effect: Page # _____

Problem or Decision
Text Example:

Effect: Page # _____

Resolution
Example:

Effect: Page # _____

Point of View/Narrative Techniques
Example:

Effect: Page # _____

My Narrative

My Character and Setting
Ideas:

-
-
-

My Problem or Decision
Ideas:

-
-
-

My Resolution
Ideas:

-
-
-

My Point of View/Narrative Techniques
Ideas:

-
-
-

Step 2 | Organize Ideas

What You Need to Know | Big ideas about the important decision or event.

To develop your story:

1. Describe the character and setting of your narrative.
2. Establish the decision/event and the setting in which it will happen.

What You Need to Write | Develop a sequence of events that lead to the resolution of the narrative.

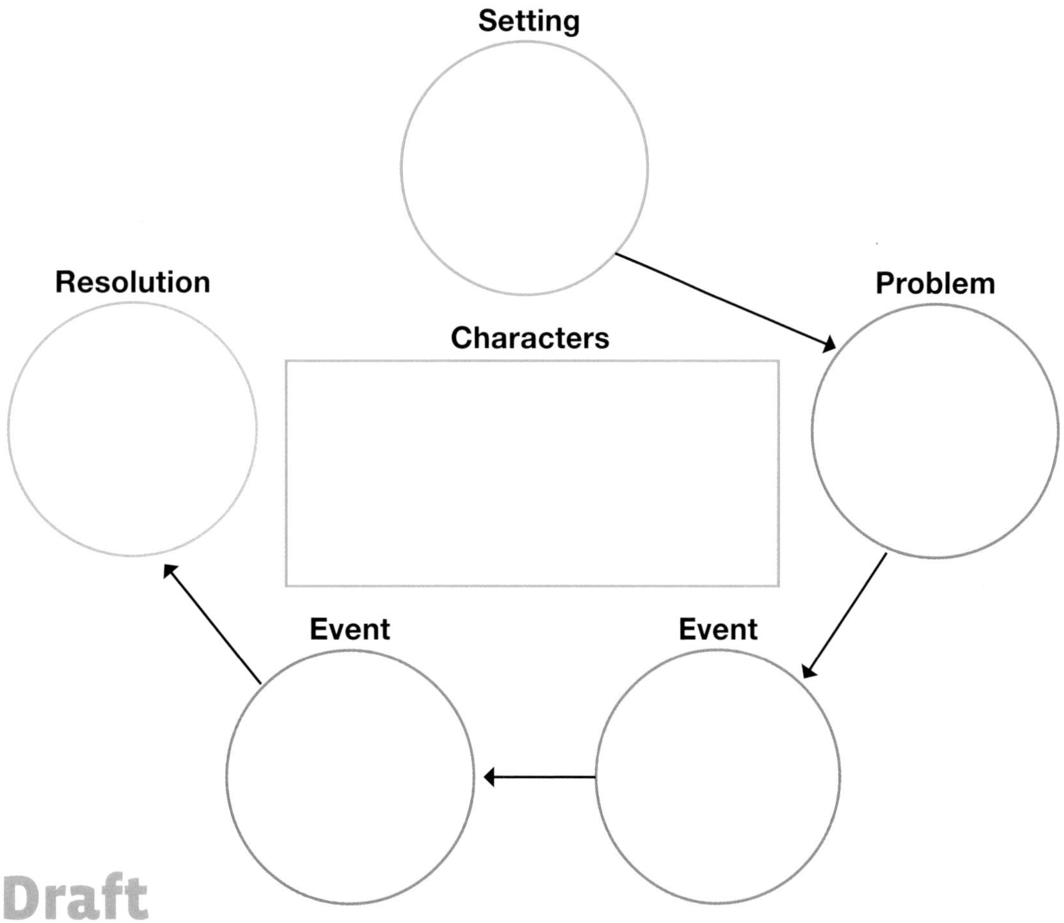

Step 3 | Draft

Write a draft of your story on the computer or on paper.

Language Study | Narrate Events with Variety

See It | **Effective writers use descriptive words and phrases to help readers understand the sequence of events in a story.**

Try It | **Read the paragraph. Find the words that help you understand the sequence of events.**

First, I heard the roar of an engine. Then, I looked out the window and saw that Grandmother had arrived. I wasn't looking forward to this visit because the last time we were together we argued. Why did we argue? Before, she kept telling me to turn down the music I was listening to. Then I had an idea. Maybe I should ask Grandmother to tell me about the type of music she listened to when she was my age. Then I think she might be more willing to listen to the music I like. Then we'll both be happier because we will have shared what we like with each other.

Use the phrases in the box below to revise the paragraph, adding more variety. Use each phrase only once.

a moment later	after a while	the last time
just after dark	a minute later	in that way

_____, I heard the roar of an engine. _____, I looked out the window and saw that Grandmother had arrived. I wasn't looking forward to this visit because the last time we were together we argued. Why did we argue? _____, she kept telling me to turn down the music I was listening to. _____, I had an idea. Maybe I should ask Grandmother to tell me about the type of music she listened to when she was my age. _____ I think she might be more willing to listen to the music I like. _____, we'll both be happier because we will have shared what we like with each other.

Apply It | Use a variety of sentence patterns to describe events, people, and insights in your narrative.

Beginning of the Story

1. When ____________ (character's name or pronoun) was ____________ (age), ____________ (detail about character).

2. A few years ago, ____________ (introduce character and action).

3. On a brisk morning when ____________ (character's name or pronoun) ____________ (action).

Middle of the Story

4. ____________ (character's name), after several days/months/years, ____________ (explain what happened).

5. One of the first things ____________ (character's name and action).

6. Later that day/month/year, ____________ (character's name and action).

7. Then, all of a sudden, ____________ (character's name and action).

End of the Story

8. As a result, ____________ (character's name) ____________ (explain what character learned/insight).

9. It's interesting ____________ (what character learned/insight).

10. From now on, ____________ (what character learned/insight).

Conventions Study | Using Phrases and Clauses

See It

Phrases and **clauses** are groups of words that show relationships in sentences. A **phrase** does not contain a verb and cannot stand on its own as a sentence. Example: *After the movie, we ate pizza.*

A **clause** contains a verb. An **independent clause** can stand on its own as a sentence. Example: *I was tired, so I went to sleep.* A **dependent clause** cannot stand on its own. Example: *Although I was tired, I stayed up and read my favorite book.*

Try It

Find the phrases and clauses the writer used in the sentence below, taken from the model. How did she summarize the problem and what changed? Then explain the effect this turning point had on her life.

> I noticed that some students always got good grades, so one day I approached one of the smartest girls in class. I asked her how to study. She was very happy to help me. She explained that while she was reading, she underlined important facts and took notes. Before a test, she reread the relevant chapters.

Apply It

Now revise the middle of your story. Use phrases and clauses to identify a cause-and-effect relationship and to signal time.

Step 4 | Revise and Edit

Revise your draft with a partner.

Organization and Clarity		
Establish the narrator and setting at the beginning of the story.	Self	1 2 3 4
	Partner	1 2 3 4
Establish the decision that must be made in the middle of the story.	Self	1 2 3 4
	Partner	1 2 3 4
Organize events in a clear and logical order, and include phrases and clauses that connect events.	Self	1 2 3 4
	Partner	1 2 3 4
Explain how the conflict or decision is resolved, and what the narrator learns, at the end of the narrative.	Self	1 2 3 4
	Partner	1 2 3 4
Evidence and Reasoning		
Establish and maintain a consistent point of view.	Self	1 2 3 4
	Partner	1 2 3 4
Develop the conflict and resolution by describing the thoughts and actions of key characters.	Self	1 2 3 4
	Partner	1 2 3 4
Develop characters and plot with narrative techniques such as simile, metaphor, and sensory details.	Self	1 2 3 4
	Partner	1 2 3 4
Language and Conventions		
Use transition words and clauses and phrases to connect events in the narrative and show the passage of time.	Self	1 2 3 4
	Partner	1 2 3 4
Vary sentences throughout the narrative.	Self	1 2 3 4
	Partner	1 2 3 4
Correctly spell all words and use punctuation and capitalization correctly.	Self	1 2 3 4
	Partner	1 2 3 4

Scoring Guide | ① needs improvement ② average ③ good ④ excellent

Step 5 | Publish

Publish your story either in print or digital form.

Publish

Publish your story either in print or digital form. Use the rubric below to assess your final performance task.

PERFORMANCE TASK RUBRIC			
Score Point	Organization and Clarity	Evidence and Reasoning	Language and Conventions
Exemplary ④	• beginning of story **effectively and creatively** introduces the main character(s) and describes the setting • middle of the story **clearly** develops the conflict • includes **well-chosen** phrases and clauses that connect events in the story • ending of story **expertly explains** how the conflict is resolved and **thoughtfully explains** what the character(s) learn(s)	• **clearly establishes** a point of view and maintains that point of view throughout the story • develops the conflict and its resolution by **carefully describing** the actions of key characters • **meaningfully** uses narrative strategies such as dialogue, figurative language, and foreshadowing to develop the plot • **convincingly describes** what the character(s) learn(s)	• **demonstrates a strong command** of the conventions of standard English grammar and usage, as well as of standard English capitalization, punctuation, and spelling • vocabulary is appropriate to the plot (a variety of words and phrases are used to narrate story events; some figurative language; vocabulary that describes the insight the character[s] gain[s])
Meets Standards ③	• beginning of story **effectively** introduces the main character(s) and setting • middle of story **develops** the conflict or problem in the story • includes phrases and clauses that connect story events • ending **clearly resolves** the conflict and **explains** what the character(s) learn(s)	• **adequately establishes** and maintains a point of view • develops the conflict and its resolution by **describing** the actions of key characters • **adequately uses narrative strategies** such as dialogue, figurative language, and foreshadowing to develop the plot • **describes** what the character(s) learn(s)	• **demonstrates a near command** of the conventions of standard English grammar and usage, as well as of standard English capitalization, punctuation, and spelling **with some errors** • vocabulary is **appropriate** to the development of the plot (a variety of words and phrases to narrate story events; some figurative language; vocabulary that describes the insight the character[s] gain[s])

PERFORMANCE TASK RUBRIC			
Score Point	**Organization and Clarity**	**Evidence and Reasoning**	**Language and Conventions**
Needs Work ②	• beginning of story **introduces** the main character(s) and setting • middle of story **somewhat develops** the conflict or problem in the story • includes **limited** phrases and clauses that connect story events • ending **attempts to resolve** the conflict and **explain** what the character(s) learn(s)	• fails to establish a consistent point of view • develops the conflict and its resolution by **describing** the actions of key characters • **uses some narrative strategies** such as dialogue, figurative language, and foreshadowing to develop the plot • **states but does not fully develop** what the character(s) learn(s)	• demonstrates a **marginal command** of the conventions of English grammar and usage, as well as of standard English capitalization, punctuation, and spelling • there are **many errors; however, the text is still understandable** • includes only **one or two examples of** vocabulary that is appropriate to the plot (a variety of words and phrases to narrate story events; some figurative language; vocabulary that describes the insight the character[s] gain[s])
Does Not Meet Standards ①	• beginning of story **does not establish** the main characters and setting • middle of story is **disorganized and/or does not establish** the conflict • includes **limited phrases** and clauses that connect story events • ending is **unclear and/or does not explain** how the conflict is resolved or what the character learns	• **partial story development** without a clear presentation of the conflict, its resolution, or what the character(s) learn(s)	• demonstrates **almost no command** of the conventions of standard English grammar and usage, as well as of standard English capitalization, punctuation, and spelling • there are **many errors that disrupt** the reader's understanding of the text • **does not include** vocabulary that is appropriate to the plot (a variety of words and phrases to narrate story events; some figurative language; vocabulary that describes the insight the character[s] gain[s])

Questions

Key Ideas and Details

1. Why does Sotomayor draw a contrast between the encyclopedia salesman and the other men who had previously rung her doorbell?

Words and Phrases in Context

2. What does Sotomayor mean when she writes that she and her brother, surrounded by the new encyclopedias, were like "explorers at the base of Everest"?

from *My Beloved World*

by Sonia Sotomayor

¶1 One day the doorbell rang, and my mother opened the door to a man carrying two big briefcases. It wasn't the man who made the rounds of the projects selling insurance. It wasn't the old man who came to collect two dollars every Saturday for the drapes he'd sold us months before. My mother sat down with the salesman at the kitchen table, and they talked for a very long time, looking at books, adding up numbers. I was in the other room, overhearing bits and pieces: "priceless gift of knowledge . . . like a library of a thousand books . . . easy monthly payments . . ."

¶2 When the two big boxes labeled *Encyclopaedia Britannica* arrived, it was Christmas come early. Junior and I sat on the floor surrounded by piles of books like explorers at the base of Everest. Each of the twenty-four volumes was a doorstop, the kind of book you'd expect to see in a library, never in someone's home and certainly not twenty-four of them, including a whole separate book just for the index! As I turned the densely set onionskin pages at random, I found myself wandering the world's geography, pondering molecules like daisy chains, marveling at the physiology of the eye. I was introduced to flora and fauna, to the microscopic structures of cells, to mitosis, meiosis, and Mendel's garden of peas. The world branched out before me in a thousand new directions, pretty much as the salesman had promised, and when it became overwhelming, all I had to do was close the book. It would wait for me to return.

¶3 Not all of my mother's efforts to expand our horizons were as welcome as the encyclopedias. Ballet class was a brief torture that I managed to whine my way out of.

Words to Know

onionskin: *(n.)* very thin, light paper
molecules: *(n.)* the smallest units into which any substance can be divided and still keep its own nature
physiology: *(n.)* the way the body of a person or an animal works
flora and fauna: *(n.)* plants and animals
mitosis: *(n.)* a process by which a cell divides
meiosis: *(n.)* a process by which a cell divides

I was too gangly and uncoordinated; end of story. Piano wasn't much better, and just as brief. I still can't hold a beat, even though the metronome mesmerized me. Guitar lessons, which Junior and I took together, were the worst of all. The real problem was getting there and back through a neighborhood on White Plains Road where a gang of taunting bullies made clear Puerto Rican kids were not welcome. I got smacked by one of them and tried to fight back, but eventually we just made a run for it: no way I could actually beat them.

¶4 My cousin Alfred had an answer for this menace: he would teach us self-defense, just the way he learned in the army reserves. We had to do push-ups with him shouting orders like a crazed drill sergeant. He slapped me. Again and again. He counted the slaps, fifty in all. This would build up my courage and resistance, he said. I didn't have the heart to tell him no amount of basic training was going to toughen me enough to take on a gang of much bigger kids just for the sake of playing guitar badly. Sometimes you have to cut your losses.

¶5 There was one more reason, beyond the pleasure of reading, the influence of English, and my mother's various interventions, that I finally started to thrive at school. Mrs. Reilly, our fifth-grade teacher, unleashed my competitive spirit. She would put a gold star up on the blackboard each time a student did something really well, and was I a sucker for those gold stars! I was determined to collect as many as I could. After the first As began appearing on my report card, I made a solemn vow that from then on, every report card would have at least one more A than the last one.

¶6 A vow on its own wasn't enough; I had to figure out how to make it happen. Study skills were not something that our teachers at Blessed Sacrament had ever addressed <u>explicitly</u>. Obviously, some kids were smarter than others; some kids worked harder than others. But as I also noticed, a handful of kids, the same ones every time, routinely got the top marks. That was the camp I wanted to join. But how did they do it?

Words to Know

<u>explicitly</u>: *(adv.)* clearly and directly

Questions

Key Ideas and Details

3. Why does Sotomayor describe the neighborhood she and Junior walk through on their way to and from guitar lessons? What do these details add to the narrative?

Words and Phrases in Context

4. What does Sotomayor mean when she writes in **paragraph 6** that study skills were not "addressed explicitly" at her school? How is Sotomayor affected by the school's lack of addressing study skills?

Questions

Key Ideas and Details

5. How does Sotomayor achieve her goal of getting more gold stars? What "critical lesson" does she learn from the experiences she describes in **paragraph 7**?

Text Structure

6. Sotomayor includes a flash forward in **paragraph 9**. What words indicate that the events are a flash forward? What is Sotomayor's purpose in including a flash forward?

¶7 It was then, in Mrs. Reilly's class, under the allure of those gold stars, that I did something very unusual for a child, though it seemed like common sense to me at the time. I decided to approach one of the smartest girls in the class and ask her how to study. Donna Renella looked surprised, maybe even flattered. In any case, she generously divulged her technique: how, while she was reading, she underlined important facts and took notes to condense information into smaller bits that were easier to remember; how, the night before a test, she would reread the relevant chapter. Obvious things once you've learned them, but at the time deriving them on my own would have been like trying to invent the wheel. I'd like to believe that even schools in poor neighborhoods have made some progress in teaching basic study skills since I was in the fifth grade. But the more critical lesson I learned that day is still one too many kids never figure out: don't be shy about making a teacher of any willing party who knows what he or she is doing. In retrospect, I can see how important that pattern would become for me: how readily I've sought out mentors, asking guidance from professors or colleagues, and in every friendship soaking up eagerly whatever that friend could teach me.

¶8 At the time, all I knew was that my strategy worked. Soon Mrs. Reilly had moved me to the row next to the window, which was reserved for the top students. My pleasure was diluted, however, when I found out that Junior's teacher had assigned him to the farthest row from the window, where the slowest kids sat. Naturally, Junior was upset, and the unfairness irked me too. It's true that I called him stupid, but that was a big sister's prerogative, and I knew that he wasn't really. He studied almost as hard as I did. He was quiet, but he listened and paid attention; nothing slipped by him.

¶9 "He's a boy," said Mami. "He'll get there when he does." The Sisters of Charity held a pessimistic view of male children: they were trouble for the most part, often in need of a good thrashing, and unlikely to amount to much. There was more wisdom in my mother's open-ended encouragement. She would never push Junior and me to get better grades, never crack the whip regarding homework or lecture us about setting our goals high, the way Tío Benny did with my cousin Nelson. When I brought my report card home for her to sign, I could tell she was delighted to see that I was getting As.

Words to Know

diluted: *(v.)* made something weaker
prerogative: *(n.)* a right that someone has because of their importance or position

That same proud smile greeted the news in later years that I'd made valedictorian or was graduating summa cum laude. It didn't matter that she didn't understand exactly what I'd accomplished to earn her pride. She trusted me, and Junior too. "Just study," she would say. "I don't care what grade you get, just study. *No me importa si trabajan lavando baños. Lo importante es hacerlo bien.*" I don't care if you clean toilets, just do it well. Achievement was all very well, but it was the process, not the goal, that was most important.

***

¶**10** Sitting in the waiting room at the clinic, I wondered, did it never occur to anyone at the Albert Einstein College of Medicine that kids who might not have long to live shouldn't have to wait endless hours with nothing to read but stacks of old *Highlights*? I should have brought my Nancy Drew book, I grumbled.

¶**11** But when my turn came, they gave me something else to read—a pamphlet about choosing a profession. I am ten years old, I thought. Isn't it a little early to be worrying about this? *You can be a famous actress, the pamphlet assured me, like Mary Tyler Moore. You can be a professional athlete. You can be:*

a doctor
a lawyer
an architect
an engineer
a nurse
a teacher . . .

¶**12** The list of possibilities for a diabetic didn't seem very long. And then, more darkly, there was a list of professions that were out-of-bounds. You couldn't be an airline pilot or a bus driver. Fair enough, I thought: you don't want someone flying a plane who might pass out. You couldn't serve in the military. Fine: I'd had enough of boot camp for a lifetime thanks to Alfred. And you couldn't be a police officer . . . uh-oh. That one stopped me like a slap in the face.

Words to Know

valedictorian: *(n.)* the student who has received the best marks all through school
diabetic: *(n.)* someone who has diabetes, a serious disease in which there is too much sugar in the blood

Questions

Key Ideas and Details

7. How does including a scene in a clinic add to our understanding of Sotomayor?

Text Structure

8. Why does the author include text in italics? What does this text indicate?

Questions

Key Ideas and Details

9. Why was it a catastrophe that Sotomayor couldn't be a detective? Why did Sotomayor think she would make a good detective?

Words and Phrases in Context

10. Find the word *quandary* in **paragraph 18**, and define it using context clues. What is Sotomayor's quandary?

¶13 You couldn't be a police officer? That meant you couldn't be a detective. This was a catastrophe! It's true that Nancy Drew manages without being a police officer, but she is an exception. She was also fictional. I knew enough about the real world to know that detectives are normally cops and not eighteen-year-old girls with charmed lives. And yet Nancy Drew had a powerful hold on my imagination. Every night, when I'd finished reading and got into bed and closed my eyes, I would continue the story, with me in Nancy's shoes until I fell asleep.

¶14 The young sleuth tools around in her little blue roadster with the top down. She is an incurable optimist who cleverly turns obstacles to her own advantage. Nancy Drew's father is a lawyer. He talks to her about his cases and gives her tips that help her solve crimes. They are like partners, father and daughter.

¶15 The world they live in is a kind of fairy tale, where people own houses on winding, tree-shaded driveways; visit summer homes at the lake; and attend charity balls at the country club. Nancy travels, too. She's even been to Paris. What I wouldn't have given to see the Eiffel Tower one day! But even though Nancy Drew is rich, she isn't a snob. And even though it is fiction, I knew such a world did exist. It wasn't Cinderella and pumpkins turning into carriages. It was real, and I was hungry to learn about it.

¶16 I was convinced I would make an excellent detective. My mind worked in ways very similar to Nancy Drew's, I told myself: I was a keen observer and listener. I picked up on clues. I figured things out logically, and I enjoyed puzzles. I loved the clear, focused feeling that came when I concentrated on solving a problem and everything else faded out. And I could be brave when I needed to be.

¶17 I could be a great detective, if only I weren't diabetic.

***

¶18 "Junior, change the channel! *Perry Mason*'s on." Okay, so I couldn't be a police officer or a detective, but it occurred to me that the solution to my quandary appeared on that small black-and-white screen every Thursday night.

¶19 <u>Perry Mason</u> was a lawyer, a defense attorney. He worked alongside a detective, Paul Drake, but even so it was Perry Mason who untangled the real story behind the crime, which was never what it seemed. And it was once the trial started that things got really interesting. You assume, of course, that Perry Mason is the hero. He's the one the show is named after, the one who gets the close-up shots, who wins the case almost every time and gets the hugs and tears of gratitude at the end. But my sympathies were not entirely <u>monopolized</u> by Perry Mason. I was fond of Burger, the prosecutor, too. I liked that he was a good loser, that he was more committed to finding the truth than to winning his case. If the defendant was truly innocent, he once explained, and the case was dismissed, then he had done his job, because justice had been served.

¶20 Most of all it was the judge who fascinated me. A minimal but vital presence, he was more of an abstraction than a character: a personification of justice. At the end of the hour, when Perry Mason said, "Your Honor, I move to dismiss the charges against my client and release him," it was the judge who made the final decision—"case dismissed" or "motion granted"—that wrapped up the episode. You had to watch carefully because it was over in a flash, but I knew that was the most important moment in the show. And even before that final decision, it was the judge who called the shots, who decided whether it was "overruled" or "sustained" when a lawyer said, "Objection!"

¶21 There was a whole new vocabulary here. And though I wasn't sure what every detail meant, I followed the gist of it. It was like the puzzles I enjoyed, a complex game with its own rules, and one that intersected with grand themes of right and wrong. I was intrigued and determined to figure it out.

¶22 I could be a great lawyer, I decided. But a part of me, I knew, would have preferred to be the judge rather than Perry Mason. At the time, with no knowledge of what either aspiration might entail, the one didn't seem any more outlandish than the other.

Words to Know

***Perry Mason*:** *(n.)* the main character of *Perry Mason*, a television show that aired from 1957–1966

monopolized: *(v.)* took all of someone's time or attention

Questions

Key Ideas and Details

11. How does the *Perry Mason* show offer a solution to the *quandary* Sotomayor describes in **paragraphs 16–18**?

Literature Circle Leveled Novels

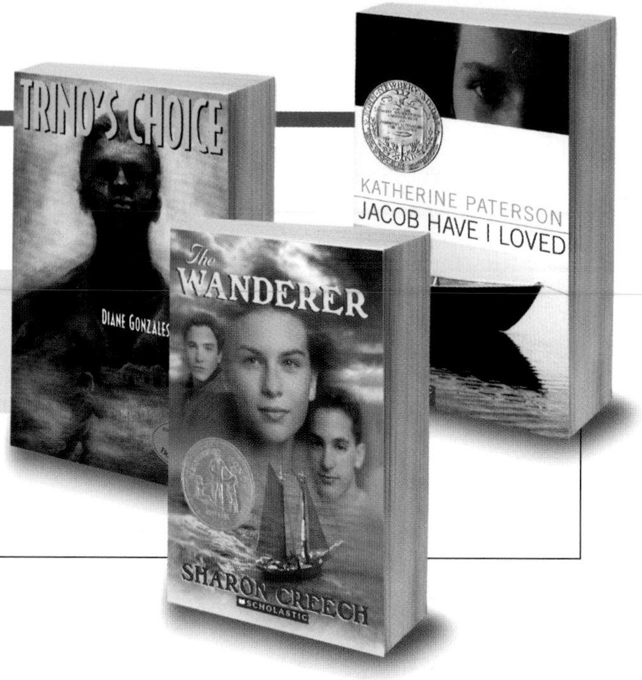

Trino's Choice *by Diane Gonzales Bertrand*
A young boy named Trino must make a difficult choice about his future: join a gang of teenage thieves to get money for his family or stay in school to make a better life for himself. **Lexile**® measure: 780L

The Wanderer *by Sharon Creech*
Thirteen-year-old Sophie and her cousin Cody record stories in their journals as they sail across the Atlantic and learn more about each other. **Lexile**® measure: 830L

Jacob Have I Loved *by Katherine Paterson*
Sara Louise is jealous of her beautiful, talented sister, but is able to figure out her own identity —and step out of her sister's shadow—by focusing on her own strengths and talents. **Lexile**® measure: 880L

Fiction, Nonfiction, Poetry, and Novels

An Island Like You: Stories of the Barrio *by Judith Ortiz Cofer.* Twelve short stories weave a picture of life in a diverse Puerto Rican barrio and the choices young residents must make about their futures. **Lexile**® measure: 910L

The Pact: Three Young Men Make a Promise and Fulfill a Dream *by Drs. Sampson Davis, George Jenkins, and Rameck Hunt.* Read about how hard work and friendship help three young men overcome obstacles to reach their goals. **Lexile**® measure: 940L

What Color Is Your Parachute for Teens: Discovering Yourself, Defining Your Future *by Richard Nelson Bolles, et al.* Learn how teens can use their strengths to set their paths for the future. **Lexile**® measure: 1090L

Poetry for Young People: Robert Frost *edited by Gary D. Schmidt.* Learn more about the life of Robert Frost and read more than 20 of his poems. **Lexile**® measure: NP

Rocket Boys *by Homer H. Hickam.* Read Hickam's memoir about his childhood in Coalwood and his decision to build a rocket and become a NASA engineer.

Think Big: Unleashing Your Potential for Excellence *by Ben Carson.* A successful surgeon shares his philosophy about how to overcome obstacles and meet goals.

What Do You Really Want? How to Set a Goal and Go for It! *by Beverly K. Bachel.* Read advice about how to set goals and pursue them.

What Teens Need to Succeed: Proven, Practical Ways to Shape Your Own Future *by Peter L. Benson, et al.* Learn about the positive assets that every teen can use to achieve success.

Films and TV

King (The History Channel, 2008) Learn more about the life and work of Dr. Martin Luther King, Jr., and consider how his message is relevant in today's world. (94 min.)

October Sky (Universal Studios, 1999) Homer Hickam's early interest in rockets and science are brought to life in this film adaptation of his memoirs. (108 min.)

The Outsiders (Warner Home Video, 1983) This film adaptation of the 1967 novel follows a group of young men who must make decisions about their loyalties and their futures. (91 min.)

The Pact (WGBH Boston, 2006) Follow the journey of the Three Doctors as they encourage each other to achieve their goals and later inspire other young people to do the same. (85 min.)

Robert Frost: New England in Autumn (Monterey Video, 2006) Hear the poems of Robert Frost, including "The Road Not Taken," read against the backdrop of a New England autumn day. (29 min.)

The Sally Ride Story: A Woman Space Pioneer (Global Science Productions, 2000) Learn how Sally Ride trained and studied to achieve her goal of flying in space. (50 min.)

Selma, Lord, Selma (Disney,1999) Follow a young girl who chooses to resist segregation in the hope of promoting the message of Dr. Martin Luther King, Jr. (94 min.)

Stand and Deliver (Warner Home Video, 1988) This film is based on the true story of a teacher who challenges his students to set goals and prove their abilities. (103 min.)

Websites

Homer Hickam's Official Web Site Follow links to learn more about Homer Hickam's life as well as his projects and published works.

NASA Career Corner Learn about the many different careers at NASA and find out what it takes to work in the space program.

Teen Business Link Students can search this US Small Business Association resource for tips and advice about how to start a business.

The Three Doctors Learn more about the Three Doctors, their experiences, their work to inspire and motivate young people, and their current projects.

Magazines

Muse Students can explore their own personal interests by searching for articles on subjects ranging from science to history.

National Geographic Kids Find articles about the NASA space program and other important science topics.

Odyssey Students who are interested in science can explore topics about space, life sciences, and technology.

Time for Kids Students can search for articles about the issues that affect the decisions that they make about their futures.

UNIT 2

SPORTS REPORT

What can we learn about ourselves from studying sports and athletes?

Unit Introduction

In an essay and an excerpt from a nonfiction book, learn how two writers view the thought process behind athletic performance and the roles of both physical prowess and mental power in sports.

In the sports article "What Could Be Better Than a Touchdown?" Kelefa Sanneh examines how an easy touchdown generated endless fan debate about the wisdom of usually uncontroversial football play.

In an excerpt from his book *Why We Run,* author Bernd Heinrich explores the physical, mental, and evolutionary processes that drive humans to run.

WRITING PERFORMANCE TASK

"Sports performance has just as much to do with mental strength and agility as with physical prowess." Develop or refute this claim in an argumentative essay.

SPORTS ARTICLE/INFORMATIONAL EXCERPT

"What Could Be Better Than a Touchdown?"
by Kelefa Sanneh

Language
- Academic Vocabulary
- Word Study: Word Families

Reading an Essay
- Identify Evidence
- Key Ideas and Details
- Craft & Structure

from ***Why We Run***,
by Bernd Heinrich

Language
- Academic Vocabulary
- Word Study: Context Clues

Reading a Nonfiction Excerpt
- Identify Evidence
- Key Ideas and Details
- Craft and Structure

SPEAKING AND LISTENING

Present a Speech
- Collaborate and Present

Checklist: Speech
- Scoring Guide

WRITING

Writing: Argumentative Essay
- Student Model
- Analyze the Model
- Examine the Topic
- Organize Ideas
- Language Study: Thesis Statements
- Conventions Study: Sentence Patterns
- Revise, Edit, and Publish
- Performance Task Rubric

EXTENDED READING

Science Article
"Confessions of a Doper"
by Jonathan Vaughter

Poem
"Casey at the Bat"
by Ernest L. Thayer

Academic Vocabulary

"What Could be Better Than a Touchdown?"
by Kelefa Sanneh

Rate your understanding of each word. Then read its meaning and write a sample sentence.

Word	Meaning	Example
intercepts *(v.)* p. 57 ① ② ③ ④	prevents something from reaching the person or place to which it was sent	If the spy intercepts the message, his enemies won't be able to read it.
modest *(adj.)* p. 58 ① ② ③ ④	not dramatic, limited in size	
forsworn *(v.)* p. 59 ① ② ③ ④	rejected strongly	
sentimental *(adj.)* p. 59 ① ② ③ ④	full of emotion, appealing to feelings	
contest *(v.)* p. 59 ① ② ③ ④	challenge; argue or disagree with	
confirming *(v.)* p. 59 ① ② ③ ④	showing or making sure that something is true or correct	

Rating Scale | ① I don't know the word. ② I've seen it or heard it. ③ I know its meaning. ④ I know it and use it.

Word Study

Word Family

A **word family** is a group of words that share the same base word and have related meanings. Word webs help you visualize how to find base words.

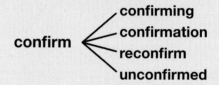

confirm → confirming, confirmation, reconfirm, unconfirmed

Complete each sentence using the correct word form from the *confirm* word family.

1. Try not to include any ____________ facts in your research paper.

2. Check the dictionary to ____________ the spelling of this word.

3. I think my answer is right, but I'll check the answer key for ____________.

4. Please call him one more time to ____________ the date.

5. I am tired of ____________ everything she tells me!

What Could Be Better Than A TOUCHDOWN?

by Kelefa Sanneh

from THE NEW YORKER Online

¶**1** It's third and five, with less than two minutes left in the game. The Minnesota Vikings have the ball at their own twenty-one yard line, down by two, with no timeouts. Brett Favre rolls out to his right and throws to his tight end, Visanthe Shiancoe. But one of the New York Jets safeties, Dwight Lowery, has been watching the play unfold. He breaks toward the ball, **intercepts** it, and dashes twenty-six yards into the end zone. Touchdown!

¶**2** And also, perhaps, a mistake? There are a few situations in football where scoring an easy touchdown is the wrong thing to do. Might this have been one of them?

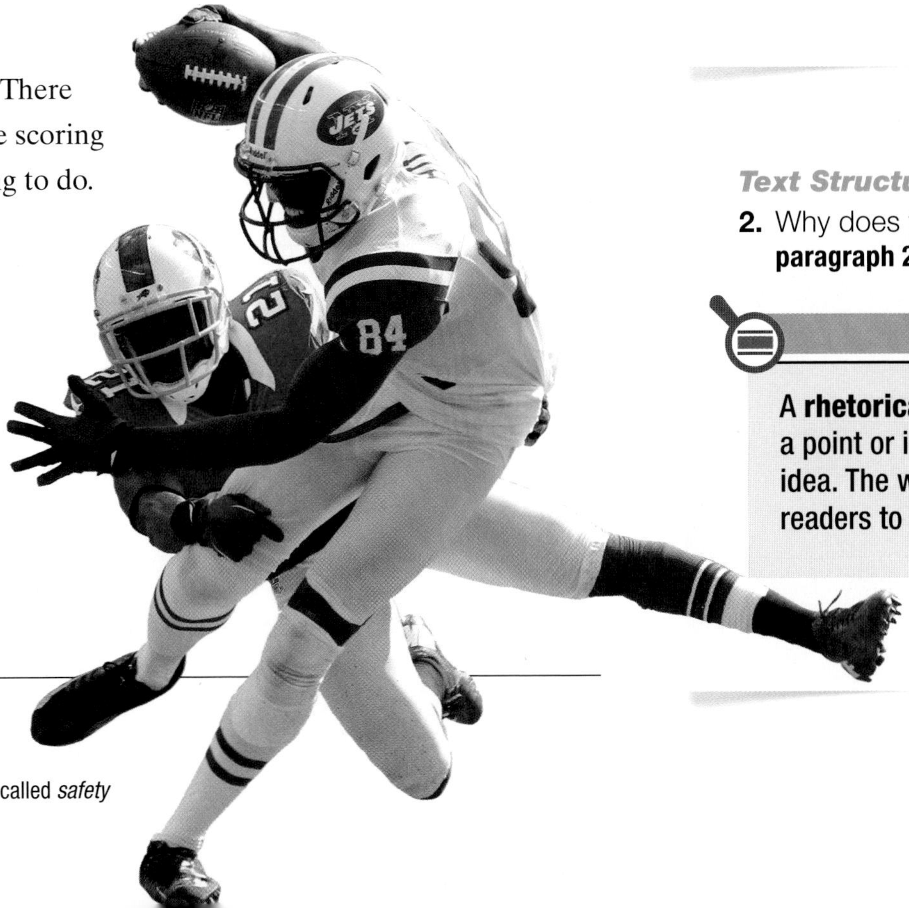

Words to Know

down by two: *(adj.)* losing by two points

safeties: *(n.)* defensive players who play a position called *safety*

Close Reading

Key Ideas and Details

1. What is this paragraph about? Find evidence in **paragraph 1** that identifies its subject.

Jargon

Jargon is the language used by people in a particular profession or group.

Text Structure

2. Why does the author begin and end **paragraph 2** with questions?

Rhetorical Question

A **rhetorical question** emphasizes a point or introduces a topic or idea. The writer does not expect readers to answer the question.

Close Reading

Key Ideas and Details

3. Who won the football game? Find details that indicate which team won.

Academic Vocabulary

4. What made the Viking's kickoff return modest? What might a less modest kickoff return have accomplished?

Text Structure

5. Why does the author begin this paragraph with *if*? What issue does he begin to write about here?

Key Ideas and Details

6. How many points is a touchdown worth? How is that important to the scenario described here?

¶**3** As it happened, Jets fans had nothing to worry about. Nick Folk kicked the extra point, putting the Jets ahead by nine. After a **modest** kickoff return, the Vikings got the ball at their own twenty-three yard line with a minute and a half left; after a pair of completed passes and a smattering of incomplete ones, the game was over.

¶**4** But if Folk had missed the extra point, then the Jets would have been ahead by only eight points, and the Vikings would have been able to tie the game with a touchdown drive and a two-point conversion. (Unlikely, but certainly not impossible.)

Words to Know

extra point: *(n.)* a point that may be scored after a touchdown by kicking the football between the goal posts

two-point conversion: *(n.)* an unusual football play that allows a team to score two points after a touchdown

¶**5** If the Vikings had scored a quick touchdown—on the kickoff return, say, or on a bomb to Randy Moss—then they would have been able to try an onside kick, giving them a small but real chance of getting the ball back. And, of course, if Lowery had fumbled during his interception return, then Favre and the Vikings offense would have got the ball back immediately, still down by only two.

¶**6** On the other hand, if Lowery had **forsworn** the end zone and dropped to one knee as soon as he caught Favre's pass, the game would have been over: the Jets could have run out the clock with three pro-forma snaps.

¶**7** Within minutes, Jets fans were debating Lowery's touchdown at Jetsinsider.com, in a chat thread called, "Dwight Lowery—TAKE A KNEE!" One argued that the risk of fumbling was low—"there were no Vikings in the area." (But then, aren't fumbles often caused by the player you don't see?) Another said, "Dude, you're arguing scenarios that have less than a 1% chance of happening." (It's true that Folk had never, in a hundred and forty-three attempts, missed an extra point. But what about a botched snap?) There was a **sentimental** argument: "Let the kid have his moment." And, more convincing, a financial one: "Gotta cover the Jets spread I bet on!!!" (Many oddsmakers had the Jets favored by four.) But how do you calculate the odds of a Jets defender getting injured on a Vikings drive that never would have happened if Lowery had refused to score? The debate was still roiling the next day, and one commentator claimed to have the latest update, straight from Rex Ryan, the Jets head coach: "Rex just said 'no biggie' (paraphrasing). He said, once you go up 2 scores, it's over. He also said you guys are nerds." It's probably impossible to **contest** the first part without **confirming** the second part.

Words to Know

fumbled: *(v.)* dropped or lost control of the ball
pro-forma: *(adj.)* moving along in a heated, agitated way

Close Reading

Words and Phrases In Context

7. Why does Sanneh use the metaphor "bomb" to describe a long pass to Vikings' player Randy Moss? How did Lowery's touchdown open up the possibility of such a play?

Key Ideas and Details

8. Why do some fans argue that Lowery should have "forsworn the end zone"?

Text Structure

9. What do the quotation marks and the parentheses throughout this paragraph indicate?

Writing

10. What does the author say is "impossible to contest" without confirming "you guys are nerds"? Why does he end the article this way?

The author cannot contest ___.

He probably concludes this way because ___.

Identify Evidence | Analyze Individuals, Events, and Ideas

Reread **"What Could Be Better Than a Touchdown?"** identifying reasons and evidence that Sanneh cites to introduce, illustrate, and elaborate the claim that a touchdown isn't always the smartest play in a football game.

- As you read, use the Evidence column to record examples from the text that reveal Sanneh's argument.
- In the Explanation column, explain how the evidence introduces, illustrates, or elaborates Sanneh's claim.

Evidence	Source	Page	Explanation
1. ". . . Dwight Lowery, has been watching the play unfold. He breaks toward the ball, **intercepts** it, and dashes twenty-six yards into the end zone. Touchdown!"	Sanneh	57	Here, the author sets the scene for the rest of the article by describing the controversial play he will discuss as a possible example of when there is some action better than a touchdown.
2. "There are a few situations in football where scoring an easy touchdown is the wrong thing to do. Might this have been one of them?"	Sanneh		The author introduces the claim that scoring an easy touchdown is not always a good idea.
3. The attitude of the fans			

Evidence	Source	Page	Evidence
4.			
5.			

Key Ideas and Details

Determining the Central Idea

1. Use the evidence you collected to summarize the key idea of Sanneh's essay. What is the central argument he makes?

2. List three key individuals or groups that Sanneh introduces in this essay. Explain why each individual is important to the central argument.

Individual	Significance
Dwight Lowery	scored a touchdown that Sanneh argues might have been a mistake

3. List three key events that did not really happen, but could have, according to Sanneh. Explain why each is important to Sanneh's argument.

Event	Significance
Nick Folk misses extra point	might have allowed the Vikings to tie game

Craft and Structure

Structure of the Essay

1. How does Sanneh begin this essay?

2. What argument does the author introduce in the second paragraph? How does it relate to the opening anecdote?

3. How does the author support his claim about touchdowns in paragraphs 4–6?

4. How does the author conclude his argument?

Author's Purpose

5. What can you conclude about the author's purpose in writing this text? Who was his intended audience for the article? Cite text evidence in your response.

Author's Purpose

Author's purpose is the reason that an author wrote a text: to inform, to entertain, or to persuade.

Academic Vocabulary

from *Why We Run* by Bernd Heinrich

Rate your understanding of each word. Then read its meaning and write a sample sentence.

Word	Meaning	Example
communal (*adj.*) p. 65 ① ② ③ ④	done together as a group	
insights (*n.*) p. 66 ① ② ③ ④	understandings of how someone or something behaves and why	
amalgamate (*v.*) p. 66 ① ② ③ ④	to blend or combine	
elongating (*v.*) p. 67 ① ② ③ ④	stretching; growing longer	
ingenious (*adj.*) p. 67 ① ② ③ ④	very clever; showing great skill or imagination	
involuntary (*adj.*) p. 69 ① ② ③ ④	automatic; impossible to control	

Rating Scale | ① I don't know the word. ② I've seen it or heard it. ③ I know its meaning. ④ I know it and use it.

Word Study

Context Clues

Context clues are words in a text that help you figure out the meaning of an unfamiliar word. Sometimes words are defined in the text or their meanings are suggested.

The sentences below are from Bernd Heinrich's nonfiction excerpt. Find the context clues to determine the meanings of the bold words.

1. The problem was: how to prepare to run that far? . . . it seemed only natural for me to look to other "**endurance** athlete" species to see why and how it's done, and for tips on how to train.

2. These hunters were running in one direction, from left to right across the rock face . . . But then I noticed something more . . . It was the figure farthest to the right, the one leading the **progression**.

from

WHY WE RUN

by Bernd Heinrich

¶**1** The human experience is populated with dreams and aspirations. For me, the animal totem for these dreams is the antelope, swift, strong, and elusive. Most of us chase after "antelopes," and sometimes we catch them. Often we don't. But why do we bother to try? I think it is because without dream-"antelopes" to chase we become what a lapdog is to a wolf. And we are inherently more like wolves than lapdogs, because the **communal** chase is part of our biological makeup.

¶**2** For me, the glimpse of a new "antelope" on the horizon came in early May 1981. I had seen a fresh sign, and I had to give chase. I had just run my first ultramarathon, a 50-kilometer race, a short race that barely qualifies as an ultramarathon. But in the final half mile I had passed the then-current U.S. National 100-kilometer record holder, which made me wonder if, just possibly, I had the potential to race well at long distances. The North American 100-kilometer championships were to be held on October 4 that year in Chicago. Although at that moment I could just barely have run another step further, I began to dream about the potential of racing in the 100 km, twice as far as I had ever run before.

Words to Know

populated: *(adj.)* filled

aspirations: *(n.)* goals or dreams

Close Reading

Words and Phrases in Context

1. What does Heinrich compare to an antelope? According to the author, how are humans who don't chase "antelopes" like lapdogs instead of wolves? Explain the author's use of metaphor and analogy to introduce a key idea about human nature.

Analogy

An **analogy** is a comparison between two things or ideas. By pointing out how they are similar, the writer hopes to clarify the more complicated or less familiar thing.

Key Ideas and Details

2. What is the author's "antelope" in **paragraph 2**?

Close Reading

Words and Phrases in Context

3. What is a *zoologist*? Identify context clues that helped you figure it out.

Key Ideas and Details

4. Why did Heinrich write this book? Why does he emphasize purposes he did not write for?

Key Ideas and Details

5. Why will Heinrich "never, never forget" the 100-km race in Chicago?

Writing

6. Compare and contrast Heinrich's childhood run with the race in Chicago.

   As a child, Heinrich ran ____ on ____, where he ____.

   In Chicago, Heinrich ran wearing ____ on ____, with ____.

   These very different memories are intertwined in Heinrich's mind because ____.

¶**3** The problem was: how to prepare to run that far? As a zoologist by profession, it seemed only natural for me to look to other "endurance athlete" species to see why and how it's done, and for tips on how to train. However, I did not write this book as a training manual, nor did I write it to highlight my running exploits, which are puny relative to those of others. I wrote to show what is involved in running an ultramarathon race, and to pull together the race experience with the **insights** I gained from my studies of animals. My intent is to **amalgamate** the race experience with human biology to explore what makes us different from other animals, and in what ways we are the same. In the process, I discovered some possibly new perspectives on human evolution.

¶**4** We are all natural-born runners, although many of us forget this fact. I will never forget when I first ran barefoot as a child on the warm sand of a lonely wooded road in Germany, where I smelled the pines, heard wood pigeons coo, and saw bright green tiger beetles running or flying ahead of me. I will never, never forget running on asphalt pavement on October 4, 1981, more than thirty years later. On that day I raced a 100-kilometer distance in Chicago with 261 other men and women. Each of them was in one way or another, like me, chasing a dream antelope. When I began to think about what running is all about for us humans, and why I raced, I was surprised at the vividness of my distant memories, and at my new revelations. There were many worlds between the small boy running barefoot on the sand and the forty-one-year-old biologist wearing Nikes on the Chicago pavement. But now these memories were intertwined in my mind with the larger scheme of human existence that relates to our kinship with animals and goes back to the dawn of humankind. Those thoughts gave new meaning to this race.

Words to Know

exploits: *(n.)* great deeds, activities that are noble or heroic

human evolution: *(n.)* human development, from early man to modern humans

¶**5** Movement is almost synonymous with life. With **elongating** stems and twirling tendrils, plants race one another toward light. Similarly, the seeds of many plants compete to be first on the right piece of ground. Some may travel hundreds of miles by **ingenious** and diverse mechanisms: being carried by wind or water, or being ferried by berry-eating birds or fur-bearing mammals.

¶**6** Animals move primarily on their own power: they harness chemical energy by means of muscles. But like plants, we humans have recently harnessed the wind, water, and other animals to carry us. And increasingly, our species, unlike any other, is tapping the energy from coal, oil, and the atom for locomotion.

¶**7** Throughout the hundreds of millions of years of animal evolution, there has been selective pressure on some species to be able to travel farther and quicker, and to do it more economically and under ever more adverse conditions than either their competitors or their predators. Both predators and prey have to move faster or die. An anonymous runner captured the notion in this now-famous aphorism: "Every morning in Africa, an antelope wakes up. It knows it must outrun the fastest lion, or it will be killed. Every morning in Africa, a lion wakes up. It knows it must run faster than the fastest antelope, or it will starve. It doesn't matter whether you're a lion or an antelope—when the sun comes up, you'd better be running." Of course, these animals don't need to know—they must only be fast.

Words to Know

synonymous: *(adj.)* the same or almost the same

adverse: *(adj.)* difficult, harsh, or unfavorable

Close Reading

Academic Vocabulary

7. Why do plants elongate? How does this detail support the author's claim that "movement is almost synonymous with life"?

Key Ideas and Details

8. How are plants and animals alike and different in the ways they travel? Why does the author include these details?

Text Structure

9. Why does the author include the anecdote about the antelope and the lion in this paragraph?

Close Reading

Words and Phrases in Context

10. What is *locomotion*? Identify clues that helped you determine its meaning.

Key Ideas and Details

11. What does the author mean when he says "we are, deep down, still runners, whether or not we declare it by our actions"? Why does he believe that "our mind, as much as our lungs and muscles . . . empowers our running"?

Writing

12. What is the effect of the author's descriptions of the national park in Zimbabwe? How does the description tie into the key ideas he is exploring in this text?

In this paragraph, the author describes _____.

The imagery he creates supports the idea that ___________.

¶**8** With the help of our <u>infinite</u> imagination and the technologies it has produced, we now travel faster, more economically, and well beyond the range of our muscle power. But for millions of years, our ultimate form of locomotion was running. We are, deep down, still runners, whether or not we declare it by our actions. And our minds, as much as our lungs and muscles, are a vital force that empowers our running. Whenever one of us jogs down a road or when we line up to race in a marathon, we are not only celebrating life in general and our individual aliveness but we are also exercising our fantasies while acknowledging reality. We are secure in the knowledge that there is no magic. Which is not to say the world is only of simple logic, because although it may be simple in its design, it is awesomely complex in its details.

¶**9** Several years ago in Matopos (now Matobo) National Park, Zimbabwe, I was on a research trip to study how body temperature affects the running and fighting ability of scarab dung beetles. On the rolling hills, their rock outcrops covered by short grass, I saw and smelled white and yellow flowering acacia trees that were abuzz with bees, wasps, and colorful cetoniid beetles. Giraffes were peaceably grazing on the flat-topped acacias. Baboons and impalas, each in their respective groups or bands, roamed in the miombe bush. Tens of thousands of wildebeest and zebra can, at the right time of year, still be seen in such a landscape, thundering by during their massive migration. Elephants and rhinoceros lumber like prehistoric giants over the land, ever on the move. <u>Serendipitously</u>, I looked under a rather inauspicious and small rock overhang and was taken aback by what I saw.

Words to Know

<u>infinite</u>: *(adj.)* never ending; going on forever

<u>serendipitously</u>: *(adv)* having great luck

¶**10** Painted onto the wall under the overhang was a <u>succession</u> of small, stick-like human figures in clear running stride. All were clutching delicate bows, quivers, and arrows. These hunters were running in one direction, from left to right across the rock face. In itself, this two- or three-thousand-year-old pictograph was not particularly extraordinary. But then I noticed something more, and it sent my mind reeling. It was the figure farthest to the right, the one leading the progression. It had its hands thrown up in the air in the universal runners' gesture of triumph at the end of a race. This **involuntary** gesture is reflexive for most runners who have fought hard, who have breathed the heat and smelled the fire, and then felt the exhilaration of triumph over adversity. The image of the Bushmen remains for me an iconic reminder that the roots of our running, our competitiveness, and our striving for excellence go back very far and very deep.

¶**11** Looking at that African rock painting made me feel that I was witness to a kindred spirit, a man who had long ago vanished yet whom I understood as if we'd talked just a moment earlier. I was not only in the same environment and of the same mind as this unknown Bushman running hunter, I was also in the place that most likely produced our common ancestors. The artist had been here hundreds of generations before me, but that was only the blink of an eye compared to the eons that have elapsed since a <u>bipedal intermediate</u> between our apelike and our recognizably human ancestors left the safety of the forest for the savanna some 4 million years ago, to start running. There is nothing quite so gentle, deep, and irrational as our running—and nothing quite so savage, and so wild.

Close Reading

Key Ideas and Details

13. What is it about the image of the Bushmen that leaves the author's "mind reeling"? Why?

Academic Vocabulary

14. What does the author imply by calling the stick figure's gesture "involuntary"?

Key Ideas and Details

15. Who is the "kindred spirit" that the author describes? What makes him feel he understands this person? Who are their "common ancestors"?

Words to Know

<u>succession</u>: *(n.)* a series of items that follow one another

<u>bipedal intermediate</u>: *(n.)* a creature that walked on two feet, like humans, but had not yet evolved into a human

Close Reading

Key Ideas and Details

16. What is the difference between why humans run and why animals run? How does the Bushman painting embody the difference?

Words and Phrases in Context

17. What did runner Steve Prefontaine mean when he said "a race is like a work of art . . ."? How does this simile help develop Heinrich's ideas about running?

Key Ideas and Details

18. What does Heinrich mean when he says, "All I knew was: it was not magic"?

¶**12** For me, the Bushman painting **embodies** the connection between running, hunting, and humanity's striving toward excellence for its own sake. All other animals are much more strictly utilitarian. They lack that artistic drive which is detached from ulterior motives and rewards. Looking at the Bushman painting, I thought of the late Steve Prefontaine, from Coos Bay, Oregon, former University of Oregon runner who was one of the greatest and gutsiest all-time middle-distance racers ever. Pre put it this way: "A race is like a work of art that people can look at and be affected by in as many ways as they're capable of understanding." Yes, the key to appreciation is in the understanding.

¶**13** As I was growing up, my gods were runners like Herb Elliott, Jim Ryun, and the now-anonymous men on competing teams who could outrun me. These weren't just people. Some of them seemed to defy natural laws. My appreciation came from the understanding that what they did was extraordinary, and not readily understood. All I knew was: it was not magic. I wanted to know what they ate and breathed and how they lived, what made them so different from other humans and so much like some of the animals I admired.

Above is a detail from the rock painting in Matobo National Park in southern Zimbabwe that inspired Bernd Heinrich.

Words to Know

utilitarian: *(adj.)* useful and practical

appreciation: *(n.)* recognition of something's beauty or value

¶**14** Seeing a great performance, whether by a human or another animal, still inspires me to no end. I'm moved by others' dreams and by their devotion and courage in the pursuit of excellence. I get choked up when I see a kid, or anyone else, fighting hopeless odds—someone who goes out there to run the lonely roads with a dream in the heart, a gleam in the eye, and a goal in mind. I admire those who have the courage to step up to the line of a great race to run their heart out for a dream. I empathize with a heart touched by fire during this Dream Time of youth, when as runners we were still undefeated in spirit, felt invincible, and thought the world was pure.

The lead runner is a member of the Tarahumara, Native Americans from northwestern Mexico who are known for their long-distance running prowess.

Words to Know

empathize: *(v.)* to understand and share someone's feelings

invincible: *(adj.)* impossible to defeat or stop

Close Reading

Writing

19. How does a great running performance inspire the author? Why does he empathize "with a heart touched by fire"?

Great performances inspire the author because ____.

When the author says he empathizes "with a heart touched by fire," he means ____.

Key Ideas and Details

20. On page 66, at the end of **paragraph 3**, Heinrich states that in writing this book, he "discovered some possibly new perspectives on human evolution." Now that you have reached the end of the text, what do you think those new perspectives might be?

Identify Evidence | Analyze Individuals, Events, and Ideas

In the excerpt from ***Why We Run***, Heinrich discusses why humans run and how our motivations differ from those of other animals. How does he introduce, illustrate, and elaborate claims about the connections among running, biology, and human evolution?

- In the Evidence column, record important details from the excerpt that present Heinrich's claims about running.
- In the Explanation column, explain how the details illustrate or elaborate a key idea, event, or individual.

Evidence	Source	Page	Explanation
1. "Most of us chase after 'antelopes,' and sometimes we catch them. Often we don't. But why do we bother to try?"	Heinrich	65	The author uses the metaphor of the antelope to explain that running is about chasing dreams.
2. ". . . we are inherently more like wolves than lapdogs because the communal chase is part of our biological makeup."	Heinrich	65	The author asserts that wolves chase prey instinctively, similar to humans chasing dreams instinctively.
3. "Movement is almost synonymous with life. With elongating stems and twirling tendrils, plants race one another toward light."	Heinrich		
4.			

Imagery	Source	Page	Significance
5.			
6.			
7.			
8.			

Key Ideas and Details

Determining the Central Idea

1. Use the evidence you have collected to summarize the key idea of this excerpt.

2. List three key events that Heinrich discusses. Explain why each event is important to the central idea.

Event	Significance
In May, 1981, the author ran in his first ultramarathon.	This event made him want to run an even longer race and got him thinking about the topic of this book.

Individual or Group	Significance
Heinrich	The author's own experiences as a runner and a zoologist led him to write his book.

Craft and Structure

Structure of the Memoir

1. What recurring metaphor does the author introduce in the first paragraph?

2. How did the author's experiences lead him to write *Why We Run*? (paragraphs 2–3)

3. Discuss the claim that the author makes and develops in paragraphs 5–7.

4. At what point does the author shift from discussing the reasons that all animals run to discussing reasons unique to humans? What story does he tell to introduce this shift?

Author's Perspective

What is the author's perspective on the relationship between our minds and our bodies?

Collaborate and Present

Plan and Deliver a Speech

In this Unit, you read an essay titled "What Could Be Better Than a Touchdown?" and an excerpt from a nonfiction book titled *Why We Run*. So, what could be better than a touchdown? Why do we run?

Assignment: Choose one of the questions above. Plan and deliver a short speech that answers the question. Base your answer on evidence from the related text.

Analyze the Content

1. Consider the following questions:
   - How does the author of the text answer the question?
   - Which examples from the text reveal his answer?
2. Choose at least two examples from the text that reveal the author's opinion on the question you chose. Record your examples on the chart.

Question	Examples

3. Use details from your chart as talking points for your speech. Draft what you will say in your speech. Remember to introduce your topic at the beginning of the speech and to close with a conclusion summarizing your main points.

Report

4. Deliver your speech.

Seeking Clarification

- Are you saying that . . .
- I think what you mean is . . .
- Can you give an example of . . .
- If I understand you correctly, you are saying that . . .

Reporting Ideas

- _____ suggests that _______.
- _____ seems to be implying that _________.
- _____ argues that ________.

Presentation

- Be still and use good posture.
- Speak loudly and clearly.
- Make eye contact with your audience.

Speech Checklist

Use the checklist below to evaluate your collaboration skills, reasoning, and final presentation. Think carefully about your work. If you know you completed an item thoroughly, give yourself a check (✓).

COLLABORATE AND PRESENT CHECKLIST		
Comprehension & Collaboration	**Evidence & Reasoning**	**Presentation of Knowledge & Ideas**
☐ Come to discussions prepared, having read and studied material. ☐ Refer to evidence when contributing to the discussion. ☐ Follow rules for discussions and lead by example. ☐ Ask and answer specific questions. ☐ Make comments that contribute to the topic under discussion. ☐ Review the key ideas under discussion and demonstrate understanding of multiple perspectives through reflection and paraphrasing.	☐ Explain the purpose of the presentation. ☐ Present information relevant to the task. ☐ Explain how the author answers the question you chose. ☐ Discuss how the author supports his claims. ☐ Use at least two examples from the text. ☐ Synthesize the key ideas from your speech with a conclusion.	☐ Adapt language to a variety of contexts and tasks to demonstrate knowledge of formal English. ☐ Include multimedia components (e.g., graphics, images, music, sound) and visual displays. ☐ Use appropriate volume/tone (clear, not too fast, too slow, or too loud) and avoid using "like" or "ummm." ☐ Have strong posture, a confident stance, and make frequent eye contact. ☐ Occasionally move from one spot to another without fiddling. ☐ Smile and act relaxed.
Number of ✓s in this category: ___	**Number of ✓s in this category: ___**	**Number of ✓s in this category: ___**
Total # of ✓s: __		

Add up the total number of checks (✓) in each category. Then use the scoring guide below to calculate your final score.

Scoring Guide			
16 to 18 ✓s	**13 to 15 ✓s**	**11 to 12 ✓s**	**10 or less ✓s**
④ **Exemplary**	③ **Meets Standards**	② **Needs Work**	① **Does Not Meet Standards**

Read the Model

Writers use many strategies to craft ideas, share information, and persuade readers. The writer of this argumentative essay uses logical reasoning and text evidence to develop the claim that mental strength and agility are just as important as physical prowess in sports. Read and discuss the model essay below.

Argumentative Essay

An **argument** is a reasoned, logical way of exploring a question or issue.

The introduction introduces the issue and the claim the author is making about that issue.

- Identify the author's claim.

The body paragraphs contain reasons and evidence that support the author's claim.

- Find two pieces of text evidence the author uses to support her claim.

The conclusion restates the thesis and offers the writer's final response to the question or issue.

- Identify the author's response to the question she explores.

Sports Success Requires Brawn *and* Brains

by Marcia Navone

Does sports performance depend as much on mental strength and agility as physical prowess? After reading "What Could Be Better Than a Touchdown?" and "Confessions of a Doper" I say yes—mental power is as important as physical power in sports.

In "Confessions of a Doper," Jonathan Vaughters describes how he used drugs to increase his physical strength and achieve "that last 2 percent" that an elite athlete needs (90). But first, Vaughters had to achieve the other 98%. That achievement required at least as much mental as physical strength. As Vaughters puts it, those athletes who "end up living their dreams are not necessarily" the most physically "gifted, but those who are stubborn, resolute, and willing to sacrifice" (89).

In "What Could Be Better Than a Touchdown?" Kelefa Sanneh describes a feat of physical prowess: New York Jets' safety Dwight Lowery "breaks toward the ball, intercepts it, and dashes twenty-six yards into the end zone" (57). But as Sanneh explains, that touchdown, while exciting, might have been "the wrong thing to do" (57). "With less than two minutes left in the game" and the Minnesota Vikings "down by two," a mentally agile player would have understood the many ways the touchdown could go wrong—"if the Vikings had scored a quick touchdown," for instance, or "if Lowery had fumbled during his interception return" (57 and 59). Sanneh's analysis shows that the ability to think on your feet is as important as the ability to run on your feet!

Sports success requires physical strength and skills, it's true. But Sanneh's and Vaughters's essays show that an athlete's mind is equally important. Mental strength and agility are just as important as physical prowess in sports.

Analyze the Model

An argumentative essay supports a position with logical reasoning and relevant evidence.

Thesis Statement

What is the writer's position? What evidence will be presented?

Body Paragraph 1 Topic Sentence:
"But first, Vaughters had to achieve the other 98% and that took at least as much mental as physical strength."

Reason/ Evidence

Reason/ Evidence

Reason/ Evidence

Body Paragraph 2 Topic Sentence:
"Sanneh's analysis shows that the ability to think on your feet is as important as the ability to run on your feet!"

Reason/ Evidence

Reason/ Evidence

Reason/ Evidence

Conclusion

How does the writer conclude the essay?

Text Strategy

In a **block-by-block analysis**, this writer discusses relevant evidence from one text in the first body paragraph and relevant evidence from the second text in the second body paragraph.

The thesis statement presents a clear plan for the essay.

- Identify the thesis statement.

The topic sentence of each body paragraph clearly states the main idea of that paragraph.

- Identify the topic sentence of each body paragraph.
- Evaluate whether each topic sentence supports the thesis.

Relevant Evidence includes logical reasoning, such as direct quotations from the text, that support the writer's ideas.

- Evaluate whether all sentences in each body paragraph support the topic sentence.

The conclusion sums up or restates the thesis and why it matters.

- Describe how the writer concludes her essay.

Step 1 | Gather Evidence

Use evidence from two texts in this Unit to develop or refute the claim that mental strength and agility are just as important as physical prowess in sports.

What You Need to Know | Examine the evidence you have collected showing how evidence from two authors' writings support your position. (See pages 60 and 72.)

What You Need to Write | Note evidence from each text that supports your thesis statement.

"What Could Be Better Than a Touchdown?"

Evidence:

Page # _____

Evidence:

Page # _____

Evidence:

Page # _____

excerpt from *Why We Run*

Evidence:

Page # _____

Evidence:

Page # _____

Evidence:

Page # _____

Step 2 | Organize Ideas

What You Need to Know | To write an effective argument, you must develop your thesis with specific and relevant text evidence.

To develop your thesis:

1. List the ways you think each author's writing supports or refutes the claim about mental agility vs. physical prowess.
2. Cite at least three direct quotes from each text that support your position regarding the claim.

What You Need to Write | Study the evidence you have gathered and organize the text evidence that best supports your thesis.

Body Paragraph 1 (Text 1)

Evidence from Text	How It Supports My Thesis

Body Paragraph 2 (Text 2)

Evidence from Text	How It Supports My Thesis

Step 3 | Draft

Write a draft of your argumentative essay on the computer or on paper.

Language Study | Construct a Thesis Statement

See It | **A thesis statement summarizes your entire essay. When writing thesis statements:**

- Present your opinion on an issue.
- Preview the reasons outlined in your body paragraphs that support this opinion.

Try It | **Read each pair of sentences. Write a thesis statement by combining the sentence that states the writer's position with the sentence that previews the writer's evidence.**

1. **Position:** Sports organizations must address the use of performance-enhancing drugs.

   Evidence: At least 30% of pro athletes use anabolic steroids.

2. **Position:** Going for the easy touchdown in football is almost always a good idea.

   Evidence: To lose because of your own teammate's touchdown requires a rare and unlikely series of events.

3. **Position:** All animals are driven to be runners.

   Evidence: For both predators and prey, running is essential to survival.

Apply It | Choose one of the frames below to revise your thesis statement.

1. In the debate over whether success in sports comes from physical prowess or mental agility, ____________ (author 1) and ____________ (author 2) have **opposing** views, with ____________ (author 1) supporting the idea that ____________ (author's position) in ____________ (title of text 1) and ____________ (author 2) suggesting that ____________ (author's position) in ____________ (title of text 2).

2. In the debate over whether success in sports comes from physical prowess or mental agility, ____________ (author 1) and ____________ (author 2) have **similar** views, with ____________ (author 1) supporting the idea that ____________ (author's position) in ____________ (title of text 1) and ____________ (author 2) suggesting that ____________ (author's position) in ____________ (title of text 2).

Now, **go back to your draft** and reread your conclusion. Remember that a strong conclusion restates the thesis. Rephrase your thesis statement to use in your revised conclusion.

____

____

____

Conventions Study | Vary Sentence Patterns

See It

Sentence patterns describe how the parts of a sentence are organized. As with word choice, writers should use clauses and vary their sentence lengths in order to add variety and avoid repetition in their writing.

Try It

Examine the paragraph below and note how the author varies sentence length, uses clauses, and avoids repetition.

In "Confessions of a Doper," Jonathan Vaughters describes how he used drugs to increase his physical strength and achieve "that last 2 percent" that an elite athlete needs. But first, Vaughters had to achieve the other 98%. That achievement required at least as much mental as physical strength. As Vaughters puts it, those athletes who "end up living their dreams are not necessarily" the most physically "gifted, but those who are stubborn, resolute, and willing to sacrifice."

Apply It

Now read through your draft and analyze your sentence patterns. Revise two sentences to add variety and avoid repetition. Use the following questions to help you:

- Can I add more descriptive details?
- Can two or more sentences be combined?
- Could I provide extra information using dashes or commas?
- Can I use pronouns to avoid repetition?

Step 4 | Revise and Edit

Revise your draft with a partner.

Organization and Clarity					
Introduce a claim and support it with clear, organized reasons and relevant evidence.	Self	1	2	3	4
	Partner	1	2	3	4
Use words, phrases, and clauses to clarify the relationship between the claim and supporting reasons.	Self	1	2	3	4
	Partner	1	2	3	4
Establish and maintain a formal style.	Self	1	2	3	4
	Partner	1	2	3	4
Provide a concluding statement that follows from the evidence presented.	Self	1	2	3	4
	Partner	1	2	3	4
Evidence and Reasoning					
Develop or refute the claim that mental strength and agility are just as important as physical prowess in sports.	Self	1	2	3	4
	Partner	1	2	3	4
Support the claim using evidence from the unit texts, correctly citing the author and page number for each piece of evidence.	Self	1	2	3	4
	Partner	1	2	3	4
Language and Convention					
Recognize and adjust variations from standard English.	Self	1	2	3	4
	Partner	1	2	3	4
Correctly punctuate, capitalize, and spell all words and phrases.	Self	1	2	3	4
	Partner	1	2	3	4
Vary sentence patterns for meaning, reader interest, and variety.	Self	1	2	3	4
	Partner	1	2	3	4

Scoring Guide | ① needs improvement ② average ③ good ④ excellent

Step 5 | Publish

Publish your essay either in print or digital form.

Publish

Publish your argument either in print or digital form. Use the rubric below to assess your final performance task.

PERFORMANCE TASK RUBRIC			
Score Point	**Organization and Clarity**	**Evidence and Reasoning**	**Language and Conventions**
Exemplary ④	• introductory paragraph includes a **strong thesis statement** that **takes a position** and **previews** the argument • body paragraphs are **effectively organized** and **present logical reasons and evidence** to support the position • includes **well-chosen** text evidence, precise language, and effective use of phrases and clauses that tie ideas together • concluding statement **restates the thesis statement** and **summarizes** the argument	• **accurately explains and convincingly argues** what it takes to be successful in sports • includes **relevant** factual evidence from the texts to support each logical reason	• demonstrates a **strong command** of the conventions of standard English grammar and usage, as well as of standard English capitalization, punctuation, and spelling • vocabulary is **appropriate** to the topic (vocabulary about sports; accurate vocabulary for writing a thesis statement and a convincing argument; a variety of phrases and clauses that tie key ideas together)
Meets Standards ③	• introductory paragraph **includes an adequate thesis statement** that **previews** the argument • body paragraphs are **logically organized** and **present reasons and evidence** to support the position • includes **some** text evidence, precise language and phrases and clauses that tie ideas together • concluding statement **restates the thesis statement** and **summarizes** the argument	• **adequately explains and argues** what it takes to be successful in sports • includes **some relevant** factual evidence from the texts to support each logical reason	• demonstrates **a near command** of the conventions of standard English grammar and usage, as well as of standard English capitalization, punctuation, and spelling **with some errors** • vocabulary is **appropriate** to the topic (vocabulary about sports; accurate vocabulary for writing a thesis statement and a convincing argument; a variety of phrases and clauses that tie key ideas together)

PERFORMANCE TASK RUBRIC			
Score Point	**Organization and Clarity**	**Evidence and Reasoning**	**Language and Conventions**
Needs Work ②	• introductory paragraph **includes a weak thesis statement that attempts to preview** the argument • body paragraphs are **somewhat logically organized** and **partially present reasons and evidence** to support the position • includes **a limited amount** of text evidence, precise language and effective use of phrases and clauses that tie ideas together • concluding statement **restates the thesis statement and attempts to summarize** the argument	• **partially explains and minimally argues** what it takes to be successful in sports • includes **one or two examples of relevant** factual evidence from the magazine article and nonfiction text to support each logical reason	• demonstrates a **marginal command** of the conventions of English grammar and usage, as well as of standard English capitalization, punctuation, and spelling • there **are many errors; however, the text is still understandable** • includes only **one or two examples** of vocabulary that is appropriate to the topic (vocabulary about sports; accurate vocabulary for writing a thesis statement and a convincing argument; a variety of phrases and clauses that tie key ideas together)
Does Not Meet Standards ①	• introductory paragraph is **unclear** and does not include a thesis statement that states a position • body paragraphs are **not organized logically** and/or **do not present reasons and evidence** • essay includes **little text evidence** and minimal use of phrases and clauses to tie ideas together • concluding statement is **unclear**	• response is **partial or inaccurate argument** about what it takes to be successful in sports • includes **no factual textual evidence** from the texts	• demonstrates **almost no command** of the conventions of standard English grammar and usage, as well as of standard English capitalization, punctuation, and spelling • there **are many errors that disrupt** the reader's understanding of the text • **does not include** vocabulary that is appropriate to the topic (vocabulary about sports; accurate vocabulary for writing a thesis statement and a convincing argument; a variety of phrases and clauses that tie key ideas together)

Questions

Text Structure

1. Explain the purpose of this introduction to Jonathan Vaughters's essay. Did Vaughters write the introduction? Identify clues that indicate whether Vaughters is the author.

Words and Phrases in Context

2. What is the meaning of *prestigious* in **paragraph 2**? Use context clues to determine its meaning.

"Confessions of a Doper"

by Jonathan Vaughters

¶1 ***Baseball great Barry Bonds, track star Marion Jones, and now cyclist Lance Armstrong: These superstar athletes have all been disgraced in doping scandals.***

¶2 ***Armstrong was not only a cycling legend, but also an inspiration because he had overcome cancer. In August, after 13 years of denying he'd used any performance-enhancing drugs, he announced that he'd stop fighting charges of illegal doping. His decision means he will be stripped of his seven titles in the Tour de France, cycling's most prestigious event, and barred from competitive cycling for life.***

¶3 ***Doping isn't limited to professional sports. While the use of performance-enhancing drugs among college and high school athletes is believed to be decreasing, it remains a serious problem. In the last few years, sports leagues at all levels have tried to address the issue, tightening rules and increasing penalties for doping.***

¶4 ***In this essay, former professional cyclist and doper Jonathan Vaughters explains why athletes take drugs and what could be done to stop it.***

Words to Know

disgraced: *(v.)* shamed; dishonored.

doping: *(n.)* using steroids or other performance-enhancing drugs to do better in sports

¶5 Why does an athlete dope? I know why, because I faced that choice.

¶6 My life on a bike started in middle school. At 5:30 every morning, I popped out of bed with excitement and purpose. Into the dark, freezing Colorado morning I rode. For the next 30 miles, I pushed my heart rate and the pedals as high and as fast as they would go.

¶7 These early rides make up many of my memories from my teenage years during the 1980s: the crashes, the adrenaline, and the discipline of training every day.

¶8 But the most vivid memory from those rides was how I dreamed. As I sped through suburban Denver, in my mind I was climbing the great alpine passes of the Tour de France. Erased from my head were the bullies at school, the money troubles at home, and the fact that no one wanted to go to homecoming with me. I decided there was no amount of hard work, suffering, discipline, and sacrifice that would keep me from achieving this dream.

¶9 Achieving childhood dreams is a hard road. First, there is the physical effort of riding 20,000 miles a year for 10 straight years to get within spitting distance of ever riding the Tour de France. Then comes the strain on your family. Next, the loss of friends and social contact. While most of my friends were at prom, I was in bed early for a race the next day. And while most kids went on to college, I went to a cold-water apartment in Spain, hoping to make it big.

Words to Know

discipline: *(n.)* activity or exercise that improves a skill

sacrifice: *(n.)* the giving up of things you value or enjoy in order to focus on something else

Questions

Text Structure

3. Why does Vaughters begin his essay with a question?

Key Ideas and Details

4. Identify author's perspective in this essay. What qualifies Jonathan Vaughters to write about this topic? What informs his perspective on doping?

Key Ideas and Details

5. How does Vaughters support the claim that "achieving childhood dreams is a hard road"? Describe the physical and emotional challenges he faced.

Questions

Words and Phrases in Context

6. Why does the author use the simile *solid as concrete* to describe a top athlete's resolve?

Key Ideas and Details

7. Why does the author provide examples from multiple sports to illustrate "how much . . . that last 2 percent" really matters?

Words and Phrases in Context

8. Why did Vaughters decide to dope? Examine the language he uses to describe the probable outcome of choosing not to dope. How do his word choices appeal to readers' sympathy?

¶**10** People who end up living their dreams are not necessarily those who are lucky and gifted, but those who are stubborn, resolute, and willing to sacrifice. Now imagine you've paid the dues, you've done the work, you've got the talent, and your resolve is as solid as concrete. At that point, the dream is 98 percent complete, but there is that last little bit you need to become great.

¶**11** Then, just short of finally living your childhood dream, you are told either straight-out or implicitly, by some coaches, mentors, even the boss—that you aren't going to make it, unless you cheat. Doping can be that last 2 percent.

¶**12** How much does that last 2 percent really matter? In elite athletics, 2 percent of time or power or strength is an eternity. It's the difference between running 100 meters in 9.8 seconds and 10 seconds. In swimming it's the difference between first and ninth place in the 100-meter breast stroke. And in the Tour de France, 2 percent is the difference between first and 100th place in overall time. If you "just said no" back when the antidoping regulations weren't enforced, then you were deciding to end your dream, because you could not be competitive.

¶**13** The choice to kiss your childhood dream goodbye or live with a dishonest heart is horrid. I chose to lie over killing my dream. I chose to dope. I am sorry for that decision, and I deeply regret it.

Words to Know

implicitly: *(adv.)* not directly or openly

regulations: *(n.)* rules or laws

enforced: *(v.)* put into force; not allowed to be broken or ignored.

¶**14** When I was racing in the 1990s and early 2000s, the rules were easily circumvented—and if you wanted to be competitive, you first had to keep up. This environment is what we must work to prevent. It destroys dreams. It destroys our finest athletes.

¶**15** Since then, huge strides have been made to rid sports of doping. Antidoping enforcement is 1,000 percent better than in my era of competition, and that brings me great satisfaction. But we must support these efforts even more.

¶**16** Athletes must know, without doubt, that they will have a fair chance by competing clean. Every sport at every level—from middle school on up to the pros—should strictly enforce antidoping rules to give our young athletes a level playing field.

¶**17** Let's put our effort and resources into making sports fair so that no athlete ever again faces the decision I faced. We put so much emotion into marketing and idolizing athletes; let's put that same zeal into giving them what they really want: the ability to live their dreams without compromising their morals.

Questions

Key Ideas and Details

9. According to Vaughters, what needs to happen to stop athletes from doping? What does he claim "destroys dreams" and "destroys our finest athletes"?

Writing

10. Summarize this essay, providing Vaughters's reasons for doping and his proposed solution to the problem of doping in sports.

Words to Know

circumvented: *(v.)* broken or gotten around

level playing field: *(n.)* a metaphor for a situation in which everyone has an equal chance to succeed

zeal: *(n.)* passion and enthusiasm

Questions

Text Structure

1. What is a ballad? Locate features that identify "Casey at the Bat" as an example of narrative poetry.

Words and Phrases in Context

2. How does the author use a metaphor to explain the situation that the "Mudville nine" were in as a "sickly silence fell upon" their fans?

Literary Analysis

3. How does the author build excitement and suspense as the fans wait to see if Casey gets to bat?

"Casey at the Bat"

by Ernest L. Thayer

The outlook wasn't brilliant for the Mudville nine that day;
The score stood four to two with but one inning more to play.
And then when Cooney died at first, and Barrows did the same,
A sickly silence fell upon the patrons of the game.

A straggling few got up to go in deep despair. The rest
Clung to that hope which springs eternal in the human breast;
They thought if only Casey could get but a whack at that—
We'd put up even money now with Casey at the bat.

But Flynn preceded Casey, as did also Jimmy Blake,
And the former was a lulu and the latter was a cake;
So upon that stricken multitude grim melancholy sat,
For there seemed but little chance of Casey's getting to the bat.

But Flynn let drive a single, to the wonderment of all,
And Blake, the much despised, tore the cover off the ball;
And when the dust had lifted, and the men saw what had occurred,
There was Jimmy safe at second and Flynn a-hugging third.

Then from 5,000 throats and more there rose a lusty yell;
It rumbled through the valley, it rattled in the dell;
It knocked upon the mountain and recoiled upon the flat,
For Casey, mighty Casey, was advancing to the bat.

There was ease in Casey's manner as he stepped into his place;
There was pride in Casey's bearing and a smile on Casey's face.
And when, responding to the cheers, he lightly doffed his hat,
No stranger in the crowd could doubt 'twas Casey at the bat.

Ten thousand eyes were on him as he rubbed his hands with dirt;
Five thousand tongues applauded when he wiped them on his shirt.
Then while the writhing pitcher ground the ball into his hip,
Defiance gleamed in Casey's eye, a sneer curled Casey's lip.

And now the leather-covered sphere came hurtling through the air,
And Casey stood a-watching it in haughty grandeur there.
Close by the sturdy batsman the ball unheeded sped—
"That ain't my style," said Casey. "Strike one," the umpire said.

From the benches, black with people, there went up a muffled roar,
Like the beating of the storm-waves on a stern and distant shore.
"Kill him! Kill the umpire!" shouted someone on the stand;
And it's likely they'd have killed him had not Casey raised his hand.

With a smile of Christian charity great Casey's visage shone;
He stilled the rising tumult; he bade the game go on;
He signaled to the pitcher, and once more the spheroid flew;
But Casey still ignored it, and the umpire said, "Strike two."

"Fraud!" cried the maddened thousands, and echo answered fraud;
But one scornful look from Casey and the audience was awed.
They saw his face grow stern and cold, they saw his muscles strain,
And they knew that Casey wouldn't let that ball go by again.

The sneer is gone from Casey's lip, his teeth are clenched in hate;
He pounds with cruel violence his bat upon the plate.
And now the pitcher holds the ball, and now he lets it go,
And now the air is shattered by the force of Casey's blow.

Oh, somewhere in this favored land the sun is shining bright;
The band is playing somewhere, and somewhere hearts are light,
And somewhere men are laughing, and somewhere children shout;
But there is no joy in Mudville—mighty Casey has struck out.

Questions

Literary Analysis

4. How does Casey's manner change from the moment he comes to bat until he strikes out? What point is the poet making about an athlete's performance?

Writing

5. Create a summary that a sports reporter could use to write an article about the game described in "Casey at the Bat."

Literature Circle Leveled Novels

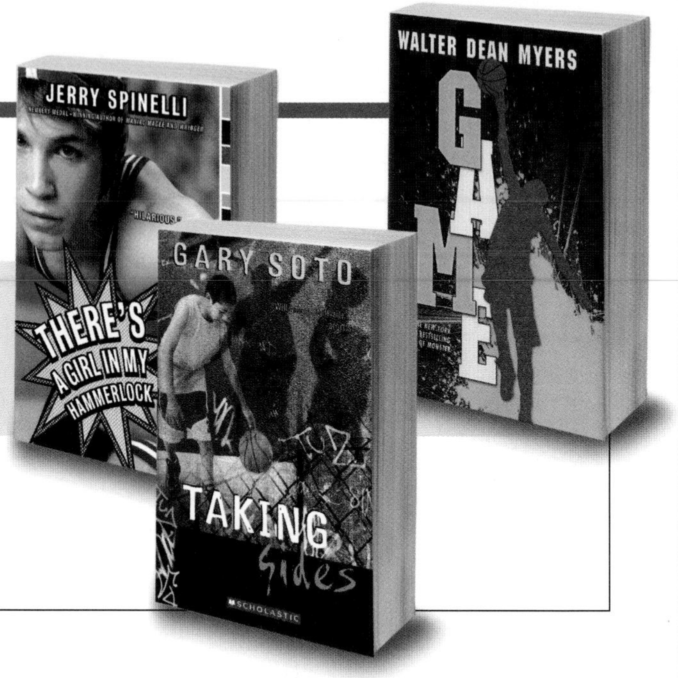

There's a Girl in My Hammerlock *by Jerry Spinelli*
When Maisie Potter decides to join the wrestling team at her school, she faces opposition from the coach, her best friend, and other students. Can she win a match and fit in on the team? **Lexile**® measure: 520L

Taking Sides *by Gary Soto*
When Lincoln Mendoza moves from his tough Mexican-American neighborhood into an affluent, mostly white suburb, his loyalties are tested. The big game between his old and new schools is coming up, and Lincoln must decide which side he is on. **Lexile**® measure: 750L

Game *By Walter Dean Myers*
Game: Drew has plenty of it, and he hopes his skills can carry him to the pros. But his confidence begins to waver when Tomas, a Czech newcomer, becomes the center of the coach's plans. Soon, Drew begins to realize that there are bigger games than the ones played on the court. **Lexile**® measure: 800L

Fiction, Nonfiction, and Novels

Heart of a Champion *by Carl Deuker.* Seth Barham, a boy who lost his father, learns about baseball, friendship, and coping with loss when he begins to play baseball with Jimmy Winters and his father. **Lexile**® measure: 650L

Sports Shorts *by Joseph Bruchac, et al.* This anthology collects sports-related short stories that most students will be able to relate to. **Lexile**® measure: 880L

And Nobody Got Hurt!: The World's Weirdest, Wackiest True Sports Stories *by Len Berman.* Read about the most bizarre-but-true stories in sports history, written by an Emmy Award–winning sportscaster. **Lexile**® measure: 960L

Stotan! *by Chris Crutcher.* Four members of the high school swim team find that more than just their physical abilities are put to the test during a week-long endurance challenge. **Lexile**® measure: 1020L

Game On *by Tom Farrey.* An insightful exploration of an intensifying youth sports landscape. Go to http://www.tomfarrey.com/farrey-reading-groups.htm to arrange a discussion of the book's themes with the author.

Knights of the Hill Country *by Tim Tharp.* Hampton Green, star linebacker of his high-school football team, carries the weight of the town's hopes for the football season on his shoulders, along with changes at home.

Sports Best Short Stories *by Paul D. Staudohar.* Twenty-four short stories from some of the world's best writers tell heart-pounding, nail-biting stories of what happens when players take to the field, court, track, rink, etc.

Sports Illustrated for Kids: The Amazing World of Sports *by Editors of Sports Illustrated.* Students can see some of the most incredible photographs in sports in this book.

Films and TV

Bend It Like Beckham (20th Century Fox, 2002) Jess is an Indian girl born in England who wants nothing more than to become a soccer star like David Beckham, despite the fact that her family does not approve. (112 min.)

Cool Runnings (Walt Disney, 1993) Based on a true story, this movie tells the story of how a team of Jamaican sportsmen go on to compete as a bobsled team in the 1988 Winter Olympics. (98 min.)

Hoosiers (MGM, 1986) Watch as the Hickory Huskers, a basketball team from a tiny Indiana high school, beat the odds to make it all the way to the state championship. (114 min.)

Invincible (Buena Vista, 2006) Watch the true story of Vince Papale unfold. Vince beats the odds when he shows up to an open audition for his hometown NFL team and lands a spot on the team. (104 min.)

Miracle (Walt Disney, 2004) This movie tells the true story of the U.S. hockey team's historic victory over the Soviet team in the 1980 Olympic Games. (136 min.)

Remember the Titans (Walt Disney, 2000) In an effort to integrate a high school in Virginia in 1971, an African-American coach is brought in, demoting the beloved coach to assistant. Together, they must lead their team to victory. (114 min.)

Rudy (Sony, 1993) Rudy is determined to play football for Notre Dame, despite people telling him he's not good enough, smart enough, or big enough. Nothing can stop Rudy from achieving his dream. (116 min.)

We Are Marshall (Warner, 2006) When the football team at Marshall University is wiped out in a place crash, Jack Lengyel takes on the job of rebuilding the program with inexperienced players. Based on a true story. (131 min.)

Websites

Guinness World Records: Gamer's Edition Browse through world records, read about the people who set them, and see videos of the record holders.

The National Baseball Hall of Fame and Museum Look up information about your favorite Hall of Famer or find news articles related to baseball.

Olympic.org Find information on current and past Olympic games on this official Web site of the Olympic Movement.

Sports Illustrated for Kids This site includes plenty of up-to-date stories on students' favorite sports, along with activities and games.

Magazines

Baseball Youth In this baseball magazine for teens, students will find interviews with baseball stars, as well as interesting stories and news about baseball.

ESPN, The Magazine Find photographs, previews, reviews, interviews, and other related coverage of the sports world.

Inside Gymnastics Keep up with the most current news in the sport of gymnastics, including competition and tournament coverage, and analysis and interviews.

UNIT 3

YOUR VOTE! YOUR RIGHTS!

How do people express opinions in meaningful ways?

Unit Introduction

Through drama and poetry, discover how authors use characters' conflicts to express perspectives about democracy, government by the people.

In an excerpt from the drama "Twelve Angry Men" by Reginald Rose, twelve jurors deliberate on a verdict. This classic jury-room drama follows the jury's decision making in a murder trial.

Two poems called "Democracy," one by Sara Holbrook and one by Langston Hughes, present different perspectives on the role of the individual. One speaker follows society's rules. The other speaker protests accepted beliefs about democracy.

WRITING PERFORMANCE TASK

Compare and contrast two writers' perspectives on democracy. Analyze the strategies they use to convey their perspectives.

PLAY EXCERPT/POETRY

from **"Twelve Angry Men"**
by Reginald Rose

Language
- Academic Vocabulary
- Word Study: Context Clues

Reading a Play
- Identify Evidence
- Key Ideas and Details
- Craft and Structure

"Democracy"
by Langston Hughes

"Democracy"
by Sara Holbrook

Language
- Academic Vocabulary
- Word Study: Word Families

Reading Poetry
- Identify Evidence
- Key Ideas and Details
- Craft and Structure

SPEAKING AND LISTENING

Present a Speech
- Collaborate and Present

Checklist: Speech
- Scoring Guide

WRITING

Writing: Informative Essay
- Read the Model
- Analyze the Model
- Gather Evidence
- Organize Ideas
- Language Study: Use Concise Language
- Conventions Study: Transitions
- Revise, Edit, and Publish
- Performance Task Rubric

EXTENDED READINGS

Speech
"Ain't I a Woman?"
by Sojourner Truth

Op-Ed
"Telling Americans to Vote, or Else" by William A. Galston

Academic Vocabulary

from "Twelve Angry Men" by Reginald Rose

Rate your understanding of each word. Then read its meaning and write a sample sentence.

Word	Meaning	Example
reasonable (*adj.*) p. 100 ① ② ③ ④	fair and sensible	
impression (*n.*) p. 100 ① ② ③ ④		It's important to leave a good first impression on a first date or interview.
drive (*n.*) p. 100 ① ② ③ ④	a strong desire for success	
customary (*adj.*) p. 101 ① ② ③ ④	according to the customs or usual practices of a society	
preliminary (*adj.*) p. 101 ① ② ③ ④	happening before something that is more important, often in order to prepare for it	
accused (*n.*) p. 101 ① ② ③ ④	a person who is charged with a crime	
resumes (*v.*) p. 102 ① ② ③ ④	to go back to the seat, place, or position where you were before	

Rating Scale | ① I don't know the word. ② I've seen it or heard it. ③ I know its meaning. ④ I know it and use it.

Word Study

Context Clues

Context clues are words in a text that help you figure out the meaning of an unfamiliar word. Sometimes words are defined in the text or meaning is suggested.

The sentences below are from Rose's play. Find the context clues to determine the meaning of the bold words.

1. 7th JUROR: . . .[*He turns to the* **FOREMAN.**] Where do you want us to sit?
   FOREMAN: Well, I was thinking we ought to sit in order . . .

2. 12th JUROR: What was your impression of the prosecuting attorney? . . . I thought he was really **sharp**. I mean, the way he hammered his points home, one by one, in logical sequence. It takes a good brain to do that. I was very impressed.

from

TWELVE ANGRY MEN

by Reginald Rose

Characters	
1st Juror (Foreman)	8th Juror
2nd Juror	9th Juror
3rd Juror	10th Juror
4th Juror	11th Juror
5th Juror	12th Juror
6th Juror	Guard
7th Juror	Judge's Voice
Setting	
The jury room on a New York Court of Law	
Time	
1957	

FOREMAN: All right, gentlemen. Let's take seats.

7TH JUROR [*to the* **2ND JUROR**]: This better be fast. I got tickets to a ball game tonight. Yankees– Cleveland. We got this new kid pitching, Modjelewski, or whatever his name is. He's a bull, this kid. [*He shoots his hand forward and out to indicate the path of a curve ball.*] Shhooooom. A real jug handle. *There is no reaction at all from the* **2ND JUROR**.
You're quite a ball fan, aren't you? [*He turns to the* **FOREMAN.**] Where do you want us to sit?

Words to Know

<u>he's a bull, this kid</u>: *(metaphor)* strong, skilled baseball player

<u>A real jug handle</u>: *(metaphor)* he throws a good curve ball

Close Reading

Text Structure

1. Describe which details on this page let you know this text is a drama. Who are the characters? What can you tell about the setting?

Words and Phrases in Context

2. The 7th juror says, "This better be fast. I got tickets to a ball game tonight." What does this tell you about how he feels about his role as a juror?

Drama

A **drama** is a story written in play format performed for an audience.
A drama has several elements:
a cast of characters, scenes, setting, dialogue with speaker tags, and stage directions.

Close Reading

Writing

3. Describe what the following characters are doing and thinking about: the foreman, the 7th juror, and the 12th juror.

The foreman is ____, which he shows by ____. The 7th juror is ____, which he shows by ____. The 12th juror is ____, which he shows by ____.

Literary Analysis

4. Use the stage directions ("sits on chair 10," "continues to stare out the window," "is still in the lavatory") in lines 14–16 to describe the setting.

Words and Phrases in Context

5. Determine the connotations of the adjectives that the jurors use to describe the prosecutor in lines 20–24 ("sharp," "logical," "good," and "expert.")

Connotation

Connotation is the feeling or emotion associated with a word.

FOREMAN: Well, I was thinking we ought to sit in order, by jury numbers. [*He points with each number.*] Two, three, four, and so on, if that's OK with you gentlemen?

10th JUROR: What's the difference?

4th JUROR: I think it's **reasonable** to sit according to number.

10th JUROR [*rising*]**:** Let it be. [*He moves and sits on chair 10.*] *The* JURORS *begin to take their seats. The* 8TH JUROR *continues to stare out of the window. The* 9TH JUROR *is still in the lavatory.*

12th JUROR [*to the* 11TH JUROR]**:** What was your **impression** of the prosecuting attorney?

11TH JUROR [*with a German accent*]**:** I beg pardon?

12TH JUROR: I thought he was really sharp. I mean, the way he hammered his points home, one by one, in logical sequence. It takes a good brain to do that. I was very impressed.

11TH JUROR: Yes, I think he did an expert job.

12TH JUROR: I mean, he had a lot of **drive**, too. Real drive.

7TH JUROR: OK, let's get this show on the road.

FOREMAN [*to the* 8TH JUROR]**:** How about sitting down?

The 8TH JUROR *does not hear the* FOREMAN. The gentleman at the window.

The 8TH JUROR *turns, startled.*

How about sitting down?

Words and Phrases to Know

prosecuting attorney: *(n.)* a lawyer who tries to prove that the person charged with a crime is guilty

hammered his points home: *(idiom)* he supported his ideas one-by-one, as a hammer hits nails

let's get this show on the road: *(idiom)* something that you say in order to tell people you want to start an activity

8TH JUROR: Oh, I'm sorry. [*He moves to his chair and sits.*]

The 9TH JUROR *enters the washroom from the lavatory and washes his hands.*

10TH JUROR [*across the table to the* 4TH JUROR]**:** It's pretty tough to figure, isn't it? A kid kills his father. Bing! Just like that.

12TH JUROR: Well, if you analyze the figures . . .

10TH JUROR: What figures? It's those people! I'm tellin' you they let the kids run wild up there. Well, maybe it serves 'em right. Know what I mean? *The* FOREMAN *crosses to the washroom door.*

7TH JUROR [*to the* 5TH JUROR]**:** Hey, you a Yankee fan?

5TH JUROR: No. Milwaukee.

7TH JUROR: Milwaukee! That's like being hit on the head with a crowbar once a day. Listen, who they got–I'm asking you, who they got besides great grounds keepers?

FOREMAN: All right. Now you gentlemen can handle this any way you want to. I mean, I'm not going to have any rules. If we want to discuss first and then vote, that's one way. Or we can vote right now to see how we stand. [*He pauses and looks around.*] Well, that's all I have to say.

4TH JUROR: I think it's **customary** to take a **preliminary** vote.

7TH JUROR: Yeah, let's vote. Who knows, maybe we can all go home.

FOREMAN: It's up to you. Just let's remember we've got a first degree murder charge here. If we vote "guilty," we send the **accused** to the electric chair. That's mandatory.

4TH JUROR: I think we all know that.

Words and Phrases to Know

crowbar: *(n.)* a metal bar that has a thin flat edge at one end and is used to open or lift things; sometimes used as a weapon

grounds keepers: *(n.)* workers who keep the ballpark well-groomed

to see how we stand: *(idiom)* to hear people's opinion about a topic

Close Reading

Literary Analysis

6. How seriously is the 7th juror taking his responsibility to decide this case? Use evidence from **lines 39–43** and **line 49** to explain.

Literary Analysis

7. Why does the 7th juror say "A kid kills his father. Bing! Just like that" in **line 34**?

Onomatopoeia

Onomatopoeia is the use of words that sound like the things they represent, such as *buzz* or *rattle*.

Words and Phrases in Context

8. What is the meaning of the word *charge* in **line 51**?

Writing

9. Reflect on the role of a jury in a democracy. What do they decide?

In a democracy, a jury decides ____.

Close Reading

Literary Analysis

10. Why does the 8th juror say "I guess we talk" in **line 70**? What evidence in the play indicates to you that the 8th juror would vote "not guilty" in **line 64**?

Words and Phrases in Context

11. Define *man* as used in **line 77**. Why does the 8th juror emphasize the word *man*? Why does he question the 3rd juror's statement, "The man's a dangerous killer," in **line 76**?

3RD JUROR: Come on, let's vote.

10TH JUROR: Yeah, let's see who's where.

FOREMAN: Anybody doesn't want to vote? [*He looks around.*] *The others are silent.*

All right. This has to be a twelve-to-nothing vote either way. That's the law. OK, are we ready? All those voting "guilty" raise your hands.

Seven or eight hands go up immediately. Several others go up more slowly. Everyone looks around the table as the FOREMAN *rises and begins to count hands.*

The 9TH JUROR's *hand goes up now, and all hands are raised except* **the 8TH JUROR's**. . . . Nine–ten–eleven. That's eleven for "guilty." OK. "Not guilty?"

The 8TH JUROR *slowly raises his hand.*

One. Right. OK, eleven to one--"guilty." Now we know where we are. [*He* ***resumes*** *his seat.*]

10TH JUROR: Boy-oh-boy! There's always one.

7TH JUROR [*after a pause*]**:** So, what do we do now?

8TH JUROR: Well, I guess we talk.

10TH JUROR: Boy-oh-boy!

3RD JUROR [*leaning over to the 8TH JUROR*]**:** Well, look, do you really think he's innocent?

8TH JUROR: I don't know.

3RD JUROR: I mean, let's be reasonable. You sat in court and heard the same things we did. The man's a dangerous killer. You could see it.

8TH JUROR: The man! He's sixteen years old.

3RD JUROR: Well, that's old enough. He knifed his own father. Four inches in the chest.

Words to Know

let's see who's where: *(idiom)* let's see who thinks what about a topic

6TH JUROR [*to the* 8TH JUROR]: It's pretty obvious. I mean, I was convinced from the first day.

3RD JUROR: Well, who wasn't? [*To the* 8TH JUROR.] I really think this is one of those open and shut things. They proved it a dozen different ways. Would you like me to list them for you?

8TH JUROR: No.

10TH JUROR: Then what do you want?

8TH JUROR: Nothing, I just want to talk.

7TH JUROR: Well, what's there to talk about? Eleven men here agree. Nobody had to think twice about it, except you.

10TH JUROR: I want to ask you something. Do you believe his story?

"Twelve Angry Men" *was performed during April 2010 at Raven Theatre in Chicago.*

Words to Know

one of those open and shut things: *(idiom)* if a legal case or problem is open and shut, the facts are very clear and it is easy to make a decision or find a solution

Close Reading

Literary Analysis

12. In **lines 80–81**, the 6th juror announces that he was "convinced" of the accused person's guilt "from the first day." What does that say about the juror's attitude toward the duties of a juror?

Writing

13. Compare and contrast the 8th juror's and the 3rd juror's perspectives about how obvious the accused's guilt is.

The 8th juror believes ___. He shows this by mentioning ___. However, the 3rd juror believes ___.

Perspective

Perspective is a personal opinion or attitude about something.

Close Reading

Literary Analysis

14. Explain how the 8th juror is defending his position. Provide textural evidence.

Literary Analysis

15. Explain the effect of the 7th juror saying "You couldn't change my mind if you talked for a hundred years" in **lines 97–98** and "suppose this whole building fell on my head in **lines 102–103**?

Hyperbole

Hyperbole is an obvious exaggeration or overstatement.

8TH JUROR: I don't know whether I believe it or not. Maybe I don't.

7TH JUROR: So what'd you vote "not guilty" for?

8TH JUROR: There were eleven votes for "guilty." It's not easy for me to raise my hand and send a boy off to die without talking about it first.

7TH JUROR: Who says it's easy for me?

8TH JUROR: No one.

7TH JUROR: What, just because I voted fast? I think the guy's guilty. You couldn't change my mind if you talked for a hundred years.

8TH JUROR: I'm not trying to change your mind. It's just that we're talking about somebody's life here. I mean, we can't decide in five minutes. <u>Suppose</u> we're wrong?

7TH JUROR: Suppose we're wrong! Suppose this whole building fell on my head. You can suppose anything.

8TH JUROR: That's right.

7TH JUROR [*after a pause*]**:** What's the difference how long it takes? We honestly think he's guilty. So suppose we finish in five minutes? So what?

Words to Know

<u>suppose</u>: *(v.)* to think of (something) as happening or being true in order to imagine what might happen; consider, imagine

8TH JUROR: Let's take an hour. The ball game doesn't start till eight o'clock.

7TH JUROR [*smiling*]**:** OK, slugger, be my guest. *There is a silence.*

FOREMAN [*hesitantly*]**:** Well, who's got something to say?

He looks at the 2ND JUROR. How about you?

2nd JUROR: Not me.

9TH JUROR: I'm willing to give it an hour.

You can share the claustrophobia of the 12 men sitting in a cramped jury room on a hot summer day in July.

Words to Know

slugger: *(n.)* someone who hits someone or something hard

Close Reading

Literary Analysis

16. In **line 113**, the 9th juror says, "I'm willing to give it an hour." What has his participation on the jury been so far?

Writing

17. In this section, all of the jurors are talking directly to the 8th juror, and some are becoming argumentative, such as when the 7th juror says, "Who says it's easy for me?" Describe the mood and how the author creates it in this section.

To sum up, the mood in this section is ___. The ___ mood is illustrated by ___.

Mood

The mood is the overall atmosphere the author creates in a story. It is the feeling a reader gets from reading. Authors create a mood through word choices, descriptive details, dialogue, and sensory language.

Identify Evidence | Analyze Individuals, Events, and Ideas

What does this excerpt from **"Twelve Angry Men"** reveal about Rose's perspective on democracy?

How does he use his characters' dialogue and actions to introduce, illustrate, elaborate, and explore conflicting ideas about democracy and our judicial system?

- As you read, use the Evidence column to record examples from the text that reveal Rose's perspective on democracy.
- In the Explanation column, explain how the evidence introduces, illustrates, or elaborates ideas about democracy and our judicial system.

Evidence	Source	Page	Explanation
1. **12th JUROR:** What was your impression of the prosecuting attorney? . . . I thought he was really sharp. I mean, the way he hammered his points home in a logical sequence. It takes a good brain to do that. I was very impressed.	12th juror	100	The 12th juror's perspective shows that the jurors, even in a murder trial, can be affected by the skill of the attorneys rather than the facts of the case.
2. **7TH JUROR:** OK, let's get this show on the road.	7th juror	100	The 7th juror shows that some people who serve on a jury want to finish the case quickly so that they can get back to their regular lives. (The 7th juror previously mentioned a baseball game.)
3. **10th JUROR** [across the table to the 4TH JUROR]**:** It's pretty tough to figure, isn't it? A kid kills his father. Bing! Just like that.	10th juror	101	
4. **FOREMAN:** . . . Just let's remember we've got a first degree murder charge here. If we vote guilty we send the accused to the electric chair. That's mandatory. . . . This has to be a twelve-to-nothing vote either way. That's the law.	foreman	101	

Evidence	Source	Page	Explanation
5.	stage directions	102	
6.	3rd juror	102	
7.	8th juror	102	
8.	3rd juror	103	
9.	8th juror	104	

Key Ideas and Details

Determining the Central Idea

1. Use the evidence you collected to summarize the key idea of this excerpt from Rose's play.

2. List the three characters that appear in this excerpt. Explain how each character's words and actions help to develop the central idea.

Character	Importance to Central Idea
Foreman	The foreman takes his role seriously in making sure that the jury follows the rules for deciding the case, and that the jury members know the effect their decision will have on the accused.

Craft and Structure

Structure of the Play

1. Use a T-chart to examine stage directions and what they teach us about a character.

Stage Directions	Observations

Perspective

2. Explain what each character in this excerpt from "Twelve Angry Men" believes about democracy and justice in America. Provide textual evidence.

Character	Perspective	Examples

3. Describe the advantages and disadvantages of presenting this story as a drama, with no narrator.

4. Based on the author's depictions of each character, what is the author's perspective on democracy and inequality.

Academic Vocabulary

"Democracy" by Langston Hughes and "Democracy" by Sara Holbrook

Rate your understanding of each word. Then read its meaning and write a sample sentence.

Word	Meaning	Example
compromise *(v.)* p. 111 ① ② ③ ④	to reach an agreement	
procedure *(n.)* p. 114 ① ② ③ ④	a way of doing something	
privilege *(n.)* p. 114 ① ② ③ ④	a special advantage or benefit given only to one person or group	
reluctant *(adj.)* p. 114 ① ② ③ ④		My brother is often reluctant to stop playing video games and do his homework.
self-conscious *(adj.)* p. 115 ① ② ③ ④	worried and embarrassed about what you look like or what other people think of you; aware of one's self	
embrace *(v.)* p. 115 ① ② ③ ④	to contain or include	
retreat *(v.)* p. 115 ① ② ③ ④	to move away from something or someone	

Rating Scale ① I don't know the word. ② I've seen it or heard it. ③ I know its meaning. ④ I know it and use it.

Word Study

Word Family

A **word family** is a group of words that share the same base word and have related meanings. Word webs help you visualize how to find base words.

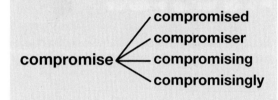

compromise → **compromised**, **compromiser**, **compromising**, **compromisingly**

Complete each sentence using the correct word form from the *compromise* word family.

1. **We accepted a ___________ in order to avoid a fight.**
2. **Ruby and Clara ____________ and split the last slice of pizza.**
3. **Henry Clay is known in history as "The Great ____________."**
4. **It was a difficult task to get the politicians to ______________ agree.**
5. **Henry is tired of ____________ with Francine, so he broke up with her.**

DEMOCRACY

by Langston Hughes

Democracy will not come
Today, this year
Nor ever
Through ***compromise*** *and fear.*
I have as much right
As the other fellow has
To stand
On my two feet
And own the land.

Poet Langston Hughes

Close Reading

Literary Analysis

1. Identify who the "other fellow" represents in **line 6**.

Literary Analysis

2. Define the idiomatic phrase "To stand On my two feet" in **lines 7–8**.

Idiom

An **idiom** is a phrase or expression that has a meaning different from the meaning of the individual words. Read the entire phrase in context to help you figure out the meaning.

Close Reading

Writing

3. Explain what **lines 20–21** mean. How do these lines explain why the narrator is tired of hearing that he should "let things take their course"?

The narrator is tired of hearing ___ because ___.

Literary Analysis

4. Describe Hughes's theme.

Theme

Theme is a message about life or human nature that the author wants the reader to understand.

I <u>tire</u> so of hearing people say,
<u>Let things take their course.</u>
Tomorrow is another day.
I do not need my freedom when I'm dead.
I cannot live on tomorrow's bread.
Freedom
Is a strong seed
Planted
In a great need.
I live here, too.
I want freedom
Just as you.

Words to Know

<u>tire</u>: *(v.)* to become tired of, or bored or impatient with, something

<u>let things take their course</u>: *(idiom)* to allow events to happen on their own, without trying to change, affect, or control them

Democracy

by Sara Holbrook

My office is government issue.
The basics, one metal desk, one chair, a stack of folders,
four rubber stamps and a whole lot of paper
in need of baling wire, or a match.
A gray office beside a multicolored room
full of folks waiting on government basics.

Thump.
Thump.
A large woman thumps, thumps.
Thumps past my office.
Thump. Thump, down the hall to the ladies room.
Sounds of running water, a squeaky door slaps against
the wall and oozes toward a bumpy close.
Thump. Thump. I look up as she passes again.
Dark hallway.
Dark clothing.
White toilet paper.
Thump. Thump.
I watch after her passing.
Thump. Thump.
She stole the toilet paper.
Also government issue, two rolls per day.

Words to Know

basics: *(n.)* necessary items, such as office supplies at work, or food and shelter to live

Close Reading

Literary Analysis

1. Describe the narrator. Provide textual evidence from the first stanza.

Imagery

Imagery is the use of descriptive words and phrases to create pictures in the reader's mind.

Text Structure

2. Explain the effect of the short one- or two-word sentences such as "thump," "Dark hallway," and "Dark clothing."

Onomatopoeia

Onomatopoeia is the use of words that sound like the things they represent, such as *buzz, click,* or *rattle.*

Close Reading

Writing

3. Interpret what the narrator means in **lines 24–26** and **lines 27–29**.

Lines 24–26 mean ___ as revealed by ___. Lines 27–29 mean ___ as shown by ___. The author uses these lines to convey ___.

Text Structure

4. Explain the effect of alliteration in **lines 25–26**.

Alliteration

Alliteration is the repeated use of words that share the same beginning sound, such as "branches full of bright blue blossoms."

Writing

5. Interpret what the narrator means by the phrase "go once more against the mountain" in **line 39**. What feeling does this use of this metaphor create?

The narrator feels ___, as revealed by ___.

Metaphor

A **metaphor** is a comparison of two things without using *like* or *as*, as in "Lucy was a walking encyclopedia."

Issued by the same government that will
murder a mountain of forest for the confusion
of paper it takes to purchase a pencil through
proper procurement **procedures**.
The same government that offers tax abated housing to
for-profit football teams and levies income tax on
where's-the-profit unemployment compensation.

The same government that issues food stamps for
koolaid, popsicles, and tater tots, but not for toilet paper,
like it's some **privilege** that poor folks don't need.
That same government issues us two rolls per day,
94% of the days since our last 6% cut.
Two rolls.

I rub at the crow's feet, which are deepening into my mother's face.
She stole the toilet paper.
The clock silently mouths that it's just 3:05.
I wait for a moment, **reluctant** to go once more against the mountain,
knowing the thin air makes me lightheaded.
Finally I move.

Words to Know

abated: *(v.)* to reduce, decrease, lessen

levies: *(v.)* to demand and collect

unemployment compensation: *(n.)* money the government may provide, for a limited time period, to workers who have lost their job

crow's feet: *(n)* figurative term for small wrinkles near the eyes

"Ma'am, did you take our toilet paper?"
She looks straight ahead, two rolls propped on knees flung wide
She is slow to acknowledge my presence,
slow looking up at the **self-conscious** stand I have taken
beside her over-filled chair in this over-filled room.
And then, in a glance, she reminds me that I am too tall,
too thin, too well-dressed, and too bless-ed white.

"I need it," she replies.
And that need, I know, is not entirely selfish,
that need **embraces** the needs of her children,
her grandchildren, maybe a neighbor.

But it does not embrace the needs of the neighbors
with whom she shares this waiting room.
"I have to ask for it back," I say, citing the needs of others.
Reluctant herself, she complies.
Practically speaking, she *is* a republican.

I **retreat** to return the basics to the necessary place,
dizzy with democracy.

Words to Know

acknowledge: *(v.)* to show someone that you have noticed them or heard what they have said

citing: *(v.)* to mention (something) especially as an example or to support an idea or opinion

Close Reading

Literary Analysis

6. Describe the narrator's perspective of the government she works for. Provide textual evidence.

Literary Analysis

7. Explain why the narrator is reluctant to ask for the toilet paper back. Why does she do it anyway?

Connotation

Connotation is the feeling or emotion associated with a word.

Words and Phrases in Context

8. Define the meaning of *complies* as it is used in **line 56**. Which context clues help you to figure out the meaning? What is the connotation of *retreat*?

Writing

9. Summarize the narrator's personal moral dilemma when confronted with poverty and our government's response to it.

The narrator's job is to ____. When she notices ____, the narrator ____. Then she ____.

Identify Evidence | Analyze Individuals, Events, and Ideas

What do these poems reveal about the authors' perspectives on democracy?

How do the authors use imagery, figurative language, and other poetic devices to introduce, illustrate, and elaborate on their ideas about democracy and its flaws and limitations?

- As you read, use the Evidence column to record examples from the text that reveal Hughes's and Holbrook's perspectives on democracy.
- In the Explanation column, explain how the evidence introduces, illustrates, or elaborates on ideas about democracy.

Evidence	Source	Page	Explanation
1. "Democracy will not come Today, this year Nor ever Through **compromise** and fear."	Hughes/ narrator	111	The narrator expresses the perspective that democracy—and the right to participate fully in it—can't come as the result of compromise or intimidation. Until everyone can participate freely, it's not really democracy.
2. "I have as much right As the other fellow has To stand On my two feet And own the land."	Hughes/ narrator	111	
3. "I do not need my freedom when I'm dead. I cannot live on tomorrow's bread."	Hughes/ narrator	112	
4. "I live here, too. I want freedom Just as you."	Hughes/ narrator	112	

Evidence	Source	Page	Explanation
5.			
6.			
7.			
8.			
9.			

Key Ideas and Details

Determining the Central Idea

1. Use the evidence you collected to summarize the key idea of Hughes's poem.

2. Use the evidence you collected to summarize the key idea of Holbrook's poem.

3. List two events from Holbrook's "Democracy." Explain how each event is important to the central idea of the text.

Event	Significance

Craft and Structure

Structure of the Poems

1. Both poets use figurative language, such as imagery, onomatopoeia, alliteration, and metaphor, to represent concepts and express ideas. List some examples of the figurative language found in each poem, and discuss what each example means.

Poem	Figurative Language	Meaning

Narrator's Perspective

2. Using examples from each text, explain how the narrator of each poem views democracy.

Poem	Narrator's Perspective	Examples

Collaborate and Present

Plan and Deliver a Speech

Reginald Rose, Langston Hughes, and Sara Holbrook use drama and poetry to present their perspectives on democracy. What is your perspective on democracy? Why? How was your perspective influenced and supported by the texts you have read in this Unit?

Assignment: Work with a partner to plan and write a two-minute speech justifying your perspective on democracy, supporting it with reasons and with evidence from the texts. Follow the steps below to create a speech and deliver it to the class.

Analyze the Content

1. Consider the following questions:
   - How does each author view democracy? How does text evidence reveal his or her perspective?
   - In what ways does text evidence support—or differ from—your perspective on democracy?
2. Go back to the text and choose at least one piece of evidence per text that supports, or helped shape, your perspective. Create a chart of reasons and text evidence that supports and justifies your perspective of democracy.

My Perspective	Reasons I Think So	Evidence

Write Your Speech

3. Use the items on your reasons and evidence chart as talking points for the body of your speech.
   - Draft your speech on paper or on the computer.
   - Remember to introduce yourself to your audience and add a conclusion.

Present

4. Deliver your speech.

Speech Checklist

Use the checklist below to evaluate your collaboration skills, reasoning, and final presentation. Think carefully about your work. If you know you completed an item thoroughly, give yourself a check (✓).

COLLABORATE AND PRESENT CHECKLIST		
Comprehension & Collaboration	**Evidence & Reasoning**	**Presentation of Knowledge & Ideas**
☐ Come to discussions prepared, having read and studied material. ☐ Refer to evidence when contributing to the discussion. ☐ Follow rules for discussions and lead by example. ☐ Ask and answer specific questions. ☐ Make comments that contribute to the topic under discussion. ☐ Review the key ideas under discussion and demonstrate understanding of multiple perspectives through reflection and paraphrasing.	☐ Explain the purpose of the presentation. ☐ Present information relevant to the task. ☐ Explain your view on democracy. ☐ Include a clear thesis and multiple reasons. ☐ Use at least one example from each text. ☐ Synthesize the key ideas with a conclusion.	☐ Adapt language to a variety of contexts and tasks to demonstrate knowledge of formal English. ☐ Include multimedia components (e.g., graphics, images, music, sound) and visual displays. ☐ Use appropriate volume/tone (clear, not too fast, too slow, or too loud) and avoid using "like" or "ummm." ☐ Have strong posture, a confident stance, and make frequent eye contact. ☐ Occasionally move from one spot to another without fidgeting. ☐ Smile and appear to be relaxed.
Number of ✓s in this category: ___	**Number of ✓s in this category: ___**	**Number of ✓s in this category: ___**
Total # of ✓s: __		

Add up the total number of checks (✓) in each category. Then use the scoring guide below to calculate your final score.

Scoring Guide			
16 to 18 ✓s	**13 to 15 ✓s**	**11 to 12 ✓s**	**10 or less ✓s**
④ Exemplary	**③ Meets Standards**	**② Needs Work**	**① Does Not Meet Standards**

Read the Model

Writers use many strategies to craft ideas and share information. The writer of this informative essay compares and contrasts format and language to show how two authors approach similar topics in different ways. Read and discuss the model essay below.

Informative Essay

An informative essay provides an overview of the key topics and ideas of a text.

The introduction states the title and author of the text that the writer will analyze.

- Describe how the writer introduced the topic.

The two body paragraphs express the writer's main points about the text.

- Find two examples of text citations.
- Find two examples of the writer's use of concise language.

Transition words or phrases organize and link ideas, sentences, and paragraphs.

- Identify transition words and explain their function.

The conclusion sums up or restates the thesis.

- Identify the conclusion.

Two Sides of the Same Point of View

by Latisha Folger

In "Democracy" by Sara Holbrook and "Ain't I a Woman?" by Sojourner Truth, both speakers want equality. However, Holbrook's speaker confides to readers while Truth's speech publicly addresses the issue to a live audience. Although they share the same opinion, the two women speak from opposite sides of society's borders.

"Democracy" tells of people divided. The poem's speaker describes her government office in dull language. She serves a diverse or "multicolored" community, "folks waiting on government services" (Holbrook 113). They deserve more, she thinks, but does not show that in her actions. That is why they view her as an enemy, "too well-dressed" and too white" (Holbrook 115). In the end, the speaker says "I retreat . . ." (Holbrook 115). She feels defeated. Holbrook reveals her point of view that people are divided through her speaker's thoughts and actions.

In "Ain't I a Woman?" Sojourner Truth, a former slave, speaks out against discrimination at a women's convention. In her speech, her voice is full of conviction. A speech contains no private thoughts, so what we read is what she tells the audience. Truth frankly describes brutalities she suffered. Her forceful language joins people in a shared message. She publicly demands her "half measure full" (Truth 132). She has the courage to ask people who enjoy privilege to turn the world "right side up again!" (Truth 133).

Holbrook and Sojourner Truth share a similar point of view. They both want equality. However, Holbrook's poem describes a bad situation with no solution. Truth's speech makes an optimistic demand for change. Using different literary formats, the two women reveal their own perspectives about the importance of equality in a democracy.

Analyze the Model

A compare/contrast essay explains similarities and differences between two texts.

Introduction	
Thesis Statement	

Body	
Topic Sentence Speaker in "Democracy" believes in equality but is unable or unwilling to do anything about it.	**Relevant Evidence**
Topic Sentence	**Relevant Evidence**

Conclusion
Restate and why it matters

Text Strategy

In a **block-by-block comparison,** the writer discusses all the relevant characteristics of one text in the first body paragraph and all the relevant characteristics of the second text in the second body paragraph.

The thesis sentence presents a clear plan for the essay.

- Identify the thesis statement.

The topic sentence of each body paragraph clearly states the main idea of that paragraph.

- Identify the topic sentence of each body paragraph.
- Evaluate whether each topic sentence supports the thesis.

Relevant evidence includes logical reasoning, such as direct quotations from the text, that support the writer's ideas.

- Evaluate whether all sentences in each body paragraph support the topic sentence.

The conclusion sums up or restates the thesis and why it matters.

- Describe how the writer concluded her essay.

Step 1 | Gather Evidence

Compare and contrast two writers' perspectives on democracy. Analyze the strategies they use to convey their perspectives.

What You Need to Know | Examine the evidence you have collected (see pages 106 and 116).

What You Need to Write | Note the key ideas you have drawn based on your evidence. Select the key ideas you will include in your essay.

excerpt from "Twelve Angry Men"

Point:

Evidence:

Page # _____

Point:

Evidence:

Page # _____

Point:

Evidence:

Page # _____

"Democracy" by _________

Point:

Evidence:

Page # _____

Point:

Evidence:

Page # _____

Point:

Evidence:

Page # _____

Step 2 | Organize Ideas

What You Need to Know | When you compare, you describe similarities. When you contrast, you point out differences.

To develop your topic:

1. Describe Rose's perspective and strategies.
2. Describe Hughes's or Holbrook's perspectives and strategies.

What You Need to Write | Determine how the authors' perspectives and strategies are the same and how they are different.

Introduction
Thesis Statement

Body	
Topic Sentence	**Relevant Evidence**
Topic Sentence	**Relevant Evidence**

Conclusion
Restate and why it matters

Step 3 | Draft

Write a draft of your essay on the computer or on paper.

Language Study | Use Concise Language

See It

Good writers present information clearly and in a few words. They use words that make their writing concise, which means brief but comprehensive.

To avoid wordiness, writers:

- use active, not passive voice
- avoid "to be" construction
- avoid wordy expressions

Example	Explanation
Use Active, Not Passive Voice • Passive: The drama "Fences" is written by August Wilson • Active: August Wilson wrote the drama "Fences."	In the passive voice, it takes eight words to say the same thing as six words in the active voice.
Avoid "To Be" Construction • Troy seems to be upset when he finds out that Cory quit his job. • Troy seems upset when he finds out that Cory quit his job.	Remove "to be" when it follows words such as *seems*, *appears*, and *looks* to make a sentence more concise.
Avoid Wordy Expressions • Troy is agitated over Cory's actions, given the fact that Cory didn't keep up with his chores. • Troy is agitated over Cory's actions because Cory didn't keep up with his chores.	The phrase "given the fact that" is a long-winded way of saying *because*. Eliminate wordiness by replacing wordy expressions with concise ones.

Try It

Revise the following sentences. You may use more than one strategy. Choose words that express ideas concisely, recognizing and eliminating wordiness and redundancy.

1. Troy is a good father, who wants what's best for his son, even though sometimes his words appear to be a bit harsh.
2. Cory is upset by Troy.
3. Rose appears to be supportive of Cory.

Apply It | Revise language in your essay to make it more concise.

1. Rewrite any sentences that have a passive voice.

2. Rewrite any sentences that have a "to be" construction.

3. Rewrite any sentences that are wordy.

Writing Tip

Remember that wordiness and length are not necessarily the same. A long sentence can be concise if every word is needed. As you revise your writing, look for unnecessary words to eliminate wordiness.

Wordy Writing	Concise Writing
at that point in time	then
at this point in time	now
there is no doubt that	no doubt
he is a person who	he
in today's world	today
due to the fact that	because
this day and age	today
end result	result
refer back	refer
in order to	to
in spite of the fact	although

Conventions Study | Transition Words and Phrases

See It | Transitions clarify the relationships among ideas and concepts.

Comparing	Contrasting
equally, in the same way, similarly, likewise, as with, like, compared with, in the same fashion	whereas, instead of, alternatively, otherwise, unlike, on the other hand, however, in contrast

Try It | Decide whether the transition between phrases or sentences should signal a similarity or a difference. Then choose the correct transition to go in the blank.

1. Emily Dickinson is well-known for her poems; ________, her sister Lavinia is less known for her role in publishing the poems. [in a similar fashion; however]
2. Any author might understand his or her own culture. __________, the material might be new to readers. [Similarly; In contrast]
3. For maintenance crews, snow removal is a challenge. ______________, icy sidewalks are hard to clear. [On the other hand; In the same way]

Apply It | Compare/contrast Wilson's, Hughes's, or Holbrook's perspectives and strategies. Choose a frame to jump-start your essay about these two authors.

1. ____________ [text title] by ____________ [author's name] and ____________ [text title] by ____________ [author's name] are different in that one text _____, whereas the other _____.
2. Although ____________ [author 1] and ____________ [author 2] both _____, a key difference is _____.
3. In ____________ [title 1] the author _____ while in ____________ [title 2] the author _____.

Step 4 | Revise and Edit

Revise your draft with a partner.

Organization and Clarity					
State the text titles and author names in the introductory paragraph.	Self	1	2	3	4
	Partner	1	2	3	4
Include a clear, meaningful thesis statement that emphasizes a compare/contrast relationship between each author's perspective on democracy.	Self	1	2	3	4
	Partner	1	2	3	4
Focus on only one text in each body paragraph and include information that reflects the topic sentence and supports the thesis statement.	Self	1	2	3	4
	Partner	1	2	3	4
Reflect the purpose of comparing and contrasting the texts in each body paragraph.	Self	1	2	3	4
	Partner	1	2	3	4
Restate the thesis statement in a new way in the conclusion.	Self	1	2	3	4
	Partner	1	2	3	4
Evidence and Reasoning					
Include two or more pieces of specific and relevant text evidence in each body paragraph.	Self	1	2	3	4
	Partner	1	2	3	4
Analyze how each author uses the structure of dramatic and poetic form to establish and develop his or her ideas.	Self	1	2	3	4
	Partner	1	2	3	4
Language and Conventions					
Include formal, academic language appropriate to an informative essay. Recognize and adjust variations from standard English.	Self	1	2	3	4
	Partner	1	2	3	4
Use concise language to avoid wordiness and redundancies.	Self	1	2	3	4
	Partner	1	2	3	4
Spell all words correctly. Properly use punctuation to set off parenthetical elements.	Self	1	2	3	4
	Partner	1	2	3	4

Scoring Guide | ① needs improvement ② average ③ good ④ excellent

Step 5 | Publish

Publish your essay either in print or digital form.

Publish

Publish your essay either in print or digital form. Use the rubric below to assess your final performance task.

PERFORMANCE TASK RUBRIC			
Score Point	**Organization and Clarity**	**Evidence and Reasoning**	**Language and Conventions**
Exemplary ④	• introductory paragraph **introduces** what the writer will compare and contrast and includes a **strong focus statement** • each body paragraph focuses on one text and **strongly supports** the focus **statement with relevant** characteristics • includes **well-chosen** text evidence, precise language, and concise language • concluding statement **restates** the focus statement, provides additional evidence, and summarizes each writer's point of view about democracy	• **effectively compares and contrasts** the writers' points of view on democracy and **analyzes** how the writers use the text structure to develop their ideas • includes **several examples of relevant** factual evidence from the drama or poem that supports the explanation of each writer's point of view	• demonstrates a **strong command** of the conventions of standard English grammar and usage, as well as of standard English capitalization, punctuation, and spelling • vocabulary is **appropriate** to the topic (vocabulary about democracy; accurate terms for referring to text structure of poetry and drama; vocabulary for making comparisons and contrasts)
Meets Standards ③	• introductory paragraph **introduces** what the writer will compare and contrast and includes a focus statement • each body paragraph focuses on a text and **supports** the focus statement with **some characteristics** about the text • includes **some** text evidence, precise language and concise language • concluding statement **restates** the focus statement and compares and contrasts both texts	• **adequately compares and contrasts** the writers' points of view on democracy • includes **some relevant** factual evidence from the drama or poem that supports the explanation of each writer's point of view	• demonstrates **a near command** of the conventions of standard English grammar and usage, as well as of standard English capitalization, punctuation, and spelling **with some errors** • vocabulary is **appropriate** to the topic (vocabulary about democracy; accurate terms for referring to text structure of poetry and drama; vocabulary for making comparisons and contrasts)

PERFORMANCE TASK RUBRIC			
Score Point	**Organization and Clarity**	**Evidence and Reasoning**	**Language and Conventions**
Needs Work ②	• introductory paragraph introduces what the writer will compare and contrast and includes a focus statement that **loosely identifies** what the essay will be about • body paragraphs are **somewhat organized** by text, though include some details about the second text in each paragraph • includes **a limited amount** of text evidence, precise language and concise language • concluding statement **attempts to restate** the focus statement but only partially compares and contrasts the two texts	• **attempts to compare and contrast** the writers' points of view on democracy • includes **some textual evidence** from the drama or poem to support the explanation of each writer's point of view	• demonstrates a **marginal command** of the conventions of English grammar and usage, as well as of standard English capitalization, punctuation, and spelling • there **are many errors; however, the text is still understandable** • includes only **one or two examples** of vocabulary that is appropriate to the topic (vocabulary about democracy; accurate terms for referring to text structure of poetry and drama; vocabulary for making comparisons and contrasts)
Does Not Meet Standards ①	• introductory paragraph is **unclear** and does not include a focus statement • body paragraphs are **not organized logically** and do not include information about both texts in each paragraph • essay includes **little text evidence** and little concise language • concluding statement is **unclear and does not wrap up** the ideas in the essay	• response is **partial or inaccurate explanation** of the writers' points of view on democracy • includes **no analyses of textual evidence** from the drama or poem	• demonstrates **almost no command** of the conventions of standard English grammar and usage, as well as of standard English capitalization, punctuation, and spelling • there **are many errors that disrupt** the reader's understanding of the text • **does not include** vocabulary that is appropriate to the topic (vocabulary about democracy; accurate terms for referring to text structure of poetry and drama; vocabulary for making comparisons and contrasts)

Questions

Words and Phrases in Context

1. Define *racket* as it is used in **paragraph 1**. Identify the words and phrases the author uses to describe the conversation about civil rights. Describe the tone.

Text Structure

2. Explain why the author repeats the question "And ain't I a woman?" four times in **paragraph 2**.

"Ain't I a Woman?"

by Sojourner Truth

Delivered 1851

Women's Convention, Akron, Ohio

¶**1** Well, children, where there is so much racket there must be something out of kilter. I think that 'twixt the negroes of the South and the women at the North, all talking about rights, the white men will be in a fix pretty soon. But what's all this here talking about?

¶**2** That man over there says that women need to be helped into carriages, and lifted over ditches, and to have the best place everywhere. Nobody ever helps me into carriages, or over mud-puddles, or gives me any best place! And ain't I a woman? Look at me! Look at my arm! I have ploughed and planted, and gathered into barns, and no man could head me! And ain't I a woman? I could work as much and eat as much as a man—when I could get it—and bear the lash as well! And ain't I a woman? I have borne thirteen children, and seen most all sold off to slavery, and when I cried out with my mother's grief, none but Jesus heard me! And ain't I a woman?

¶**3** Then they talk about this thing in the head; what's this they call it? [member of audience whispers, "intellect"] That's it, honey. What's that got to do with women's rights or negroes' rights? If my cup won't hold but a pint, and yours holds a quart, wouldn't you be mean not to let me have my little half measure full?

¶**4** Then that little man in black there, he says women can't have as much rights as men, 'cause Christ wasn't a woman! Where did your Christ come from? Where did your Christ come from? From God and a woman! Man had nothing to do with Him.

Words to Know

carriage: *(n.)* a large vehicle with four wheels that is pulled by a horse and that carries people

ploughed: *(v.)* to dig into or break up (dirt, soil, land, etc.) with a plow

grief: *(n.)* deep sadness caused especially by someone's death

¶5 If the first woman God ever made was strong enough to turn the world upside down all alone, these women together ought to be able to turn it back and get it right side up again! And now they is asking to do it, the men better let them.

¶6 Obliged to you for hearing me, and now old Sojourner ain't got nothing more to say.

THE SHADOW TO SUPPORT THE SUBSTANCE.
SOJOURNER TRUTH.

Words to Know

pint: *(n.)* a unit for measuring liquids that is equal to 0.473 liters

quart: *(n.)* a unit of liquid measurement equal to two US pints or 0.946 liters

obliged: *(adj.)* very grateful, thankful

Questions

Key Idea and Details

3. Describe the author's view of the relationship between intellect and rights. Explain how she uses the pint vs. quart analogy to convey her view.

Writing

4. Summarize the speech. Identify the three arguments against women's rights that Truth mentions. Explain how she counters each argument.

Questions

Test Structure

1. Determine the purpose of the **first paragraph** of the text. What does the author introduce?

Words and Phrases in Context

2. What type of "enforcement mechanism" might back up a "legal requirement"?

Text Structure

3. Explain how the author supports the claim that the results of mandatory voting in Australia were remarkable. Why did the author choose Australia's results to examine?

Telling Americans to Vote, or Else

by William A. Galston from *The New York Times*

Washington

¶**1** Jury duty is mandatory; why not voting? The idea seems vaguely un-American. Maybe so, but it's neither unusual nor undemocratic. And it would ease the intense partisan polarization that weakens our capacity for self-government and public trust in our governing institutions.

¶**2** Thirty-one countries have some form of mandatory voting, according to the International Institute for Democracy and Electoral Assistance. The list includes nine members of the Organization for Economic Cooperation and Development and two-thirds of the Latin American nations. More than half back up the legal requirement with an enforcement mechanism, while the rest are content to rely on the moral force of the law.

¶**3** Despite the prevalence of mandatory voting in so many democracies, it's easy to dismiss the practice as a form of statism that couldn't work in America's individualistic and libertarian political culture. But consider Australia, whose political culture is closer to that of the United States than that of any other English-speaking country. Alarmed by a decline in voter turnout to less than 60 percent in 1922, Australia adopted mandatory voting in 1924, backed by small fines (roughly the size of traffic tickets) for nonvoting, rising with repeated acts of non-participation. The law established permissible reasons for not voting, like illness and foreign travel, and allows citizens who faced fines for not voting to defend themselves.

Words to Know

mandatory: *(adj.)* required by law or rule

obligation: *(n.)* something that you must do because of a law, rule, or promise

materialize: *(v.)* to begin to happen or exist — usually used in negative statements

¶**4** The results were remarkable. In the 1925 election, the first held under the new law, turnout soared to 91 percent. In recent elections, it has hovered around 95 percent. The law also changed civic norms. Australians are more likely than before to see voting as an obligation. The negative side effects many feared did not materialize. For example, the percentage of ballots intentionally spoiled or completed randomly as acts of resistance remained on the order of 2 to 3 percent.

¶**5** Proponents offer three reasons in favor of mandatory voting. The first is straightforwardly civic. A democracy can't be strong if its citizenship is weak. And right now American citizenship is attenuated — strong on rights, weak on responsibilities. There is less and less that being a citizen requires of us, especially after the abolition of the draft. Requiring people to vote in national elections once every two years would reinforce the principle of reciprocity at the heart of citizenship.

¶**6** The second argument for mandatory voting is democratic. Ideally, a democracy will take into account the interests and views of all citizens. But if some regularly vote while others don't, officials are likely to give greater weight to participants. This might not matter much if nonparticipants were evenly distributed through the population. But political scientists have long known that they aren't. People with lower levels of income and education are less likely to vote, as are young adults and recent first-generation immigrants.

¶**7** Changes in our political system have magnified these disparities. During the 1950s and '60s, when turnout rates were much higher, political parties reached out to citizens year-round. At the local level these parties, which reformers often criticized as "machines," connected even citizens of modest means and limited education with neighborhood institutions and gave them a sense of participation in national politics as well. (In its heyday, organized labor reinforced these effects.) But in the absence of these more organic forms of political mobilization, the second-best option is a top-down mechanism of universal mobilization.

Words to Know

reciprocity: *(n.)* a situation or relationship in which two people or groups agree to do something similar for each other

disparities: *(n.)* a noticeable and often unfair difference between people or things

inclusiveness: *(n.)* openness to everyone

Questions

Words and Phrases in Context

4. Define *proponent* as used in **paragraph 5**. Identify context clues that helped you determine its meaning.

Key Idea and Details

5. Explain the first two arguments the author discusses. How would mandatory voting strengthen citizenship?

Key Idea and Details

6. Analyze the second argument the author presents. How would mandatory voting strengthen democracy?

Questions

Key Ideas and Details

7. Describe our "current ills." How would mandatory voting help to make them better?

Words and Phrases in Context

8. What are *quadrennial* and *biennial* elections? How do they contribute to low voter turnout?

Text Structure

9. Explain how mandatory voting would improve political campaigns. Identify the author's reasons.

¶**8** Mandatory voting would tend to even out disparities stemming from income, education and age, enhancing our system's inclusiveness. It is true, as some object, that an enforcement mechanism would impose greater burdens on those with fewer resources. But this makes it all the more likely that these citizens would respond by going to the polls, and they would stand to gain far more than the cost of a traffic ticket.

¶**9** The third argument for mandatory voting goes to the heart of our current ills. Our low turnout rate pushes American politics toward increased polarization. The reason is that hard-core partisans are more likely to dominate lower-turnout elections, while those who are less fervent about specific issues and less attached to political organizations tend not to participate at levels proportional to their share of the electorate.

¶**10** A distinctive feature of our constitutional system — elections that are quadrennial for president but biennial for the House of Representatives — magnifies these effects. It's bad enough that only three-fifths of the electorate turns out to determine the next president, but much worse that only two-fifths of our citizens vote in House elections two years later. If events combine to energize one part of the political spectrum and dishearten the other, a relatively small portion of the electorate can shift the system out of all proportion to its numbers.

¶**11** Some observers are comfortable with this asymmetry. But if you think that today's intensely polarized politics impedes governance and exacerbates mistrust — and that is what most Americans firmly (and in my view rightly) believe — then you should be willing to consider reforms that would strengthen the forces of conciliation.

¶**12** Imagine our politics with laws and civic norms that yield near-universal voting. Campaigns could devote far less money to costly, labor-intensive get-out-the-vote efforts. Media gurus wouldn't have the same incentive to drive down turnout with negative advertising. Candidates would know that they must do more than mobilize

Words to Know

dominate: *(v.)* to have control of or power over

impedes: *(v.)* to slow the movement, progress, or action of (someone or something)

exacerbates: *(v.)* to make a bad situation, a problem, etc. worse

their bases with red-meat rhetoric on hot-button issues. Such a system would improve not only electoral politics but also the legislative process. Rather than focusing on symbolic gestures whose major purpose is to agitate partisans, Congress might actually roll up its sleeves and tackle the serious, complex issues it ignores.

• • •

¶**13** The United States is not Australia, of course, and there's no guarantee that the similarity of our political cultures would produce equivalent political results. For example, reforms of general elections would leave untouched the distortions generated by party primaries in which small numbers of voters can shape the choices for the entire electorate. And the United States Constitution gives the states enormous power over voting procedures. Mandating voting nationwide would go counter to our traditions (and perhaps our Constitution) and would encounter strong state opposition. Instead, a half-dozen states from parts of the country with different civic traditions should experiment with the practice, and observers — journalists, social scientists, citizens' groups and elected officials — would monitor the consequences.

¶**14** We don't know what the outcome would be. But one thing is clear: If we do nothing and allow a politics of passion to define the bounds of the electorate, as it has for much of the last four decades, the prospect for a less polarized, more effective political system that enjoys the trust and confidence of the people is not bright.

William A. Galston is a senior fellow at the Brookings Institution.

Words to Know

distortion: *(n.)* the act of changing the natural shape, appearance, or sound of (something) in a way that is usually not attractive or pleasing

opposition: *(n.)* actions or opinions that show that you disagree with or disapprove of someone or something

bounds: *(n.)* something that shows where one area ends and another area begins, boundaries

Questions

Key Idea and Details

10. According to the author, how should we try out mandatory voting?

Test Structure

11. Describe how the author concludes his argument. Restate his position in your own words.

Literature Circle Leveled Novels

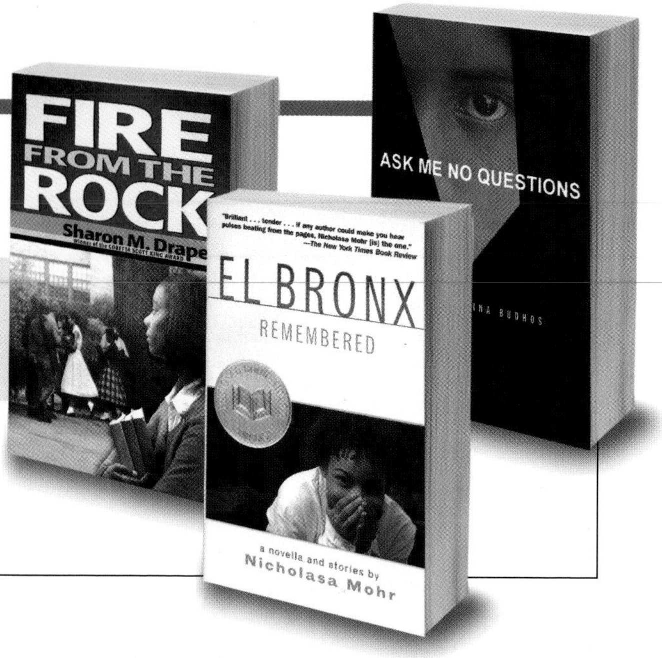

Fire From the Rock *by Sharon Draper*
Sylvia is scared when she is asked to be one of the first black students to attend Central High School in 1957 Arkansas. **Lexile**® measure: 830L

El Bronx Remembered *by Nicholasa Mohr*
This book is a collection of stories about a Puerto Rican neighborhood in the South Bronx in the 1940s and '50s. **Lexile**® measure: 610L

Ask Me No Questions *by Marina Budhos*
Nadira, fourteen, and her family come to the United States on a tourist visa and stay long after it expires. When their illegal status is discovered following 9/11, Nadira must keep her family's secret in order to avoid deportation. **Lexile**® measure: 790L

Fiction, Nonfiction, and Novels

Remember: The Journey to School Integration *by Toni Morrison.* Morrison brings eloquent words to archival photographs of the struggle for school integration during the civil rights movement. **Lexile**® measure: 660L

Weedflower *by Cynthia Kadohata.* A Japanese-American girl, Sumiko, finds that life on her family's flower farm in Southern California is turned upside down when Pearl Harbor is attacked. **Lexile**® measure: 750L

To Kill a Mockingbird *by Harper Lee.* A black man is wrongly accused of a violent crime. Scout learns from her father about prejudice and doing what's right as he defends this man. **Lexile**® measure: 870L

Warriors Don't Cry *by Melba Pattillo Beals.* One of nine black teenagers to integrate a high school in Little Rock in 1957, Beals tells her story of struggling against school segregation. **Lexile**® measure: 1000L

Freedom Walkers: The Story of the Montgomery Bus Boycott *by Russell Freedman.* This book provides in-depth history of the boycott, with an emphasis on the contributions of everyday people. **Lexile**® measure: 1110L

The Day the Women Got the Vote *by George Sullivan.* Explore this photographic record of the women's movement, including the fight for suffrage and equal rights. **Lexile**® measure: 1130L

Kids at Work: Lewis Hine and the Crusade Against Child Labor *by Russell Freedman.* In an effort to enhance his message, Hine used photography to document the appalling child labor conditions in the early twentieth century. **Lexile**® measure: 1140L

United States Preamble and First Amendment to the United States Constitution Read the introduction to the US Constitution and learn more about the freedoms allowed in the First Amendment.

Films and TV

Eyes on the Prize: America's Civil Rights Years 1954–1964 (PBS, 1987) This 14-hour documentary series on the civil rights movement chronicles the stories of people determined to fight for racial equality. (360 min.)

Free at Last: Civil Rights Heroes (Image Entertainment, 2004) Immerse yourself in the stories of some of the incredible people who fought for civil rights. (95 min.)

Martin Luther King, Jr.—I Have a Dream (MPI Home Video, 1986) See King deliver his famous speech, in addition to the opposition protesters faced that day. (60 min.)

The Rosa Parks Story (Xenon, 2002) Follow the story of Rosa Parks as her act of defiance creates an uproar and ignites the civil rights movement. (97 min.)

Ruby Bridges (Walt Disney Home Entertainment, 1998) Six-year-old Ruby is the first African-American girl to attend her local New Orleans elementary school in the racially charged 1960s. (96 min.)

Unfinished Business (New Video Group, 2005) This Oscar-nominated film was one of the first to address the Japanese-American internment camps during World War II. (58 min.)

Voices of Civil Rights (A&E Home Video, 2005) This collection of five programs includes firsthand accounts by people who lived through the civil rights movement. (243 min.)

Websites

Japanese American National Museum Explore this site to find interactive cultural activities and games, as well as information about the museum's exhibitions and collections.

National Underground Railroad Freedom Center This site includes information about the secret network that helped slaves escape to freedom. Also on this site is information about slavery that exists today.

The King Center The King Center is continuing work to carry out Dr. Martin Luther King, Jr.'s dream. Find out more about King and this organization.

Way Back: Stand Up for Your Rights Learn the personal stories of those who fought for their rights as well as the rights of others.

Magazines

The American Look for articles pertaining to groups fighting for equal rights in America.

History: The History Channel Magazine Gain insight into significant events in America's history, including the fight for equal rights.

National Geographic Find articles and videos about struggles for human rights throughout the world.

Time Search the online archives for issues and articles devoted to civil rights issues.

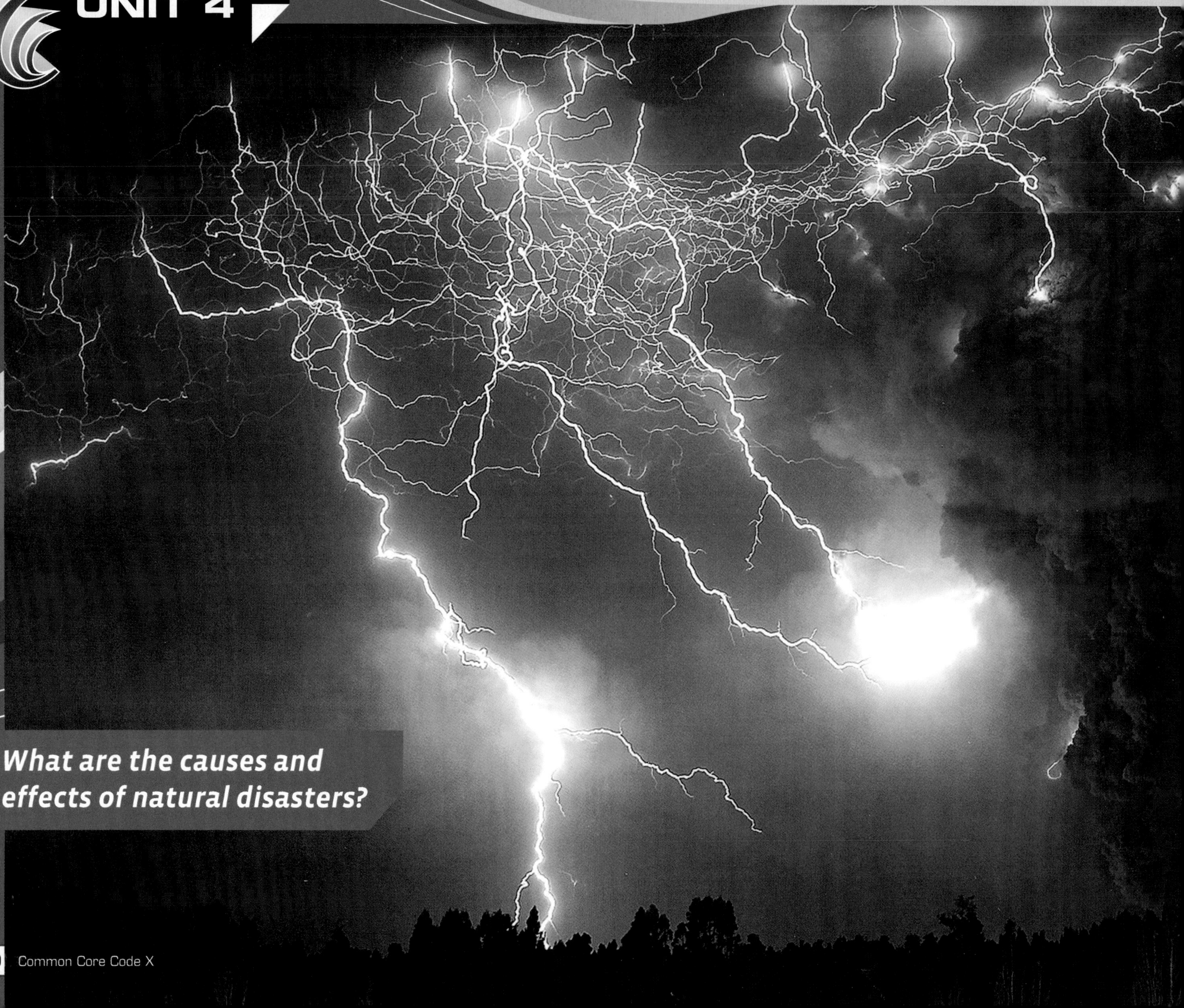

What are the causes and effects of natural disasters?

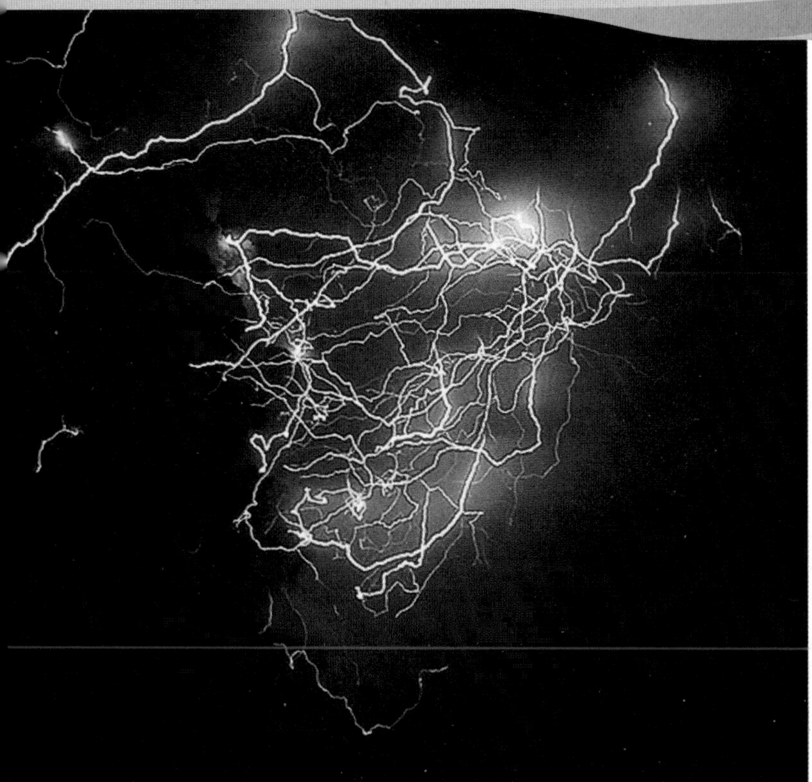

Unit Introduction

In a science article and an informational excerpt, discover how writers chronicle natural disasters and their impact on the world.

In an excerpt from the science article "Super Disasters of the 21st Century," Jacqueline Adams and Ken Kostel detail recent disasters and provide an in-depth look at how hurricanes, earthquakes, and tsunamis occur and the devastation that results.

In an excerpt from *The Perfect Storm*, Sebastian Junger combines a first-person anecdote with a factual explanation to bring to life the experience of surviving a massive storm at sea.

WRITING PERFORMANCE TASK

Compare and contrast the strategies and techniques that each author uses to describe the causes and effects of disasters. Consider text structure, choice of vocabulary, and use of data and details.

SCIENCE ARTICLE/INFORMATIONAL EXCERPT

from **"Super Disasters of the 21st Century"**
by Jacqueline Adams and Ken Kostel

Language
- Academic Vocabulary
- Word Study: Dictionary

Reading Nonfiction
- Identify Evidence
- Key Ideas and Details
- Craft and Structure

from ***The Perfect Storm***
by Sebastian Junger

Language
- Academic Vocabulary
- Word Study: Thesaurus

Reading Literary Nonfiction
- Identify Evidence
- Key Ideas and Details
- Craft and Structure

SPEAKING AND LISTENING

Present
- Collaborate and Present

Checklist: Presentation
- Scoring Guide

WRITING

Writing: Explanatory Essay
- Read the Model
- Analyze the Model
- Gather Evidence
- Organize Ideas
- Language Study: Combining Sentences
- Conventions Study: Sentence Variety
- Revise, Edit, and Publish
- Performance Task Rubric

EXTENDED READING

Science Article
from **"In Deference to Crisis, a New Obsession Sweeps Japan: Self-Restraint"**
by Ken Belson and Norimitsu Onishi

Science Article
"Submerged City"
by Jacqueline Adams

Academic Vocabulary

"Super Disasters of the 21st Century"

by Jacqueline Adams and Ken Kostel

Rate your understanding of each word. Then write its meaning and a sample sentence.

Word	Meaning	Example
displaced (*v.*) p. 144 ① ② ③ ④	to force people to leave where they live	
inevitable (*adj.*) p. 145 ① ② ③ ④	certain to happen; unavoidable	
vulnerable (*adj.*) p. 147 ① ② ③ ④		The bird and its eggs were vulnerable during the hailstorm.
intensity (*n.*) p. 148 ① ② ③ ④		The intensity of the heat in Florida in July was too much for me.
unparalleled (*adj.*) p. 152 ① ② ③ ④	having no equal; being greater than all others	
detection (*n.*) p. 155 ① ② ③ ④	the act of finding or discovering	

Rating Scale | ① I don't know the word. ② I've seen it or heard it. ③ I know its meaning. ④ I know it and use it.

Word Study

Dictionary

A **dictionary** is a reference book that contains words listed in alphabetical order and that gives information about the words' meanings, forms, and pronunciations.

Use the dictionary entry for the word *calamity* to answer the questions below:

calamity (kah•**lam**•ah•tee) *noun.* calamities. a terrible event causing much loss and distress. *Losing funding for the assistant librarians would be a calamity for the library.*

1. Is the *l* in *calamity* pronounced in the first or second syllable?

2. What part of speech is the word *calamity*?

3. What is the plural form of the word *calamity*?

from SUPER DISASTERS OF THE 21ST CENTURY

NATURAL DISASTERS TAKE COUNTLESS LIVES AND COST BILLIONS OF DOLLARS. WHY DO THESE FORCES OF NATURE HAPPEN?

***by Jacqueline Adams and Ken Kostel from* Science World**

¶**1** The 21st century has just begun, yet it has already been marked by some of the worst natural disasters in history.

¶**2** In 2005, Gulf Coast residents braced themselves for what weather experts were predicting to be a violent hurricane. When the storm hit land, it lived up to the hype. Hurricane Katrina's mighty winds tore some towns to shreds, and drowned others in floodwaters. When it was over, more that 2,500 people were dead or missing. While Katrina devastated New Orleans and other parts of the U.S.'s Gulf Coast, the storm paled in comparison to other disasters unfolding in the new century.

¶**3** In 2008, a powerful earthquake rocked China. The quake toppled hundreds of buildings and left 12,000 lifeless bodies buried beneath the rubble. It was China's most destructive earthquake in decades, but as far as disasters go, it still wasn't the deadliest.

Words to Know

braced: *(v.)* prepared for a danger or threat

devastated: *(v.)* destroyed

toppled: *(v.)* to cause something to become unsteady and fall

rubble: *(n.)* broken pieces of stone, brick, etc., from walls or buildings that have fallen

Close Reading

Key Ideas and Details

1. Based on the introductory text, what are two effects of natural disasters caused by forces of nature?

Words and Phrases in Context

2. Define the phrase *paled in comparison* as it is used in **paragraph 2**. What words or phrases do the authors use to support you in determining the meaning?

Close Reading

Key Ideas and Details

3. Do you think that the authors adequately support the claim that "the most catastrophic event . . . occurred in 2004"?

Claim

A **claim** is an arguable statement or position.

Text Structure

4. Describe what the subheading "Hurricane Katrina: New Orleans" signals about how the authors have structured this text.

Subheading

A **subheading** is a short phrase used as a title for a small part within a longer piece of writing.

¶**4** The most catastrophic event so far in the century occurred in 2004. On a quiet morning in December, the waters of the Indian Ocean rose far above sea level and traveled toward land at frightening speeds. A series of monstrous waves, called a tsunami, hit shore and destroyed everything in sight. More than 200,000 people died.

¶**5** These disasters may seem unusual, but extreme weather has been shaping the Earth for millions of years. We can't keep these events from happening, but scientists hope that by studying them we can find ways to predict and prepare for them. Take a tour of three super disasters of this century to learn what scientists have uncovered.

Hurricane Katrina: New Orleans

¶**6** Hurricane Katrina was one of the costliest hurricanes in U.S. history. Total losses exceeded $150 billion. There was also a human toll. At least 1,800 people died. Hundreds of missing people were never accounted for. Over one million people were **displaced** from their homes. Most of the victims came from New Orleans, Louisiana. The event left many asking, "Why?"

The Storm Hits

¶**7** In late August 2005, Hurricane Katrina pounded the Gulf Coast region with 225 kph (140 mph) winds. At first, it seemed that New Orleans and its surrounding areas had dodged the worst of the storm. That would soon prove untrue.

¶**8** New Orleans' flood-control methods could not handle the rising waters produced by the storm. Within a day of landfall, a few barriers that were built to protect the city from flooding broke or were washed away. Soon, most of the city was underwater. Residents fled from flooded homes. Some clung to rooftops waiting to be plucked to safety by rescue workers.

Words to Know

catastrophic: *(adj.)* relating to great loss and tragedy

dodged: *(v.)* avoided

landfall: *(n.)* the land that you see or arrive at after a long journey by sea or air, or the act of arriving there

¶9 TV viewers watched in shock as the city drowned. However, scientists were not surprised. For years, researchers had warned of exactly this type of disaster. "Something like this was pretty much **inevitable**," says Hugh Willoughby, a hurricane expert at Florida International University in Miami.

Sinking City

¶**10** Why did Willoughby and other experts expect a catastrophe like Katrina to occur? Nearly 80 percent of New Orleans sits in a bowl-shaped area between two bodies of water. Lake Pontchartrain is to the north and the Mississippi River is to the south. In some areas the city is more than 2.4 meters (8 feet) below sea level. To keep these higher waters from spilling into the "bowl," residents have relied on an extensive system of barriers called levees. These barriers stand 5.5 meters (18 feet) tall, and are made of earth and concrete.

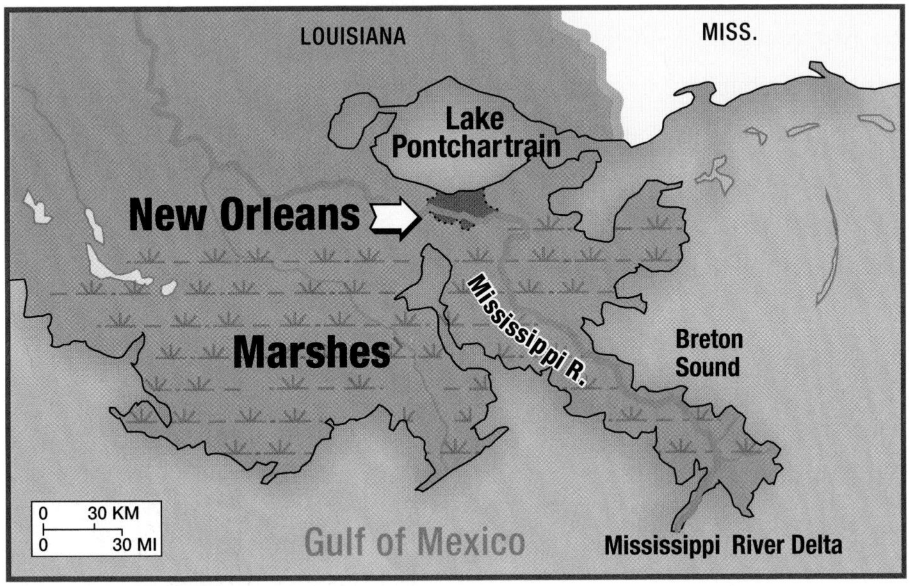

The marshes south of New Orleans absorb some of the storm surge. In recent times, these marshes have been wearing away.

Words to Know

relied: *(v.)* to depend on something in order to continue to live or exist

extensive: *(adj.)* large in size or amount : very full or complete

Close Reading

Key Ideas and Details

5. Based on details in **paragraph 8**, what caused the flooding? What were the effects of the flooding?

Key Ideas and Details

6. Do you think that the authors adequately support the claim that the flooding in New Orleans "was pretty much **inevitable**"?

Writing

7. What is the effect of comparing the location of New Orleans to a bowl?

Close Reading

Text Structure

8. Why did the authors ask the question "Why?" in **paragraph 11**? Describe the effect.

Key Ideas and Details

9. Why does Willoughby describe the Mississippi Delta as "basically a pile of mud in the gulf of Mexico" in **paragraph 12**?

¶**11** New Orleans didn't always sit so low. Since it was built in 1718, the city has sunk 2.7 meters (9 feet). Why? New Orleans sits on the Mississippi Delta, where the Mississippi River meets the Gulf of Mexico. At the Delta, the river's current slows. This causes sediment, such as mud, to fall to the bottom. Over millions of years, this sediment has built up.

¶**12** However, the resulting land is not sturdy. "The Mississippi Delta is basically a pile of mud in the gulf of Mexico," says Willoughby. The spongy ground on which New Orleans was built is slowly spreading and sinking.

¶**13** If the levees of New Orleans had not been built, the city would be sitting high, but not dry. That's because each spring, as snow upriver melts and drains into the Mississippi, the river floods the Delta. Left uncontrolled, these floods would wash over the city of New Orleans. But in the 18th century, European settlers began building levees to keep floodwater out of the city.

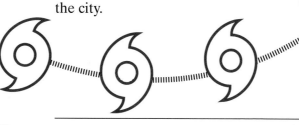

Words to Know

current: *(n.)* a continuous movement of water in the same direction

sediment: *(n.)* material, often bits of rock from weathering, that settles at the bottom of water

Disappearing Defenses

¶**14** New Orleans had another strike against it–one that made it especially **vulnerable** to Katrina's wrath. With each passing year, the sinking city's natural landscape has worn away, causing it to become defenseless against storms.

¶**15** Before the levees were built, New Orleans relied on its surrounding marshes (swamps) and barrier islands (long narrow islands that run parallel to the mainland) for protection during the hurricanes. These natural defenses have absorbed some storm surges, or rushes of ocean water pushed onshore by storms, before they reach the city. The bad news: These defenses are gradually wearing away.

¶**16** Why is this happening? The marshes require river sediment to keep them strong. Before the levees were built, this wasn't a problem. The Mississippi River would flood the area, and leave behind all the sediment needed. Now, the levees keep the river from flooding, but as a consequence, no sediment flows in to strengthen the marshes.

¶**17** The results are disastrous: About 25 to 30 square miles of Delta marshes vanish every year. "That's the size of a college football field lost every 15 minutes," says Gregory Stone, a geologist at Louisiana State University in Baton Rouge.

Words to Know

absorbed: *(v.)* to prevent (often harmful or unwanted) from passing through something

consequence: *(n.)* something that happens as a result of a particular action or set of conditions, effect

Close Reading

Academic Vocabulary

10. What was the other "strike against" New Orleans? How did it make the city more vulnerable to a hurricane?

Text Structure

11. Explain what the colon (:) signals in the last sentence in **paragraph 15**.

Writing

12. Review **paragraphs 10–17.** Summarize the effects the levees had on the city of New Orleans.

Disappearing Defenses

¶**14** New Orleans had another strike against it–one that made it especially **vulnerable** to Katrina's wrath. With each passing year, the sinking city's natural landscape has worn away, causing it to become defenseless against storms.

¶**15** Before the levees were built, New Orleans relied on its surrounding marshes (swamps) and barrier islands (long narrow islands that run parallel to the mainland) for protection during the hurricanes. These natural defenses have absorbed some storm surges, or rushes of ocean water pushed onshore by storms, before they reach the city. The bad news: These defenses are gradually wearing away.

¶**16** Why is this happening? The marshes require river sediment to keep them strong. Before the levees were built, this wasn't a problem. The Mississippi River would flood the area, and leave behind all the sediment needed. Now, the levees keep the river from flooding, but as a consequence, no sediment flows in to strengthen the marshes.

¶**17** The results are disastrous: About 25 to 30 square miles of Delta marshes vanish every year. "That's the size of a college football field lost every 15 minutes," says Gregory Stone, a geologist at Louisiana State University in Baton Rouge.

Words to Know

absorbed: *(v.)* to prevent (often harmful or unwanted) from passing through something

consequence: *(n.)* something that happens as a result of a particular action or set of conditions, effect

Close Reading

Academic Vocabulary

10. What was the other "strike against" New Orleans? How did it make the city more vulnerable to a hurricane?

Text Structure

11. Explain what the colon (:) signals in the last sentence in **paragraph 15**.

Writing

12. Review **paragraphs 10–17.** Summarize the effects the levees had on the city of New Orleans.

Close Reading

Words and Phrases in Context

13. Define *stretch* as it used in **paragraph 18**. What words or phrases did the author use to support you in determining the meaning?

Key Ideas and Details

14. What "cycle" ended in 1994 (**paragraph 19**)? Why does this mean that "more monster storms loom ahead"?

Writing

15. Why do some people suggest in **paragraph 21** "quitting the fight against nature and moving the city to a different spot"?

Hyped Up Hurricanes

¶**18** Katrina's destructive power is also the result of the cycle of powerful storms currently happening in the Atlantic. Scientists have observed that the number and **intensity** of Atlantic Ocean hurricanes run in cycles. During a particular cycle—which can last a few decades at a stretch—the frequency and strength of hurricanes are constant. One cycle may experience a greater number of high-intensity storms. This cycle would be followed by one with fewer hurricanes, and with lower wind speeds.

¶**19** Researchers believe that a cycle of fewer and lower-intensity storms ended in 1994. That means more monster storms loom ahead.

No Easy Fix

¶**20** Even today, everyone is left wondering: Is it possible to prevent a similar New Orleans nightmare from occurring again? Suggestions include toting in sediment to rebuild the marshes, raising the height of the levees, and building a second fortress of levees inside the city.

¶**21** All these proposals have been analyzed before, but the money wasn't provided to carry them out. Some people have even suggested quitting the fight against nature and moving the city to a different spot.

¶**22** There's no easy fix. But experts agree: Something must be done to keep this tragedy from recurring.

Words to Know

cycles: *(n.)* a repeated series of events or actions

loom: *(v.)* if a problem or difficulty looms, it is likely to happen very soon

toting: *(v.)* to carry something, especially regularly

proposals: *(n.)* plans or ideas

Earthquake: China

¶23 May 12, 2008, seemed like an ordinary school day in China's Sichuan province. Students studied in their classrooms while parents went to work or cared for their homes. Suddenly, the earth began to move and shudder. Schools, houses, factories, and other buildings toppled, burying thousands of people under rubble. The earthquake struck with such force that people felt the ground shake 1,900 kilometers (1,180 miles) away.

Deadly Quake

¶24 The earthquake triggered landslides that blocked roads and railways, and buried people beneath rubble. Rescuers were unable to reach many trapped victims. For weeks, aftershocks (tremors that follow a main earthquake shock) rocked the area. Terrified survivors didn't know where tragedy would strike next. By June, 69,000 people were confirmed dead with another 17,500 missing. Why was this quake so deadly? Several factors figured into the catastrophe.

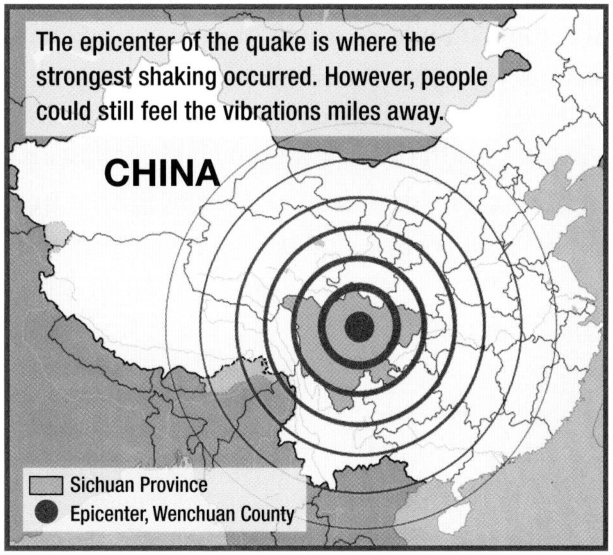
The epicenter of the quake is where the strongest shaking occurred. However, people could still feel the vibrations miles away.
CHINA
Sichuan Province
Epicenter, Wenchuan County

Pushy Plates

¶25 The trouble started far away, at the boundary of two plates—giant rock slabs that make up earth's crust. As the plates move, usually only a few millimeters each year, they can collide with earthshaking results.

Words to Know

triggered: *(v.)* to cause to start or happen

slabs: *(n.)* a thick flat piece of a hard material such as rock

collide: *(v.)* to crash together

Close Reading

Key Ideas and Details

16. How did the "ordinary school day" become horrific?

Writing

17. State the details and facts that the authors include to show how disastrous the earthquake was. How do these facts help support the central claim of their text that "The 21st century has just begun, yet it has already been marked by some of the worst disasters in history"?

Close Reading

Writing

18. Review **paragraphs 26 and 27.** Summarize the geological sequence of events that led to the monster earthquake in China in 2008.

Key Ideas and Details

19. What evidence supports the claim that the aftershocks were "powerful"?

¶**26** Shake-ups don't occur only at plate boundaries. As plates push together, they create energy. This energy can transfer through the rock to other areas, where it builds up over time. "At any given moment, the energy that's stored gets released in the form of an earthquake," says geophysicist Rafael Abreu, who studies earth physics at the U.S. Geological Survey.

¶**27** In the case of China's deadly earthquake, energy transferred to a fault (a fracture between two sections of rock) that borders the Sichuan Basin. On May 12, the fault ruptured, triggering a monster earthquake that caused massive devastation.

Shallow Shock

¶**28** There was one factor especially responsible for the great destruction in Sichuan. The earthquake was shallow, originating only 19 kilometers (12 miles) below the surface. Abreu explains, "The closer you are to the source of the earthquake, the stronger you will feel the ground shaking." The quake's vibrations traveled through the ground to other sections of the fault, where the energy built up until those sections ruptured. The result was a chain reaction of powerful aftershocks.

¶**29** The aftershocks not only interfered with rescue efforts, they also triggered landslides that blocked rivers. The trapped waters rose and threatened to flood the areas. Survivors evacuated to higher ground until engineers drained the water.

Words to Know

ruptured: *(v.)* to break or burst

massive: *(adj.)* huge; large in amount or degree

interfered: *(v.)* to prevent something from succeeding or from happening in the way that was planned

Shaky Ground

¶**30** There was another factor to blame for the damage. The ground in low-lying Sichuan is made of particles called sediment. Abreu explains that when the quake's vibrations move from solid rock into softer sediment, the effect is similar to what happens when you strike the side of a bucket of water and make waves. "The bucket itself doesn't move that much, but all that energy is transferred into the water," he says. "The same thing happens when you have a basin filled with sediment." The result is that buildings on sediment experience a more severe shaking than those built on rock.

¶**31** Add in the factors that the quake struck a highly populated area and that many buildings weren't sturdy enough to withstand such a shock, and the **calamity** was complete. Entire villages collapsed. The rubble included over 7,000 classrooms.

¶**32** Government officials have promised to build sturdier schools to avert future disasters. But the principal of Sangzao Middle School was one step ahead of them. A few years ago, he hired workers to reinforce older school buildings. When the quake struck and most buildings crumbled, all 2,323 students and teachers in his school were safe. Abreu says, "You can't prevent the earthquake from happening, but you can prevent the building from collapsing."

Words to Know

factor: *(n.)* one of several things that influence or cause a situation

populated: *(adj.)* with a lot of people

avert: *(v.)* to prevent something unpleasant from happening

Close Reading

Text Structure

20. How does Abreu explain the effect of the quake's vibrations moving from solid rock into softer sediment in **paragraph 30**?

Academic Vocabulary

21. What details support the claim that "the **calamity** was complete"?

Key Ideas and Details

22. Explain why all 2,323 students and teachers were safe at Sangzao Middle School. Provide textual evidence.

Close Reading

Text Structure

23. Compare the "ordinary school day in China's Sichuan province" to the "sunny and warm day in Sumatra, Indonesia."

Academic Vocabulary

24. Do the authors adequately support the claim that the damage from the 2004 tsunami was "unparalleled"?

Key Ideas and Details

25. Why does Emile Okal, a seismologist at Northwestern University state, "The bottom line is we can't predict tsunamis"?

Tsunami: Indonesia

¶**33** December 26, 2004, started as a sunny and warm day in Sumatra, Indonesia. But at 8:00 a.m., the seafloor off Sumatra's northwest coast suddenly buckled, generating a massive earthquake—the largest in 40 years. The quake triggered a tsunami—a series of powerful ocean waves—that flooded the coastline of a dozen countries in Southeast Asia, South Asia, and parts of East Africa. The destruction was revealed when the water receded. Many coastal communities had been destroyed. More than 280,000 people were dead or missing.

Unpredictable Earth

¶**34** "Something like this is **unparalleled** in recent history," says Emile Okal, a seismologist at Northwestern University. In the last century, only seven tsunamis are known to have resulted from earthquakes beneath the Indian Ocean. None of these rare events were very large or caused major damage. That's why no one anticipated the 2004 tsunami. "The bottom line is we can't predict tsunamis," says Okal.

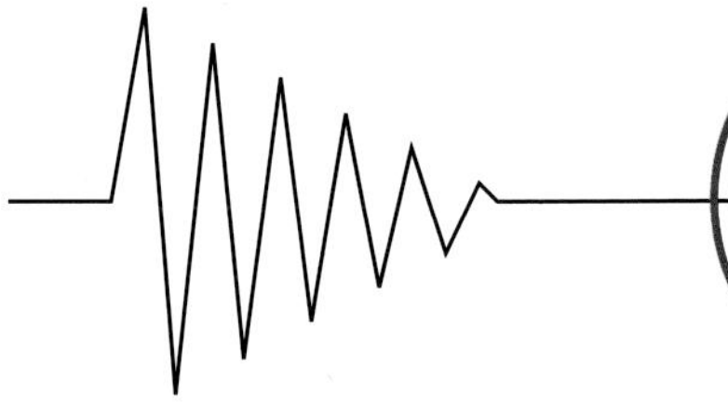

Words to Know

receded: *(v.)* if water recedes, it moves back from an area that it was covering

anticipated: *(v.)* to expect that something will happen

bottom line: *(n.)* used to tell someone what the most important part of a situation is

predict: *(v.)* to say that something will happen, before it happens

¶**35** Tsunamis are difficult to predict because they usually form after a very strong underwater earthquake. Since quakes happen out of sight, deep within the earth, scientists have yet to find a method to pinpoint when or where one will occur.

¶**36** An underwater earthquake begins deep below the seafloor, in a part of earth's hard crust. This outer layer of the planet is composed of plates. "Earth is like a hard-boiled egg with a cracked shell, except that the pieces [of earth's shell] are moving," says Steven Ward, a geophysicist at the University of California, Santa Cruz.

¶**37** Earth's plates move about 8 centimeters (3 inches) per year. But this movement causes stress along the tightly locked faults. When the stress becomes too intense, the faults rupture. The rocks on either side of the fault violently move by each other.

¶**38** This movement releases vibrating waves of energy called seismic waves. These waves move along the fault, and then gradually travel in all directions through the earth.

¶**39** The Indian Ocean quake registered a staggering magnitude of 9.3 on the Richter scale, a measure of the strength of the earthquake's seismic waves. "Earthquakes like the one that occurred in December 2004 cause a lot of shaking," says Ward. "But it's not the shaking that makes a tsunami."

Wave Maker

¶**40** So, what does cause a tsunami? The Indian Ocean earthquake occurred between the Eurasian and Indian plates along a subduction zone, an area where one plate tries to dive beneath another. When this thrust fault ruptured, it caused the plate on top to snap upward. A piece of the Eurasian Plate—about 1,000 kilometers (600 miles) long and 100 kilometers (60 miles) wide—was pushed up as much as 10 meters (30 feet). "If you have that much vertical movement [in the seafloor], you are going to move a lot of water," says Okal. "And that water has to go somewhere."

Words to Know

composed: *(v.)* to be made up of

gradually: *(adv.)* slowly, over a long period of time

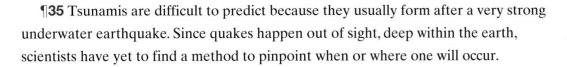

Close Reading

Key Ideas and Details

26. Explain Ward's comparison of Earth to a hard boiled egg with a cracked shell in **paragraph 36**.

Words and Phrases in Context

27. Define *staggering* as used in **paragraph 39**. What words or phrases do the authors use to support you in determining its meaning?

Text Structure

28. What does the sentence "But it's not the shaking that makes a tsunami" in **paragraph 39** suggest that the authors will discuss in the next section?

Close Reading

Words and Phrases in Context

29. What is the effect of words such as *quickly* and *raced* that the authors use to describe the movement of the 2004 tsunami in **paragraph 41**?

Key Ideas and Details

30. What words and phrases explain why it is so difficult to predict a tsunami?

Text Structure

31. What is the purpose of the diagram below?

¶**41** The displaced seafloor pushed the column of water above it upward. But gravity (the earth's pulling force) quickly pulled the bulged ocean surface back to sea level. That jolt pushed waves outward in all directions. The waves raced along the depths of the Indian Ocean at nearly 800 kilometers (500 miles) per hour. Then the waves met the sloping incline of the seafloor, known as the continental slope, and approached shallow water near shore. This caused the waves to slow down, and their peaks to scrunch together and get taller. When the tsunami hit shore, eyewitnesses in Southeast Asia saw walls of water towering as high as 12 meters (40 feet).

Uncommon Waves

¶**42** But not every strong underwater quake produces a massive tsunami. That makes predicting these deadly waves even more difficult. Just two days before the Indian Ocean tsunami occurred, a magnitude 8.1 earthquake rumbled through the seafloor of the Southern Ocean.

Tsunami Formation: **An earthquake deep in the ocean floor triggered a series of waves—a tsunami—that wiped out many coastal areas. Study the diagram to learn how it unfolded.**

1 An underwater earthquake occurs; seafloor snaps up, lifting the column of water above it. Gravity pulls the water back down, fanning waves outward.

2 Individual waves in a tsunami are spread out: The distance between two wave peaks, or wavelength, can be hundreds of kilometers long. Each wave's amplitude, or height, is typically less than 0.9 meters (3 feet).

3 As waves meet the continental slope and shallower water, wavelength decreases and amplitude rises.

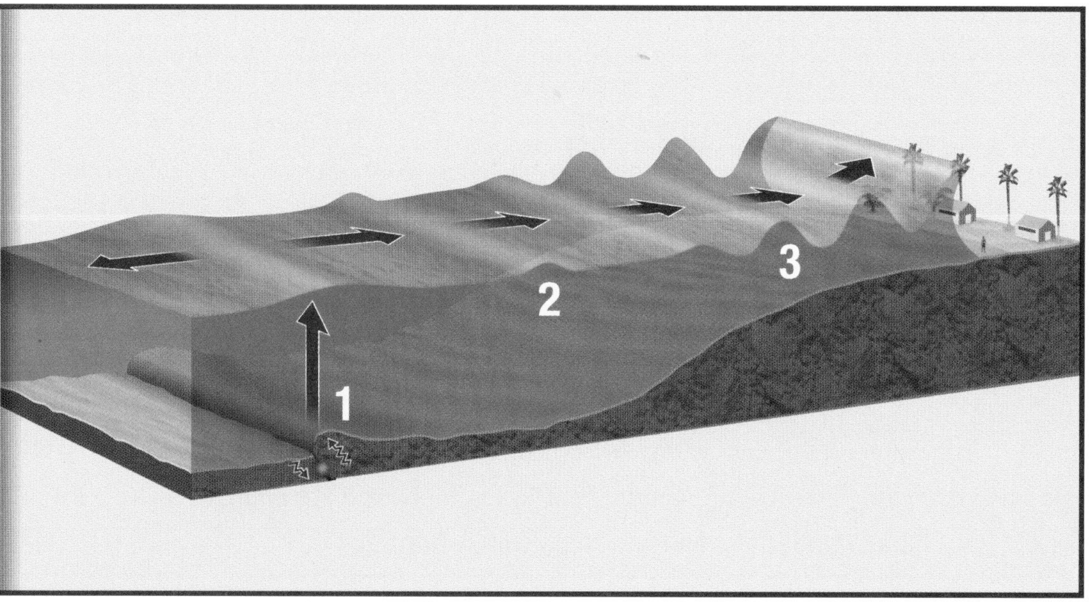

Words to Know

approximately: *(adv.)* nearly; about

¶**43** As powerful as that quake was, all it did was shake the ground of Macquarie Island approximately 400 kilometers (250 miles) away, startling a few resident penguins.

¶**44** Why didn't a tsunami occur? The quake occurred along a strike-slip fault, where two plates grind against each other in opposite directions. "Strike-slip faults are much less efficient at making tsunamis than thrust faults," says Ward. When the fault ruptured under the Southern Ocean, the two plates suddenly jolted sideways in opposite directions. There was very little vertical movement in the crust, so little water was displaced. Most of the energy just went into shaking rocks.

Monitoring the Quakes

¶**45** Scientists routinely use seismometers to monitor for seismic waves released by earthquakes. Although some scientists detected the Indian Ocean quake, no one saw the tsunami coming—and no one ordered an evacuation.

¶**46** Tsunami scientists usually focus their attention on the Pacific Ocean. That's because the area that borders that ocean, dubbed the "Ring of Fire," contains most of earth's subduction zones. That is where 90 percent of all tsunamis occur. In fact, that is why the Pacific Ocean has the earth's only network of sensors that **detects** and warns scientists of the changing water levels and pressures associated with a tsunami.

¶**47** Scientists are now analyzing records of how the Indian Ocean tsunami traveled through the water and exactly where it hit. They hope the information will help them design a tsunami **detection** and warning system for the Indian Ocean, and make the tsunami of December 2004 the final one to claim so many lives.

Words to Know

monitor: *(v.)* to carefully watch and check a situation in order to see how it changes over a period of time

associated: *(v.)* connected to; thought of as being a part of something

Close Reading

Writing

32. Explain why the earthquake with a magnitude of 8.1 didn't trigger a tsunami. What was different about the earthquake with a magnitude of 9.3 that allowed it to create a tsunami?

Key Ideas and Details

33. Discuss why no one ordered an evacuation. Provide textual evidence.

Words and Phrases in Context

34. Define *dubbed* as used in **paragraph 46.** What words or phrases do the authors use to support you in determining its meaning?

Identify Evidence | Analyze Events and Ideas

Reread the excerpt from **"Super Disasters of the 21st Century,"** highlighting details that tell about the causes and effects of the three disasters. Consider the text structure, choice of vocabulary, and use of data and details.

- After you read, use the Evidence column to record examples from the text that tell about the causes and effects of disasters.
- In the Explanation column, explain how the evidence relates to a technique or strategy that the authors used to describe the causes and effects of the disasters.

Text Structure		
Evidence	**Page**	**Explanation**
1. "At least 1,800 people died. Hundreds of missing people were never accounted for."	144	The authors structure this section by telling about the effects of Hurricane Katrina first to draw in the readers.
2.		
Vocabulary		
Evidence	**Page**	**Explanation**
3. "TV viewers watched in shock as the city drowned."	145	

Evidence	Page	Explanation
4.		

Data

Evidence	Page	Explanation
5. "Total losses exceeded $150 billion."		
6.		

Key Ideas and Details

Determining the Central Idea

1. Use the evidence you collected to summarize the key idea of Adams and Kostel's science article.

The central idea of Adams and Kostel's science article is ____

____The authors discuss ________

____ such

as ____

____

____

2. List three key effects of super disasters that the authors discuss in their text. List a solution the authors offer to minimize each effect.

Disaster: Effect:	→	Solution:
Disaster: Effect:	→	Solution:
Disaster: Effect:	→	Solution:

Craft and Structure

Structure of the Science Article

1. Make a list of words and phrases that the authors use to help the reader visualize the effects of the disasters.

Hurricane Katrina	Earthquake in Sichuan	Indian Ocean Tsunami

2. Note the comparisons the authors use to help readers understand how each disaster occurred.

Hurricane Katrina	Earthquake in Sichuan	Indian Ocean Tsunami

3. How is the tone different when the authors discuss the effects of the disasters compared to when they discuss the causes? Why do you think the authors use a different tone?

4. What solutions do the authors discuss for minimizing the effects of super disasters?

5. What is the authors' perspective toward super disasters?

Tone

Tone is the writer's attitude toward the writing and the readers. Tone is set through word choices, descriptive details, sensory language, and setting.

Perspective

Perspective is a personal opinion or attitude about something.

Academic Vocabulary

from *The Perfect Storm* by Sebastian Junger

Rate your understanding of each word. Then read its meaning and write a sample sentence.

Word	Meaning	Example
stable *(adj.)* p. 162 ① ② ③ ④	steady and not likely to move or change	
conditions *(n.)* p. 163 ① ② ③ ④		The conditions outside changed quickly from hot and sunny to cold and windy.
dynamics *(n.)* p. 164 ① ② ③ ④	the science relating to the movement of objects and the forces involved in movement	
concept *(n.)* p. 165 ① ② ③ ④		The concept for the school dance is that it is a winter wonderland.
impractical *(adj.)* p. 165 ① ② ③ ④	not sensible or possible for practical reasons	

Rating Scale | ① I don't know the word. ② I've seen it or heard it. ③ I know its meaning. ④ I know it and use it.

Word Study

Thesaurus

A **thesaurus** is a book that contains lists of synonyms. Some thesauruses also include antonyms.

Use the dictionary entry and the thesaurus entry for the word *impractical* to answer the questions below.

Dictionary Entry

impractical: (im•**prahk**•teh•kal) *adjective.* impracticality; not wise to do; not capable of being done sensibly. *Redesigning the library is impractical because of the great effort it would take.*

Thesaurus Entry

impractical: *adjective.* unwise.
synonyms: impossible, unrealistic.
antonyms: practical, sensible

1. What definition does the dictionary provide for the word *impractical*?
2. What definition does the thesaurus provide for the word *impractical*?
3. Which definition is more precise?

from

The Perfect Storm

by Sebastian Junger

Albert Johnston:

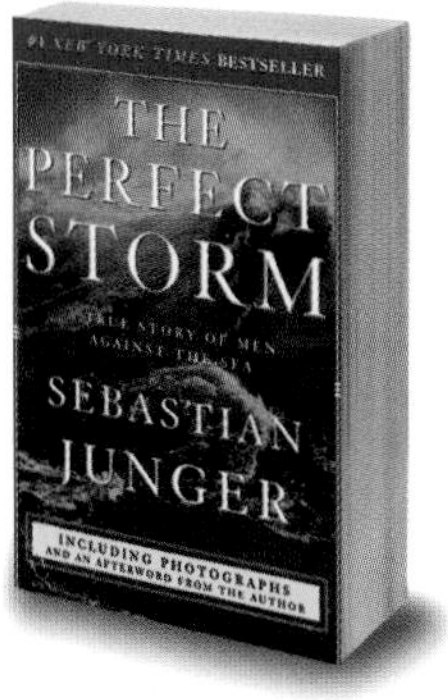

¶**1** *I was the first one to know how bad it was really gonna be. Halifax called for twenty meter seas and when we heard that we thought, Oh boy. You don't really have the time to run to land so we tried to get into the coldest water we could find. The colder the water, the denser it is and the waves don't get so big. Also, I knew we'd get a northeast-northwest wind. I wanted to make as much headway as possible 'cause the Gulf Stream was down south and that's where the warm water and fast current are.*

Words to Know

denser: *(adj.)* thicker; made of or containing a lot of things that are very close together

headway: *(n.)* to move forward or make progress

Close Reading

Text Structure

1. Describe what the use of *italics* signals to the reader.

Anecdote

A first-person **anecdote** is a short story based on a personal experience.

Key Ideas and Details

2. Why did Albert Johnson and his crew try to get into the coldest water they could find?

Close Reading

Key Ideas and Details

3. How do you know that Albert Johnston and his crew were used to being at sea during bad weather?

Words and Phrases in Context

4. Define the phrase *in retrospect* as it is used in **paragraph 3**. What words or phrases does the author use to support you in determining the meaning?

Academic Vocabulary

5. Discuss why it was important for the boat to be stable during the storm.

¶2 *There was an awful lot of electrical noise along the leading edge of this thing, there was so much noise you couldn't hear anything on the radio. I was up in the* wheelhouse*, when it's bad like that I usually stay up there. If it looks like it's settlin' down a bit and I can grab a little sleep, then I will. The crew just racks out and watches videos. Everyone acknowledged this was the worst storm they'd ever been in–you can really tell by the size of the waves, the motion of the boat, the noise, the crashing. There's always a point when you realize that you're in the middle of the ocean and if anything goes wrong, that's it. You see so much bad weather that you kind of get used to it. But then you see really bad weather. And that, you never get used to.*

¶3 *They had ship reports of thirty meter seas. That's ninety feet. I would imagine–truthfully, in retrospect–that if the whole U.S. swordfish fleet had been caught in the center of that thing, everybody would've gone down. We only saw, I don't know, maybe fifty foot waves, max. We went into it until it started to get dark, and then we turned around and went with it. You can't see those* rogue *waves in the dark and you don't want to get blasted and knock your wheelhouse off. We got the RPM tuned in just right to be* in synch *with the waves; too fast and we'd start surfing, too slow and the waves would just blast right over the whole boat. The boat was heavy and loaded with fish, very* ***stable****. It made for an amazingly good ride.*

Words to Know

wheelhouse: *(n.)* an enclosed area on a boat or ship where a person stands to steer

rogue: *(adj.)* not behaving in the usual or accepted way and often causing trouble

in synch: *(idiom)* to occur at the same time; working well together at exactly the same time and speed

¶**4** Johnston had finished his last haul late in the afternoon of the 28th: nineteen swordfish, twenty bigeye, twenty-two yellowfin, and two mako. He immediately started steaming north and by morning he was approaching the Tail of the Banks, winds out of the northeast at one hundred knots and seas twenty to thirty feet. Several hundred miles to the west, though, **conditions** have gone off the chart. The first hundred-foot wave spikes the graph at 8 p.m., and the second one spikes it at midnight. For the next two hours, peak wave heights stay at a hundred feet and winds hit eighty miles an hour. The waves are blocking the data buoy readings, though, and the wind is probably hitting 120 or so. Eighty-mile-an-hour wind can suck fish right out of the bait barrels. Hundred-foot waves are fifty percent higher than the most extreme sizes predicted by computer models. They are the largest waves ever recorded on the Scotian Shelf. They are among the very highest waves measured anywhere in the world, ever.

Words to Know

haul: *(n.)* everything collected or acquired by a single effort

peak: *(adj.)* at the highest point or level

Close Reading

Text Structure

6. Describe how the purpose and narrator of the text shifts in **paragraph 4**.

Words and Phrases in Context

7. Define the phrase *off the chart* as it is used in **paragraph 4**. What words or phrases does the author use to support you in determining the meaning?

Writing

8. Identify the data and details that the author includes to help the reader understand the effects of the storm.

Close Reading

Academic Vocabulary

9. Explain how the dynamics of water affect a boat during a storm with monster waves.

Text Structure

10. What is the effect of using verbs such as *flipped, blasted,* and *heaved* to describe bad weather?

Writing

11. Identify the reasons the author included to explain why "average wave heights are slowly rising and the freak waves . . . are becoming more common."

¶**5** A general rule of fluid **dynamics** holds that an object in the water tends to do whatever the water it replaces would have done. In the case of a boat in a breaking wave, the boat will effectively become part of the curl. It will either be flipped end over end or shoved backward and broken on. Instantaneous pressures of up to six tons per square foot have been measured in breaking waves. Breaking waves have lifted a 2,700-ton breakwater, en masse, and deposited it inside the harbor at Wick, Scotland. They have blasted open a steel door 195 feet above sea level at Unst Light in the Shetland Islands. They have heaved a half-ton boulder ninety-one feet into the air at Tillamook Rock, Oregon.

¶**6** There is some evidence that average wave heights are slowly rising, and that freak waves of eighty or ninety are becoming more common. Wave heights off the coast of England have risen an average of 25 percent over the past couple of decades, which converts to a twenty-foot increase in the highest waves over the next half-century. One cause may be the tightening of environmental laws, which has reduced the amount of oil flushed into the oceans by oil tankers. Oil spreads across water in a film several molecules thick and inhibits the generation of capillary waves, which in turn prevent the wind from getting a "grip" on the sea. Plankton releases a chemical that has the same effect, and plankton levels in the North Atlantic have dropped dramatically. Another explanation is that the recent warming trend—some call it the greenhouse effect—has made storms more frequent and severe. Waves have destroyed docks and buildings in Newfoundland, for example, that haven't been damaged for decades.

Words to Know

en masse: *(adv.)* as a single group; all together

heaved: *(v.)* to pull or lift something very heavy

converts: *(v.)* to change something into a different form of thing

inhibits: *(v.)* to prevent something from growing or developing well

¶7 As a result, stresses on ships have been rising. The standard practice is to build ships to withstand what is called a twenty-five-year stress—the most violent condition the ship is likely to experience in twenty-five years. The wave that flooded the wheelhouse of the *Queen Mary,* ninety feet up, must have nearly exceeded her twenty-five-year stress. North Sea oil platforms are built to accommodate a 111-foot wave beneath their decks, which is calculated to be a one-hundred-year stress. Unfortunately, the twenty-five-year stress is just a statistical **concept** that offers no guarantee about what will happen next year, or next week. A ship could encounter several twenty-five-year waves in a month or never encounter any at all. Naval architects simply decide what level of stress she's likely to encounter in her lifetime and then hope for the best. It's economically and structurally **impractical** to construct every boat to hundred-year specifications.

The 1991 Perfect Storm, also known as the Halloween Nor'easter of 1991, caused over $200 million dollars worth of damage.

Words to Know

exceeded: *(v.)* to go beyond the limit of (something)

statistical: *(adj.)* based on numbers and data

platform: *(n.)* a tall structure built so that people can stand or work above the surrounding area

Close Reading

Key Ideas and Details

12. Why would rising wave heights place more stress on ships?

Academic Vocabulary

13. Discuss why "the twenty-five-year stress specification is just a statistical concept."

Writing

14. Does the author provide sufficient evidence to support the claim that "it's economically and structurally impractical to construct every boat to hundred-year specifications"?

Identify Evidence | Analyze Individuals, Events and Ideas

Reread the excerpt from ***The Perfect Storm***, highlighting details that tell about the causes and effects of the storm. Consider the text structure, choice of vocabulary, and use of data and details.

- After you read, use the Evidence column to record examples from the text that tell about the causes and effects of disasters.
- In the Explanation column, explain how the evidence relates to a technique or strategy that the author used to describe the causes and effects of the disaster.

Text Structure		
Evidence	**Page**	**Explanation**
1. "I was the first one to know how bad it was really gonna be."	161	Engages the reader by beginning with a first-person anecdote of the effects of the storm.
2.		

Vocabulary		
Evidence	**Page**	**Explanation**
3. "Eighty-mile-an-hour wind can suck fish right out of the bait barrels."	163	

Evidence	Page	Explanation
4.		
Data		
Evidence	**Page**	**Explanation**
5. "Hundred-foot waves are fifty percent higher than the most extreme sizes predicted . . ."		
6.		

Key Ideas and Details

Determining the Central Idea

1. Use the evidence you collected to summarize the key idea of Sebastian Junger's text.

The central idea of Sebastian Junger's text is ______________________________

______________________________. The author includes a firsthand anecdote of

____

______________________________. The author then discusses reasons for ______________

____

2. List the key individuals, events, and ideas the author presents in each paragraph. Then explain the significance of the individual, event, or idea to the central idea.

Paragraph	Key Individuals, Events, and Ideas	Significance
1–3	Individual	
4	Event	
5	Idea	
6	Idea	
7	Idea	

Craft and Structure

Structure of Literary Nonfiction

1. Junger starts off the text with a first-person anecdote. Albert Johnston shares that "then you see really bad weather. And that, you never get used to." What idea does Junger set up in this section of the text?

2. What evidence and details does Junger use to describe the effects of monster waves?

Effect	Data and Details
• cause destruction	• boat can be "flipped end over end or shoved backward and broken on" • "blasted open a steel door 195 feet above sea level" • "destroyed docks and buildings" • "heaved a half-ton boulder ninety-one feet into the air"

3. What is Junger's attitude toward the building of ships that can withstand the force of monster waves?

Collaborate and Present

Plan and Deliver a Presentation

While both texts tell about the harrowing effects of natural disasters, there is much more to learn about each of the disasters.

Assignment: Work in small groups to research one of the disasters in greater detail. Describe the effects of the disaster on the country, city, or community. Use and compare multiple resources for information about the disaster.

Analyze the Content

1. Consider the following questions:
   - Which natural disaster was the most interesting to you? Why?
   - What else do you want to know about the natural disaster?
2. Working with your group, select one natural disaster to research. Go to the library or use the Internet to find out more about the effects of that natural disaster. Discuss the reliability of the sources you find with your group. After selecting at least three reliable sources, record your notes from those sources in a chart like this one.

Natural Disaster:

Effects	Source

Create Your Presentation

3. Use your notes to create your presentation.
   - With your group, organize the information you gathered into a logical order. Identify the disaster, discuss two or three effects, use quotations and data.
   - Decide which group members will present which parts of your presentation.
   - Practice your presentation.

Present

4. Deliver your presentation.

Seeking Clarification

- In other words, you think that . . .
- If I understand you correctly, you would like to . . .
- So you would prefer to . . .

Reporting Ideas

- _____ noticed
- _____ suggested
- _____ agreed

Presentation

- Use formal English.
- Face your audience.
- Stand up straight and speak with confidence.
- Avoid fidgeting.

Presentation Checklist

Use the checklist below to evaluate your collaboration skills, reasoning, and final presentation. Think carefully about your work. If you know you completed an item thoroughly, give yourself a check (✓).

COLLABORATE AND PRESENT CHECKLIST		
Comprehension & Collaboration	**Evidence & Reasoning**	**Presentation of Knowledge & Ideas**
☐ Come to discussions prepared, having read and studied material. ☐ Refer to evidence when contributing to the discussion. ☐ Follow rules for discussions and lead by example. ☐ Ask and answer specific questions. ☐ Make comments that contribute to the topic under discussion. ☐ Review the key ideas under discussion and demonstrate understanding of multiple perspectives through reflection and paraphrasing.	☐ Explain the purpose of the presentation. ☐ Present information relevant to the task. ☐ Explain in detail the effects of a natural disaster on a country, city or community. ☐ Compare multiple resources for information about the disaster. ☐ Use at least one example from each source. ☐ Synthesize the key ideas from the presentation with a conclusion.	☐ Adapt language to a variety of contexts and tasks to demonstrate knowledge of formal English. ☐ Include multimedia components (e.g., graphics, images, music, sound) and visual displays. ☐ Use appropriate volume/tone (clear, not too fast, too slow, or too loud) and avoid using "like" or "ummm." ☐ Have strong posture, a confident stance, and make frequent eye contact. ☐ Occasionally move from one spot to another without fidgeting. ☐ Smile and appear to be relaxed.
Number of ✓s in this category: ___	**Number of ✓s in this category: ___**	**Number of ✓s in this category: ___**
Total # of ✓s: __		

Add up the total number of checks (✓) in each category. Then use the scoring guide below to calculate your final score.

Scoring Guide			
16 to 18 ✓s	**13 to 15 ✓s**	**11 to 12 ✓s**	**10 or less ✓s**
④ **Exemplary**	③ **Meets Standards**	② **Needs Work**	① **Does Not Meet Standards**

Read the Model

Writers employ many strategies to share ideas and explain a topic. The writer of this explanatory essay compares and contrasts the use of data and details to show how two authors describe similar occurrences in different ways. Read and discuss the model essay below.

Explanatory Essay

An **explanatory essay** examines a topic and conveys ideas.

The introduction states the title and author of the text that the writer will analyze.

- Describe how the writer introduced the topic.

The two body paragraphs express the writer's main points about the text.

- Find two examples of text citations.
- Find two examples of the writer's use of concise language.

Transition words or phrases organize and link ideas, sentences, and paragraphs.

- Identify transition words and explain their function.

The conclusion sums up or restates the thesis.

- Identify the conclusion.

Different Ways to Discuss Causes and Effects

By Sara Dryden

Sebastian Junger's *The Perfect Storm* and Jacqueline Adams' "Submerged City" describe the causes and effects of nature's savagery. Each author uses similar strategies and techniques to accomplish this goal.

Junger, in *The Perfect Storm*, combines a personal anecdote with data, and scientific theories to illustrate the causes and effects of increasing wave heights. The anecdote tells the story of a ship's captain. He faced "fifty-foot waves" that were capable of blasting "right over the whole boat" (Junger 162). The data cites a few concrete examples of the effects of monster waves: "They have heaved a half-ton boulder ninety-one feet into the air at Tillamook Rock, Oregon" (Junger 164). The author also explains scientific theories about what causes these waves: a chemical in plankton "prevents the wind from getting a 'grip' on the sea,' " and plankton levels "have dropped" (164).

Like Junger, Adams in "Submerged City," describes the causes and effects of hurricanes, and she explains why they are a threat to the New York City area using extensive data but avoids using a personal anecdote. Facts explaining why New York is vulnerable to hurricanes, such as "some storms turn north and are swept up by faster winds," are highly convincing since they are validated by quotes from reliable sources, like atmospheric scientist Kerry Emanuel, who says that hurricanes "embedded in those winds, move faster" (Adams 188).

In brief, Junger and Adams both tell about the dangerous side of nature by citing data, details and descriptions. Junger also chooses to include a personal anecdote to engage the reader.

Analyze the Model

A compare/contrast essay explains similarities and differences between two texts.

Introduction

Body Paragraph 1: Junger

Purpose: describe the causes and effects of increasing wave heights

Strategies/Techniques:

Examples/Evidence:

Body Paragraph 2: Adams

Purpose:

Strategies/Techniques:

Examples/Evidence:

Conclusion

Text Strategy

In a **block-by-block comparison,** the writer discusses all the relevant characteristics of one text in the first body paragraph and all the relevant characteristics of the second text in the second body paragraph.

The thesis statement presents a clear plan for the essay.

- Identify the thesis statement.

Relevant evidence includes examples and quotations from the text, that support the writer's ideas.

- Identify the purpose, strategies/techniques, and examples/evidence of each body paragraph.
- Evaluate whether all the evidence supports the thesis sentence.

The conclusion sums up or restates the thesis.

- Describe how the writer concludes her essay.

Step 1 | Gather Evidence

Compare and contrast strategies and techniques that each author uses to describe the causes and effects of disasters. Consider text structure, choice of vocabulary, and use of data and details.

What You Need to Know | Examine the evidence you have collected about the strategies and techniques the writers use to describe the causes and effects in the Touchstone Texts. (See pages 156 and 166.)

What You Need to Write | Note the strategies and techniques.

excerpt from "Super Disasters of the 21st Century"

Point:

Evidence:

Page # _____

Point:

Evidence:

Page # _____

Point:

Evidence:

Page # _____

excerpt from *The Perfect Storm*

Point:

Evidence:

Page # _____

Point:

Evidence:

Page # _____

Point:

Evidence:

Page # _____

Step 2 | Organize Ideas

What You Need to Know | When you compare two things, you describe their similarities. When you contrast them, you focus on their differences.

To develop your topic:

1. Describe Adams's and Kostel's strategies and techniques
2. Describe Junger's strategies and techniques

What You Need to Write | Determine which of these authors' strategies and techniques are the same and which are different.

Body Paragraph 1: ______________________________
(author's name)

Purpose:

Strategies/Techniques:

Evidence:

Strategies/Techniques that are Similar:

Body Paragraph 2: ______________________________
(author's name)

Purpose:

Strategies/Techniques:

Evidence:

Strategies/Techniques that are Different:

Step 3 | Draft

Write a draft of your explanatory essay on the computer or on paper.

Language Study | Combining and Rewriting Sentences

See It

The words *because* and *since* can be used to join together sentences stating a cause-and-effect relationship. Below are examples of two sentence patterns.

1. ***Because*** or ***since*** as the first word and a comma in the middle: *Because temperatures are getting warmer, storms are more severe.*
2. ***Because*** or ***since*** in the middle and no comma: *Storms are more severe since temperatures are getting warmer.*

Try It

Combine each pair of sentences twice using the word in parentheses ( ) and both patterns.

1. So many Japanese have been displaced by the recent disasters.
   The whole country is practicing self-restraint. (because)

   Combined 1:

   Combined 2:

2. Political candidates have even taken to campaigning quietly.
   Following the spirit of jishuku means the practice should extend into public life. (since)

   Combined 1:

   Combined 2:

3. Jishuku is so widespread.
   Even the cherry blossom ceremonies that are a big part of the Japanese culture have been cancelled. (because)

   Combined 1:

   Combined 2:

Apply It | **Use the sentence frames to combine sentences about the causes and effects of the authors' strategies.**

1. Because ____________ (author's name) uses ____________________ (strategy/technique the author uses) in the ____________ (text type) titled ____________ (title), the reader ____________________ (result of author's strategy/technique).

2. The reader ____________________ (result of author's strategy/technique) because ____________ (author's name) uses ____________________ (strategy/technique the author uses) in the ____________ (text type) titled ____________ (title).

3. Since ____________ (author's name) uses ____________________ (strategy/technique the author uses) in the ____________ (text type) titled ____________ (title), the reader ____________________ (result of author's strategy/technique).

4. The reader ____________________ (result of author's strategy/technique) since ____________ (author's name) uses ____________________ (strategy/technique the author uses) in the ____________ (text type) titled ____________ (title).

Now revisit your draft and combine sentences stating a cause-and-effect relationship.

____

____

Conventions Study | Using Sentence Variety

See It

Sentence variety is the use of different sentence structures. Sentence variety makes writing less monotonous and signals different relationships among ideas.

- A **simple sentence** has one independent clause and expresses one main idea clearly and forcefully:

  Earthquakes can cause extensive damage.

- A **compound sentence** has two or more independent clauses and joins two closely related thoughts:

  Hurricanes are dangerous, but advance warning can help save lives.

- A **complex sentence** has one independent clause and at least one *subordinate clause*. It expresses one important idea and a less important idea:

  When an earthquake happens at sea, a tsunami may be created.

- A **compound–complex sentence** has two or more independent clauses and at least one *subordinate clause*. It expresses two main ideas and a subordinate thought.

  Experts knew that a hurricane could damage New York City,
  but most residents were caught off guard when the storm hit.

Try It

Identify the structure of the sentence the writer uses in the sentence below from the model. What is the relationship between the ideas?

> He faced "fifty-foot waves" that were capable of blasting "right over the whole boat."

Apply It

Revise one of your body paragraphs. Use a variety of sentence structures to make your writing more interesting and to signal different relationships among ideas. Underline independent clauses and circle subordinate clauses.

Step 4 | Revise and Edit

Revise your draft with a partner.

Organization and Clarity		
State the title and authors of the texts in the introduction.	Self	1 2 3 4
	Partner	1 2 3 4
Include a clear, meaningful thesis statement that compares and contrasts each author's strategies and techniques used to describe causes and effects of disasters.	Self	1 2 3 4
	Partner	1 2 3 4
Each body paragraph focuses on only one text and contains information that reflects the topic sentence and supports the thesis statement.	Self	1 2 3 4
	Partner	1 2 3 4
Each body paragraph reflects the purpose of comparing and contrasting the texts.	Self	1 2 3 4
	Partner	1 2 3 4
The conclusion paragraph includes a final thought about the implications of the strategies and techniques the authors used.	Self	1 2 3 4
	Partner	1 2 3 4
Evidence and Reasoning		
Include three or more pieces of specific and relevant text evidence in each body paragraph.	Self	1 2 3 4
	Partner	1 2 3 4
Language and Conventions		
Use a variety of sentence structures.	Self	1 2 3 4
	Partner	1 2 3 4
Use appropriate transition words to link sections of the essay and ideas within each paragraph.	Self	1 2 3 4
	Partner	1 2 3 4
Use precise language to convey the complexity of ideas. Use academic and domain-specific vocabulary from the texts as appropriate.	Self	1 2 3 4
	Partner	1 2 3 4
Establish and maintain a formal style and objective tone throughout the essay.	Self	1 2 3 4
	Partner	1 2 3 4

Scoring Guide | ① needs improvement ② average ③ good ④ excellent

Step 5 | Publish

Publish

Publish your essay either in print or digital form. Use the rubric below to consider the success of your final performance task.

PERFORMANCE TASK RUBRIC			
Score Point	**Organization and Clarity**	**Evidence and Reasoning**	**Language and Conventions**
Exemplary ④	• introductory paragraph **introduces** what the writer will compare and contrast and includes a **strong focus statement** • each body paragraph focuses on one text and **strongly supports** the focus **statement with relevant** strategies and techniques the writer uses • includes **well-chosen** text evidence, precise language, and sentence variety • concluding statement **restates** the focus statement	• **effectively compares and contrasts** the strategies and techniques each author uses to describe the causes and effects of natural disasters • includes **several examples of relevant** factual evidence from the science article and informational excerpt to support the explanation, including text structure, choice of vocabulary, and use of data and details	• demonstrates a **strong command** of the conventions of standard English grammar and usage, as well as of standard English capitalization, punctuation, and spelling • vocabulary is **appropriate** to the topic (vocabulary about causes and effects of natural disasters; accurate terms for referring to text structure, choice of vocabulary, and use of data and details; vocabulary for making comparisons and contrasts)
Meets Standards ③	• introductory paragraph **introduces** what the writer will compare and contrast and includes a focus statement • each body paragraph focuses on a text and **supports** the focus statement with **some strategies and techniques** the writer uses • includes **some** text evidence, precise language, and sentence variety • concluding statement **restates** the focus statement	• **adequately compares and contrasts** the strategies and techniques each author uses to describe the causes and effects of natural disasters • includes **some relevant** factual evidence from the science article and informational excerpt to support the explanation, including text structure, choice of vocabulary, and use of data and details	• demonstrates **a near command** of the conventions of standard English grammar and usage, as well as of standard English capitalization, punctuation, and spelling **with some errors** • vocabulary is **appropriate** to the topic (vocabulary about causes and effects of natural disasters; accurate terms for referring to text structure, choice of vocabulary, and use of data and details; vocabulary for making comparisons and contrasts)

PERFORMANCE TASK RUBRIC			
Score Point	**Organization and Clarity**	**Evidence and Reasoning**	**Language and Conventions**
Needs Work ②	• introductory paragraph introduces what the writer will compare and contrast and includes a focus statement that **loosely identifies** what the essay will be about • body paragraphs are **somewhat organized** by text, though include some details about the second text in each paragraph • includes **a limited amount** of text evidence, precise language and sentence variety • concluding statement **attempts to restate** the focus statement	• **attempts to compare and contrast** the strategies and techniques each writer uses to describe the causes and effects of natural disasters • includes **some textual evidence** from the science article and informational excerpt to support the explanation, including text structure, choice of vocabulary, and use of data and details	• demonstrates a **marginal command** of the conventions of English grammar and usage, as well as of standard English capitalization, punctuation, and spelling • there **are many errors; however, the text is still understandable** • includes only **one or two examples** of vocabulary that is appropriate to the topic (vocabulary about causes and effects of natural disasters; accurate terms for referring to text structure, choice of vocabulary, and use of data and details; vocabulary for making comparisons and contrasts)
Does Not Meet Standards ①	• introductory paragraph is **unclear** and does not include a focus statement • body paragraphs are **not organized logically** and/or **do not include information** about both texts in each paragraph • essay includes **little text evidence** and little sentence variety • concluding statement is **unclear and does not wrap up** the ideas in the essay	• response is **partial or inaccurate explanation** of the strategies and techniques each writer uses to describe the causes and effects of natural disasters • includes **no analyses of textual evidence** from the science article and informational excerpt	• demonstrates **almost no command** of the conventions of standard English grammar and usage, as well as of standard English capitalization, punctuation, and spelling • there **are many errors that disrupt** the reader's understanding of the text • **does not include** vocabulary that is appropriate to the topic (vocabulary about causes and effects of natural disasters; accurate terms for referring to text structure, choice of vocabulary, and use of data and details; vocabulary for making comparisons and contrasts)

Questions

Words and Phrases in Context

1. Define the term *jishuku*. What words or phrases do the authors use to support you in determining the meaning?

Key Ideas and Details

2. Compare and contrast Japanese behavior before and after the tsunami.

from **In Deference to Crisis, a New Obsession Sweeps Japan: Self-Restraint**

by Ken Belson and Norimitsu Onishi from *The New York Times*

¶**1** Even in a country whose people are known for walking in lockstep, a national consensus on the proper code of behavior has emerged with startling speed. Consider post-tsunami Japan as the age of voluntary self-restraint, or jishuku, the antipode of the Japan of the "bubble" era that celebrated excess.

¶**2** With hundreds of thousands of people displaced up north from the earthquake, tsunami and nuclear crisis, anything with the barest hint of luxury invites condemnation. There were only general calls for conservation, but within days of the March 11 [2011] quake, Japanese of all stripes began turning off lights, elevators, heaters and even toilet seat warmers.

¶**3** But self-restraint goes beyond the need to compensate for shortages of electricity brought on by the closing of the Fukushima Daiichi nuclear plant. At a time of collective mourning, jishuku also demands that self-restraint be practiced elsewhere. Candidates in next month's local elections are hewing to the ethos by literally campaigning quietly for votes, instead of circling neighborhoods in their usual campaign trucks with blaring loudspeakers.

¶**4** With aggressive sales tactics suddenly rendered unseemly, the giant Bic Camera electric appliance outlet in central Tokyo has dropped the decibels on its incessant in-store jingle, usually audible half a block away. At the high school baseball tournament in Osaka, bands put away their instruments; instead, cheering sections have been clapping by hitting plastic horns together.

¶**5** There are also doubts about whether it is proper to partake in the seasonal pleasures that regulate much of Japanese life.

¶**6** "At this time of the year, we'd usually be talking about going to see cherry blossoms," Hiroshi Sekiguchi, one of the country's best-known television personalities, said on his Sunday morning talk show.

Words to Know

displaced: *(v.)* to make a group of people or animals have to leave the place where they normally live

ethos: *(n.)* the guiding beliefs of a person, group, or organization

¶**7** In fact, cherry blossom viewing parties and fireworks festivals have been canceled. Graduations and commencements have been put off. Stores and restaurants have reduced their hours or closed. Cosmetics and karaoke are out; bottled water and Geiger counters are in.

¶**8** It is as if much of a nation's people have simultaneously hunkered down, all with barely a rule being passed or a penalty being assessed.

¶**9** "We are not forced or anything," said Koichi Nakamura, 45, who runs a karaoke shop in Kabukicho, Tokyo's famed entertainment district, where customers looking to sing their lungs out have all but vanished. "I hope it will somehow contribute to the affected areas."

¶**10** The almost overnight transformation is likely to continue for months, if not years. The hot summer ahead is expected to further strain the nation's electrical network, leading to more disruptive blackouts that make it hard for business to be conducted the Japanese way, face to face and often into the night. The vast entertainment industry that greases corporate Japan, including sushi bars and cabarets, is likely to be deeply hurt.

¶**11** As effective as the self-restraint has been—conservation measures have allowed Tokyo Electric Power to cancel some planned blackouts—the continued scaling back is likely to have a corrosive effect on Japan's sagging economy. While the government will spend heavily to rebuild the shattered prefectures to the northeast, consumer spending, which makes up about 60 percent of the economy, will probably sink; bankruptcies are expected to soar.

¶**12** Had the disasters hit a more distant corner of the country, things might have been different. But because Tokyo has been directly affected by the blackouts and the nuclear crisis, the impact has been greater. The capital and surrounding prefectures, where so many companies, government agencies and news media outlets are located, account for about one-third of the country's gross domestic product.

Words to Know

hunkered down: *(v.)* to be prepared for a difficult situation

soar: *(v.)* to increase very quickly in amount or price

Questions

Text Structure

3. Nakamura, a business man, states that "We are not forced or anything" to practice *jishuku*. Although many of his customers "have all but vanished" he hopes "it will somehow contribute to the affected areas." Why does the author include this information?

Words and Phrases in Context

4. Define *corrosive* in **paragraph 11**. What words or phrases do the authors use to support you in determining the meaning?

Questions

Key Ideas and Details

5. What evidence in this section supports the claim that *jishuku* has changed the Japanese culture in a serious way?

Words and Phrases in Context

6. Define *outliers* in **paragraph 19**. What words or phrases do the authors use to support you in determining the meaning?

¶**13** Japan has gone through spasms of self-control before, including after the death of Emperor Hirohito in 1989. This time, though, self-restraint may be a way of coping with the traumatizing scale of the loss of life as well as the spreading fears of radioactive fallout, according to Kensuke Suzuki, an associate professor of sociology at Kwansei Gakuin University in western Japan.

¶**14** "With the extensive coverage of the disaster zone, jishuku has become a way for people in Tokyo to express solidarity at a time of crisis," Professor Suzuki said in an email. "Jishuku is the easiest way to feel like you're doing something, though perhaps there isn't much thought put into how much these actions make a difference over all."

¶**15** It is not surprising then that the national obsession with self-restraint has bled into political circles. In several prefectures, like Gifu, Aomori and Akita, candidates have agreed not to campaign too aggressively, by limiting their appearances and not calling voters at home.

¶**16** In Tokyo's luxury shopping district, Ginza, on Sunday, Hideo Higashikokubaru, 53, a politician and former comedian, practiced jishuku-style campaigning by riding a bicycle and eschewing a bullhorn. "I'm trying my best in my own voice," Mr. Higashikokubaru said, surrounded by voters on an intersection overlooked by Chanel, Louis Vuitton, Cartier and Bulgari.

¶**17** Political analysts have said that such campaign constraints will favor incumbents like Shintaro Ishihara, the three-term Tokyo governor Mr. Higashikokubaru is trying to unseat.

¶**18** "That's right," Mr. Higashikokubaru said in a short interview. "That's why I have to try even harder."

¶**19** But outliers, like Japan's Communist Party, have explicitly rejected a calmer tenor to their campaigning, saying that it would rob voters of valuable information about candidates.

¶**20** Another objector was Yoshiro Nakamatsu, 82, who, despite a past draw of only tens of thousands of votes, was running for Tokyo governor for a fifth time.

Words to Know

coping: *(v.)* managing emotions in stressful situations

solidarity: *(n.)* unity based on community interests

Mr. Nakamatsu—an inventor who claims credit for hundreds of gadgets—campaigned in front of his truck in Ginza on Sunday, standing on top of what he described as a stretching machine that would prevent deep vein thrombosis.

¶**21** As a loudspeaker played a recorded speech, he described campaigning by walking or riding a bicycle as something from "another era."

¶**22** There were other opponents of self-restraint. While the ethos has been strongest in northern Japan and in the Tokyo area, western Japan appeared split. Kobe, the site of a 1995 earthquake, was firmly in favor.

¶**23** But Toru Hashimoto, the governor of Osaka, Japan's second-biggest city, said too much holding back would hurt the economy. Echoing President Bush after the attacks on Sept. 11, 2001, Mr. Hashimoto urged people to spend even more, so as to support the economy; some businesses are helping by donating part of their proceeds to affected areas.

¶**24** In Tokyo, though, there was no debate.

¶**25** At Hair ZA/ZA, a salon in the Shin Koenji neighborhood, appointments have dried up because so many school and corporate ceremonies have been canceled. The rolling blackouts could also make it hard for customers to keep reservations, according to Takayuki Yamamoto, the salon's chief hair stylist.

¶**26** This has upended Ayaka Kanzaki's plans to pass the salon's tests for new stylists. The exam includes three components: cutting, blow-drying and hair coloring. Ms. Kanzaki, 21, passed the cutting section, but to qualify for the hair coloring test, she must recruit 20 models. So far, she has managed just seven and is worried about getting 13 more.

¶**27** The salon's efforts to reduce electricity use have made it difficult to practice after hours, too. In addition to turning off the lights, training with blow dryers has been stopped. Ms. Kanzaki, however, keeps any frustration to herself.

¶**28** "I'm not the only one in this condition," she said, in a remark that typified Japanese selflessness. "Others are, too."

Words to Know

rolling blackouts: *(n.)* regularly having no electrical power

upended: *(v.)* hindered, interfered, turned her plans upside down.

Questions

Key Ideas and Details

7. Explain how the "rolling blackouts" have affected "a salon in the Shin Koenji neighborhood."

Questions

Text Structure

1. What is the purpose of the introductory text?

Words and Phrases in Context

2. Look at the word *submerged* in the title and *submerging* in **paragraph 3**. Define the word in context and explain its importance to the text.

Submerged City

by Jacqueline Adams from *Science World*

¶1 *IN A 2008* SCIENCE WORLD *ARTICLE, scientists predicted what could happen if a major hurricane were to strike New York City. In October 2012, a hurricane-turned-superstorm called Sandy hit the East Coast.*

¶2 *How did Sandy measure up to the predictions? To find out, read the text that follows. It's our 2008 article word for word. The "Sandy's Reality" boxes show how Sandy actually played out.*

¶3 Howling winds rush between New York City's skyscrapers, shattering windows and uprooting trees. A 7.6 meter (25 foot) wall of water sweeps over Lower Manhattan, submerging the financial district and popular neighborhoods like Chinatown and Little Italy. Subways fill with seawater. Millions of New Yorkers who evacuated the danger zone can't return to their devastated homes.

SANDY'S REALITY

The scenario *Science World* described in 2008 depicts potential damage from a major hurricane—a Category 3 or higher, with wind speeds of at least 179 km (111 mi) per hour. When Sandy made landfall, its sustained winds reached 129 kph (80 mph). "Sandy is not the worst-case scenario," says Kerry Emanuel, an atmospheric scientist at the Massachusetts Institute of Technology. Even so, the storm inflicted severe damage. When Sandy struck, it caused severe flooding of subways and much of lower Manhattan. In New York City, 48 people died.

Words to Know

shattering: *(v.)* breaking suddenly into very small pieces

devastated: *(adj.)* destroyed

sustained: *(adj.)* continuing for a long time

¶**4** Is this the script from a disaster movie? No, it's a scenario that experts warn could play out in real life. Hurricanes have hit the Northeast barely missing the city in the past. And a 2001 report ranked New York the third-most vulnerable U.S. city to hurricanes, right behind New Orleans and Miami.

¶**5** New Orleans found out the hard way what can happen when a major hurricane strikes a vulnerable city. In 2005, Hurricane Katrina killed 1,800 people and filled New Orleans with floodwaters, forcing the city's residents to flee their homes and take shelter in public arenas like the Astrodome in Houston, Texas. With New York City's population at more than 8 million—16 times the population of New Orleans—could such a tragedy multiply many times over?

SANDY'S REALITY

Before Sandy hit, 375,000 people had to evacuate low-lying areas of New York City. In the storm's aftermath, millions of people in New York and nearby New Jersey were without electricity for weeks. The National Guard and Federal Emergency Management Agency were mobilized to provide food and water to those who were affected.

FAST TRACK TO NEW YORK

¶**6** The reason for concern isn't that the Big Apple is a hurricane hot spot. Atlantic hurricanes form far from New York in the tropics, usually between the months of June and November. Warm water evaporating from the ocean fuels their swirling, high-speed winds. As a hurricane rotates, slow-moving streams of air called trade winds carry it across the ocean. Fortunately, most hurricanes run out of steam without reaching land. Areas in the Caribbean, Gulf of Mexico, and Southeastern U.S. are at greatest risk for an Atlantic hurricane hit since the trade winds push storms in this direction.

Words to Know

vulnerable: *(adj.)* open to attack, harm, or damage

aftermath: *(n.)* the period of time after something such as a storm, when people are still dealing with the results

Questions

Words and Phrases in Context

3. Find the phrase *run out of steam* in **paragraph 6**. What does this figure of speech mean within the context of this paragraph?

Key Ideas and Details

4. Describe the cause and effects of Hurricane Sandy.

Questions

Key Ideas and Details

5. "As Hurricane Sandy moved north, it became embedded in another powerful weather system." How did this affect New York?

Text Structure

6. What is the purpose of the "Sandy's Reality" boxes?

¶**7** The trade winds move at only 16 to 24 kilometers (10 to 15 miles) per hour, which gives people in the storm's path time to prepare. But some storms turn north and are swept up by faster winds. Kerry Emanuel, an atmospheric scientist at the Massachusetts Institute of Technology, explains, "If you get up to [higher] latitudes, the winds tend to be much stronger. And so the hurricanes, when they get embedded in those winds, move faster."

SANDY'S REALITY

As Hurricane Sandy moved north, it became embedded in another powerful weather system. "It combined forces with a winter storm," says Emanuel. This huge superstorm now included both the central, swirling winds of the hurricane and the broader-reaching winds of the winter storm.

¶**8** This means that a hurricane on track for New York could accelerate, forcing city residents to act fast. "Accelerating hurricanes will cause watches and warnings to be issued more suddenly," says Gary Conte, warning coordination meteorologist for the National Weather Service's Upton, New York office. "So people will certainly have less time to prepare for an approaching hurricane which is forecast to accelerate here across the Northeast United States."

SANDY'S REALITY

Luckily, Sandy was a slow-moving storm and sped up only slightly as it neared land, so people in the danger zone had time to evacuate.

Words to Know

embedded: *(v)* trapped inside

accelerate: *(v)* to move faster, gain speed

approaching: *(v)* to move nearer to something

FUNNEL EFFECT

¶**9** Usually, such a hurricane wouldn't strike the city directly, because land to the south of New York acts as a shield. Most strong storms pass to the east of the city. That's what happened in 1938, when New England's worst recorded hurricane struck. Although the monster storm killed hundreds of people in the Northeastern U.S., its strongest winds missed New York City.

¶**10** But the city's geographical location could also be its downfall. New York City sits on a bight, a curve in the coastline that forms New York Bay. If a hurricane were to strike this spot, the storm surge (water pushed toward shore by a hurricane) would funnel into the bay, piling up until it flooded parts of Manhattan. Emanuel explains, "For the same storm hitting New York, at least at the right angle, you could get a far bigger storm surge than that storm hitting a straight coastline, because the water has nowhere to escape."

SANDY'S REALITY

As Sandy moved north, it made an unusual move: it turned left and headed straight for the coast. "We cannot find one hurricane track that was the same as Sandy's, as far as we go back in history," says Conte. The winds came from the perfect direction to funnel water into New York Bay—and they had perfect timing. The gravitational pull of the moon on earth's waters causes tides to rise and fall, and tides rise highest when the moon is full or new. The full moon on the night of Sandy's landfall and the storm's arrival as the tide was rising maximized the storm surge.

¶**11** "That's the nightmare scenario for New York," says Greg Holland, an atmospheric scientist at the National Center for Atmospheric Research. The nightmare has happened before. In 1821 a hurricane swept into the bay. The trapped water rose into a 4 meter (13 foot) storm surge that put Lower Manhattan underwater.

Questions

Words and Phrases in Context

7. Explain how the "land to the south of New York acts as a shield" in **paragraph 9**.

Key Ideas and Details

8. What evidence does the author use to support her claim that New York City is in danger of a superstorm?

Questions

Text Structure

9. Why does Adams include quotes from Gary Conte and Greg Holland?

Key Ideas and Details

10. How did the effect of the 1821 hurricane differ from the 2012 hurricane?

¶**12** Back then, not many people lived in the flooded area. But today, this region is densely populated and includes miles of subway tunnels. If a stronger hurricane were to strike this spot, Conte says, "You could end up with surge values ranging from 20 to 25-plus feet across portions of New York City.

SANDY'S REALITY

Sandy whipped up a surge that ranged from 2.7 to 4 m (9 to 13 ft)—similar to that of the historic 1821 hurricane that also hit New York. A 7.6 m (25 ft) storm surge would likely require a strong Category 2 or 3 hurricane. "If that ever happens, that would be a complete disaster for the city," says Conte.

¶**13** This funnel effect is the reason the Big Apple ranks so high on the hurricane risk list. Holland says, "In New York, the chances of getting [a hurricane] are actually fairly remote, but when you get one, if it's anything like the right track, then the consequences are going to be enormous.

Words to Know

densely: *(adj)* containing a lot of things or people that are very close together

whipped: *(v)* to move quickly or forcefully

remote: *(adj)* very small

HURRICANE CYCLES

¶**14** There is more bad news: Atlantic hurricanes appear to run in cycles. In the mid-1990s, a new cycle started in which both the number and intensity of hurricanes have increased. Holland says, "It's the classic double whammy."

SANDY'S REALITY

This is the second year running that New York City has been directly hit by a major storm. In 2011, Hurricane Irene struck the city.

¶**15** Normally, scientists would expect the cycle to run its course and the number of hurricanes to decrease. But climate change could throw a wrench in the cycle as rising sea surface temperatures and shifting wind patterns affect hurricane formation and tracks. "Climate change is expected to affect hurricane activity in ways that we're still struggling to grasp," Emanuel says. Some studies predict that the number of hurricanes will drop but that the storms will become more intense.

¶**16** The chance of the nightmare storm hitting the Big Apple may be small, but city officials are taking it seriously. Even though New Yorkers need not live in fear, experts urge them to have a disaster plan. After all, says Holland, "it gets pretty hard to think logically once the winds start howling and the water starts running around your ankles." A little forethought can make a big difference in an emergency.

Words to Know

intensity: *(n.)* the quality of being felt very strongly or having a strong effect

throw a wrench: *(idiom)* to cause something to fail

grasp: *(v.)* to understand

forethought: *(n.)* careful thinking or planning about the future

Questions

Words and Phrases in Context

11. Find the phrase *classic double whammy* in **paragraph 14**. Determine its meaning using context clues.

Literature Circle Leveled Novels

Night of the Howling Dogs *by Graham Salisbury*
When a massive earthquake strikes Hawaii's Big Island, Dylan and Louie must rescue people trapped in the chaos that crumbles the solid earth and makes it drop "like a broken elevator." **Lexile**® measure: 530L

The Killing Sea *by Richard Lewis*
Ruslan, an Indonesian boy, and Sarah, a Western girl, are trapped in a coastal town called Ujung Karang when a massive tsunami strikes. Together, can they survive the dangers and find their families? **Lexile**® measure: 760L

The Dead and the Gone *by Susan Beth Pfeffer*
A meteor has knocked the moon from its orbit, creating tidal waves that devastate New York City. Can Alex take care of his sisters by scavenging for food and eventually escaping the city? **Lexile**® measure: 680L

Fiction, Nonfiction, Poetry, and Novels

The Long Winter *by Laura Ingalls Wilder.* The struggle to survive a fierce, endless Dakota winter with Laura and her pioneer family. **Lexile**® measure: 790L

Night of the Twisters *by Ivy Ruckman.* Tornado warnings are ordinary for Dan Hatch. But one day, a real twister strikes and devastates his Nebraska town. **Lexile**® measure: 790L

Volcano: The Eruption and Healing of Mount St. Helens *by Patricia Lauber.* See the results of the 1980 Mount St. Helens eruption and find out why it happened. **Lexile**® measure: 830L

Dark Water Rising *by Marian Hale.* In 1900, the town of Galveston, Texas, was nearly obliterated when a storm killed almost 8,000 people. Experience the story through the eyes of 16-year-old Seth. **Lexile**® measure: 970L

Fire in Their Eyes: Wildfires and the People Who Fight Them *by Karen Magnuson Beil.* Feel the intensity and danger of a forest fire through profiles of smoke jumpers and dramatic color photos of wildfires. **Lexile**® measure: 1010L

Out of the Dust *by Karen Hesse.* Fourteen-year-old narrator Billie Jo tells about living through her mother's death, her father's grief, and a daily life of loss in the dust storms of Oklahoma. **Lexile**® measure: NP

Eyewitness Books: Natural Disasters *by Claire Watts and Trevor Day.* Learn about natural disasters through photos and explanations.

Hurricane Force: In the Path of America's Deadliest Storms *by Joseph B. Treaster.* Take a scientific look at hurricanes and how they affect people.

Films and TV

Forces of Nature (National Geographic, 2004) Watch volcanoes bubble over and earthquakes split the earth—and then find out why these disasters happen. (40 min.)

Hunt for the Supertwister (NOVA, 2004) Go supertwister hunting with scientists and watch them solve the puzzle of how these killer storms form. (60 min.)

Science of Storm Chasing (Discovery, 2007) Enter the core of a tornado with meteorologist Dr. Josh Wurman and his crew of storm chasers. (86 min.)

In the Path of a Killer Volcano (NOVA, 2006) A deadly volcano in the Philippines is about to blow, and a typhoon is headed toward the area, too. What should the residents do? (56 min.)

Restless Earth (National Geographic, 2003) Experience the destruction of volcanoes, asteroid hits, and natural disasters such as earthquakes, hurricanes, tornadoes, and floods in this DVD set. (175 min.)

Storm That Drowned a City (NOVA, 2006) Relive the destruction of Hurricane Katrina through eyewitness interviews, storm footage, and analysis of how it happened. (56 min.)

Tornado Intercept (National Geographic, 2005) Plunge into the 300-mile winds of a tornado with an armor-plated tornado intercept vehicle. (60 min.)

Tsunami 2004: Waves of Death (History Channel, 2005) Follow the path of the 2004 tsunami in Thailand through the eyes of scientists and the people who lived through it. (50 min.)

Websites

Discovery Channel: Virtual Volcano Learn about different types of volcanoes by building your own and watching it spew debris, gas, rock, and lava.

Hunt for the Supertwister Learn why three-quarters of tornadoes hit in the United States, rate a tornado on the Fujita Scale, and then read interviews from scientists and people who have lived through tornadoes.

Storm Chasers Race tornadoes in an intercept vehicle, look at the vehicle in detail, or watch tornado videos on this Discovery Channel page.

Storm That Drowned a City Use interactive programs to find out how Hurricane Katrina flooded 85 percent of the city of New Orleans in 2005.

Magazines

Discover Find out about natural disasters such as tsunamis, hurricanes, thunderstorms, asteroid hits, and volcanic eruptions.

Earth Read the latest research on earthquakes, volcanoes, and other natural disasters.

National Geographic After reading an article about tornadoes, see the inside of a tornado, watch tornado simulations, and listen to interviews with scientists.

Time Find out more about Hurricane Katrina with photos, videos, and articles.

UNIT 5

Stolen Childhoods

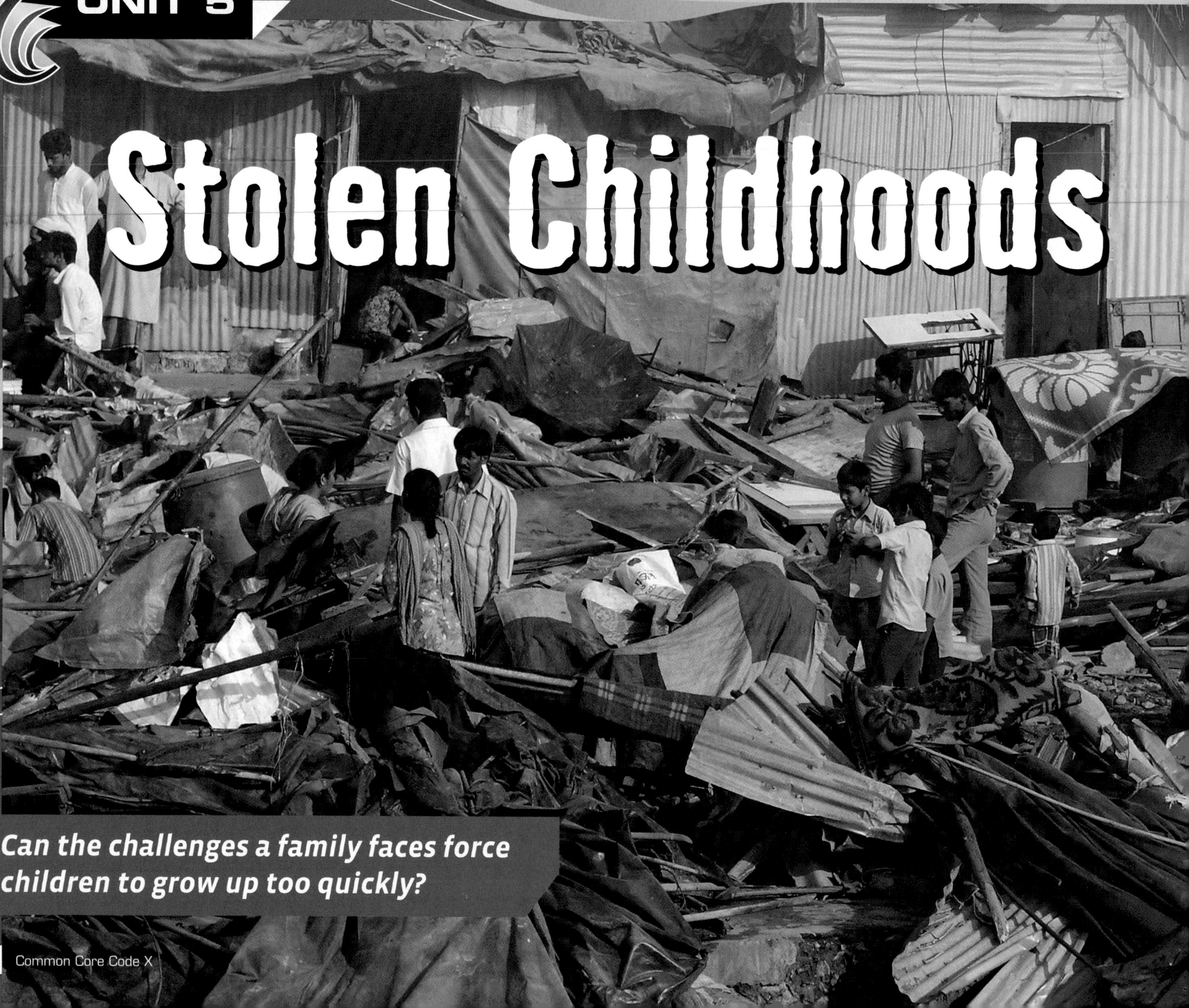

Can the challenges a family faces force children to grow up too quickly?

Unit Introduction

In these two informational text selections, writers describe the challenging family life of young people growing up during different times in history.

Rabbit-Proof Fence, by Doris Pilkington, tells of the effects of white raiders and settlers on a traditional Aboriginal family.

In *Behind the Beautiful Forevers*, Katherine Boo recounts a day in the life of Abdul, a young Indian struggling to make money to help support his family in the Mumbai slum of Annawadi.

WRITING PERFORMANCE TASK

Analyze which author conveys the challenges faced by the people or main characters most successfully. Consider the narrative techniques and the strategies that the authors use.

INFORMATIONAL EXCERPTS

from ***Rabbit-Proof Fence*** by Doris Pilkington

Language

- Academic Vocabulary
- Word Study: Word Families

Reading Informational Text

- Identify Evidence
- Key Ideas and Details
- Craft and Structure

from ***Behind the Beautiful Forevers*** by Katherine Boo

Language

- Academic Vocabulary
- Word Study: Roots and Suffixes

Reading Informational Text

- Identify Evidence
- Key Ideas and Details
- Craft and Structure

SPEAKING AND LISTENING

Give a Group Presentation

- Collaborate and Present

Checklist: Presentation

- Scoring Guide

WRITING

Writing: Argumentative Essay

- Read the Model
- Analyze the Model
- Gather Evidence
- Organize Ideas
- Language Study: Evidence
- Conventions Study: Transitions
- Revise, Edit, and Publish
- Performance Task Rubric

EXTENDED READINGS

Informational Excerpt

from ***We Were There Too! Young People in U.S. History*** by Phillip Hoose

Play Excerpt

from ***The Diary of Anne Frank*** by Frances Goodrich and Albert Hackett

Academic Vocabulary

from *Rabbit-Proof Fence* by Doris Pilkington

Rate your understanding of each word. Then read its meaning and write a sample sentence.

Word	Meaning	Example
ritual (*n.*) p. 197 ① ② ③ ④		Walking the dog has become my after-school ritual.
situate (*v.*) p. 197 ① ② ③ ④	to be in a particular place or position	
tranquil (*adj.*) p. 198 ① ② ③ ④	pleasantly calm, quiet, and peaceful	
annual (*adj.*) p. 198 ① ② ③ ④	happening once a year	
strategic (*adj.*) p. 198 ① ② ③ ④		Getting permission to use the science lab is strategic to the success of my science project.
ominous (*adj.*) p. 200 ① ② ③ ④		The dark sky looked ominous.
assure (*v.*) p. 201 ① ② ③ ④	to tell someone that something will happen so that they are less worried	

Rating Scale | ① I don't know the word. ② I've seen it or heard it. ③ I know its meaning. ④ I know it and use it.

Word Study

Word Family

A **word family** is a group of words that share the same base word and have related meanings. Word webs help you visualize how to find base words.

strategy → **strategic**, **strategist**, **strategically**

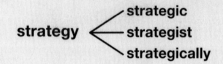

Complete each sentence using the correct word form from the strategy word family.

1. She acted __________, which helped win the game.
2. Henry was a brilliant __________, a caring mentor, and a wise friend.
3. Playing chess can develop your ________ abilities.
4. It is a good _______ to have a good education.

from

Rabbit-Proof Fence

by Doris Pilkington

¶**1** It was still very cool in the early summer morning; the fresh, clean air he breathed into his lungs felt good. He stood up and stretched his arms above his head, then dropped them to his side. He was the first to rise. This was not unusual, Kundilla always woke before anyone else and this morning was no different from any other. He looked slowly around at the sleeping forms covered by warm, animal-skin blankets, lying outside their shelters made from branches and slabs of bark. There was no shortage of trees and shrubs around here, that is why this spot was chosen for the winter camp. Kundilla walked silently to perform his early morning **rituals**, away from the camp, which was **situated** in a clearing a hundred miles from the river. On his return he stopped along the banks of the river to pull up the fish traps he had set the previous evening. How peaceful it was, with the sounds of birds twittering high above, amid the leafy branches of the giant river gums, and the occasional splash of the fish in the river. Dawn was his favorite time of day. As the sun rose he could meditate and reflect on the events of the past few days but, more importantly, he could plan future activities without interruption and distraction.

Words to Know

unusual: *(adj.)* strange; different

reflect: *(v.)* to think about something seriously and for a while

Close Reading

Text Structure

1. Identify the point of view. Who does the narrator focus on in **paragraph 1**?

Point of View

Point of view is the position from which a narrative is told.

- first person = the narrator is part of the story *(I, me, my, mine, we, ours)*
- second person = the narrator gives information or addresses someone *(you, yours)*
- third person = the narrator tells another person's story *(he, she, her, they, them)*

Writing

2. Determine the mood and how the author created it in **paragraph 1**.

The author described the ____, to create a mood of ____.

Close Reading

Text Structure

3. Explain how the phrase "Little did he know that soon" in **paragraph 2** changes the mood. Describe what the details in **paragraph 2** foreshadow.

Foreshadowing

Foreshadowing is when an author hints at what might happen later in the story. It is a way that an author creates interest, or engages the reader.

Words and Phrases in Context

4. Define *heightened* as used in **paragraph 3**. Which clues help you determine its meaning?

Writing

5. Explain the effect of the juxtaposition of "birds twittering" in **paragraph 1** and "anguished cries" in **paragraph 2**. Discuss mood, sensory language, and descriptive details. Cite textual evidence.

Juxtaposition

Juxtaposition is the arrangement of two or more ideas, characters, actions, settings, phrases, or words, side-by-side or in similar narrative moments, for the purpose of comparison, contrast, suspense, or character development.

¶2 Little did he know that soon devastation and desolation would shatter this **tranquil** environment; that this pristine forest would echo the anguished cries and ceaseless weeping of thousands of people—his people—as they were tormented by foreigners and driven off their land.

¶3 His long, wavy, grey hair and thick white beard heightened his dignified appearance as he approached the camp carrying two fish traps filled with marrons and gilgies for his family's breakfast. He had power and strength which commanded respect.

¶4 Kundilla was satisfied with the results of yesterday's **annual** scrub firing. This was a special time on the seasonal calendar when his family clans from far around would gather on their territory to set fire to areas of dense undergrowth to flush out any game, such as kangaroos and wallabies, that might be sheltering there. All the men waited in **strategic** places around the scrub as the animals dashed out in panic. They then either speared or clubbed them to death. The animal pelts were made into warm cloaks as protection against the bitterly cold winter winds of the south west. The smaller skins were made into skin bags with fur lining on the inside to be used for carrying babies and as all-purpose bags.

Words to Know

desolation: *(n.)* the state of being left without any inhabitants

marrons and gilgies: *(n.)* types of fish found in Australia

panic: *(n.)* a sudden feeling of fear or terror

¶5 Kundilla had two wives, the senior wife, Ngingana, had already lit the fire to cook the first meal of the day when he returned. She raked the coals and ashes to one side, then dropped marrons and gilgies on them. When they were cooked, she pulled them out with a long, green stick and laid them on the gum leaves. As she dusted the ashes from the food she called for everyone to come and eat. This meal was washed down with the cool water drawn from the soak under the thick bullrushes that grew along the river bank. Kundilla's second wife Mardina was breastfeeding their youngest child, Jalda.

¶6 Her two teenage sons, Wandani and Binmu, would soon be taken away to join several others who will leave the camp as boys and go through the Law and return as men. She glanced proudly at her sons and felt a pang of sadness. To her they were still boys, surely one more summer wouldn't make any difference. She was only their mother, the tribal elders had already made their decision and there was nothing she could do to change it. Mardina wiped the tears from her eyes then raised her head and continued to feed baby Jalda.

Words to Know

elders: *(n.)* older people

Close Reading

Key Ideas and Details

6. Identify whether the point of view is omniscient or limited. Who does the narrator focus on in **paragraph 5**? How does this character add to your understanding of Aboriginal culture and family life?

Point of View

Omniscient: The narrator sees and knows all, and can describe as well as analyze thought, emotions, and actions of any character.

Limited: The narrator sees and knows all about only one character.

Words and Phrases in Context

7. Define the meaning of the phrase *pang of sadness* in **paragraph 6.** How does the text support your definition?

Writing

8. Explain how Mardina feels about the decision made by the tribal elders: "Her two teenage sons . . . would soon be taken away." What did she choose not to do? What does this tell you about Aboriginal culture?

Due to ___, Mardina feels ___. In response she chooses not to ___ because ___.

Close Reading

Key Ideas and Details

9. What do the Aboriginals do during their annual trip to the coast?

Academic Vocabulary

10. Why would an *ominous* sound cause the women to run to the men for protection? Why do you think the author chose the word *ominous*? What other words could the author have chosen to describe the sound?

Writing

11. Explain the contrast that the author is setting up by describing Kundilla as reaching for "the sharpening stone to hone a spear" just as he hears the "ominous sound." Describe the effect.

¶7 Kundilla's three married sons and their families were camped to the right of them. Others camped nearby, forming a semicircle. There were about sixty people in the group and for the hunters and fishermen this was the place to be right now. Some had travelled for many days from outlying areas to join this group while the food supply was plentiful here. Kundilla had planned to move soon to the mouth of the river so that he and his family could feast on crayfish, crabs, seals and shellfish. They looked forward to this annual trip to the coast.

¶8 After breakfast, Kundilla sat under the shade of a large eucalyptus away from the camp and began checking his spears and fishing traps in preparation for the coastal trip. Behind him the sounds of normal, everyday camp life continued: mothers and grandmothers yelling orders to their offspring, children playing games, some fighting and squabbling, others delightfully splashing and diving in the pool. As he reached for the sharpening stone to hone a spear, an **ominous** sound reverberated through the forest. The peace and tranquility was shattered by a loud boom. Alarmed and frightened, the women snatched up their babies and toddlers and ran to the men.

Rocky Point near Nyinyikay Homeland, Australia

Words to Know

semicircle: *(n.)* half circle

outlying: *(adj.)* far from the main area

reverberated: *(v.)* echoed; was heard many times as it bounced back from different surfaces

¶**9** "What was that?" the people asked their leader. Even the flock of birds were squawking loudly as they sought refuge in the high canopy of the forest.

¶**10** "I don't know what that noise was or where it came from," Kundilla replied. "But we will go down and find out," he **assured** them. He called all the adult men to him and they gathered by a tea-tree clump.

¶**11** "They're back. They've come to take away our women," he said in a voice filled with passion, anxiety and fear.

¶**12** "Yes, but what can we do to stop them?" asked Bunyun, his eldest son. "You know what happened the last time they came ashore."

¶**13** The men nodded as they recalled the incident; it happened to Bunyun's Uncle Tumi and other members of his family who usually camped further along the beach, near the cove. They were shot by the white raiders when they tried to stop them from kidnapping the women. The family were still mourning their dead.

Words to Know

refuge: *(n.)* shelter or protection from someone or something

incident: *(n.)* an event, especially one that is unusual, important, or violent

Close Reading

Text Structure

12. Describe how dialogue such as "They're back" and descriptive details such as "flock of birds were squawking" help to portray challenges faced by the Aboriginals.

Key Ideas and Details

13. Identify the details in this section that help you understand that Kundilla knew exactly what the ominous sound signified.

Writing

14. Explain the mood the author creates with phrases such as "kidnapping the women" and "mourning their dead" in the last sentence in **paragraph 13.** Contrast that mood with the mood created in **paragraph 1** with phrases like "fresh, clean air he breathed into his lungs."

Identify Evidence | Analyze Individuals, Events, and Ideas

Reread the excerpt from ***Rabbit-Proof Fence,*** highlighting narrative techniques and strategies that Pilkington includes to convey the Aboriginals' way of life and the challenges they faced. How does she use the techniques and strategies to elaborate on the events and the individuals they affected?

- As you read, use the Evidence column to record examples from the text that describe Kundilla and his tribe's experiences.
- In the Explanation column, explain how the use of narrative techniques and strategies help to reveal the challenges the Aboriginals faced.

Evidence	Source	Page	Explanation
1. "How peaceful it was, with the sounds of birds twittering high above, amid the leafy branches of the giant river gums, and the occasional splash of the fish in the river."	Pilkington	197	This description shows that the Aboriginals enjoyed a peaceful existence before the white raiders showed up. The author's use of words such as "peaceful," "twittering," and "leafy" show that the mood is relaxed.
2. ". . . that this pristine forest would echo the anguished cries and ceaseless weeping of thousands of people—his people . . ."			
3. "Kundilla was satisfied with the results of yesterday's annual scrub firing."			
4. ". . . the tribal elders had already made their decision and there was nothing she could do to change it."			

Evidence	Source	Page	Explanation
5.			
6.			
7.			

Key Ideas and Details

Determining the Central Idea

1. Use the evidence you collected to summarize the key idea of this excerpt from Pilkington's text.

2. List three ways that Pilkington describes the Aboriginals' way of life. Explain the significance of each detail.

Detail	Significance

3. List three ways that Pilkington conveys the threat the white raiders pose to the Aboriginal way of life. Explain the significance of each detail.

Detail	Significance

Craft and Structure

Structure of the Literary Nonfiction Text

1. Pilkington introduces the Aboriginals before she introduces the white raiders. What makes the order in which the author introduces the characters significant or strong?

2. How does Pilkington describe the challenges faced by Aboriginals?

Author's Purpose

3. How can you summarize the events of the story to form an idea of the author's intentions in writing this piece?

Academic Vocabulary

from *Behind the Beautiful Forevers* by Katherine Boo

Rate your understanding of each word. Then write its meaning and a sample sentence.

Word	Meaning	Example
exuberantly (*adv.*) p. 207 ① ② ③ ④	with joy, energy, and excitement	
pivotal (*adj.*) p. 207 ① ② ③ ④		It is pivotal that she does well in this debate if she wants to win the election.
intimate (*adj.*) p. 208 ① ② ③ ④	relating to very private or personal matters	
companionably (*adv.*) p. 209 ① ② ③ ④		The lab partners worked companionably together.
restraint (*n.*) p. 210 ① ② ③ ④	controlled behavior, especially in a situation when it is difficult to stay calm	
stigmatized (*v.*) p. 212 ① ② ③ ④	to be treated by society as if you should feel ashamed of your situation or behavior	
predominated (*v.*) p. 213 ① ② ③ ④	to hold advantage in numbers or importance	

Rating Scale | ① I don't know the word. ② I've seen it or heard it. ③ I know its meaning. ④ I know it and use it.

Word Study

Roots and Suffixes

A **root** is the basic part of a word that shows its main meaning, to which other parts can be added. A **suffix** is a word part at the end of a word that changes its meaning. You can use word parts to determine the meaning of a word.

Adding a suffix to a root word changes its meaning.

- *-ion* is a suffix that means "the result, act, or state of something"
- *-able* is a suffix that means "capable of doing something"
- *-ly* is a suffix that changes adjectives into adverbs and means "to be like something"

Company means "people you spend time with; friends." How do the suffixes change the meaning of the word?

1. *Companion* means ____
2. *Companionable* means ____
3. *Companionably* means ____

from Behind the Beautiful Forevers

by Katherine Boo

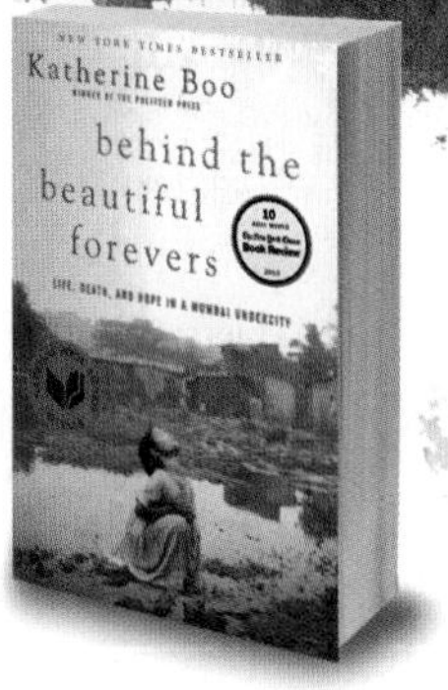

¶**1** Dawn came gusty, as it often did in January, the month of treed kites and head colds. Because his family lacked the floor space for all of its members to lie down, Abdul was asleep on the gritty maidan, which for years had passed as his bed. His mother stepped carefully over one of his younger brothers, and then another, bending low to Abdul's ear. "Wake up, fool!" she said **exuberantly**. "You think your work is dreaming?"

¶**2** Superstitious, Zehrunisa had noticed that some of the family's most profitable days occurred after she had showered abuses on her eldest son. January's income being **pivotal** to the Husains' latest plan of escape from Annawadi, she had decided to make the curses routine.

Close Reading

Key Ideas and Details

1. How does the author describe where Abdul is asleep? What does this tell you about Abdul and his family?

Writing

2. Explain Abdul's mother's tone toward Abdul when she says, "Wake up, fool!" What word helps you understand this?

Abdul's mother's tone is one of _____ as shown by _____.

Tone

Tone is the writer's (or character's) attitude toward the writing (characters, situation) and the readers. Tone is set through word choices, descriptive details, dialogue, sensory language, and setting.

Words to Know

maidan: *(n.)* an open space in South Asia in or near a town, used for public events

superstitious: *(adj.)* having irrational beliefs that doing something a certain way will affect its outcome

Close Reading

Key Ideas and Details

3. What is the tone in **paragraph 3**, which describes the "gentle going hour" when "Abdul rose with minimal whining"?

Writing

4. What descriptive details does the author use to create mood in **paragraph 3**?

Through use of ____, the author creates a ____ mood.

For instance, ____.

Mood

The **mood** is the overall atmosphere the author creates in a story. It is the feeling a reader gets from reading.

¶**3** Abdul rose with minimal whining, since the only whining his mother tolerated was her own. Besides, this was the gentle-going hour in which he hated Annawadi least. The pale sun lent the sewage lake a sparkling silver cast, and parrots nesting at the far side of the lake could still be heard over the jets. Outside his neighbors' huts, some held together by duct tape and rope, damp rags were discreetly freshening bodies. Children in school-uniform neckties were hauling pots of water from the public taps. A languid line extended from an orange concrete block of public toilets. Even goats' eyes were heavy with sleep. It was the moment of the **intimate** and the familial, before the great pursuit of the tiny market niche got under way.

Words to Know

sewage: *(n.)* waste material that is carried away from homes and other buildings in a system of pipes

discreetly: *(adv.)* carefully so that you do not offend or embarrass

market niche: *(n.)* a subset of commerce that focuses on a specific product, such as shampoo

¶4 One by one, construction workers departed for a crowded intersection where site supervisors chose day laborers. Young girls began threading marigolds into garlands, to be hawked in Airport Road traffic. Older women sewed patches onto pink-and-blue cotton quilts for a company that paid by the piece. In a small, sweltering plastic-molding factory, bare-chested men cranked gears that would turn colored beads into ornaments to be hung from rearview mirrors—smiling ducks and pink cats with jewels around their necks that they couldn't imagine anyone, anywhere, buying. And Abdul crouched on the maidan, beginning to sort two weeks' worth of purchased trash, a stained shirt hitching up his knobby spine.

¶5 His general approach toward his neighbors was this: "The better I know you, the more I will dislike you, and the more you will dislike me. So let us keep to ourselves." But deep in his own work, as he would be this morning, he could imagine his fellow Annawadians laboring **companionably** alongside him.

This photograph of a slum in Mumbai, India, was taken in September 2009.

Words to Know

day laborers: *(n.)* people who work on a day-to-day basis for another person or company

hawked: *(v.)* sold, usually by going from place to place and trying to persuade people to buy it

Close Reading

Words and Phrases in Context

5. What words or phrases does the author use to support you in determining the meaning of *approach* in **paragraph 5**?

Academic Vocabulary

6. Why do you think Abdul imagines "his fellow Annawadians laboring *companionably* alongside him"?

Writing

7. What is life like for Annawadians?

As shown by the following descriptive detail _____ the author reveals _____. Life in Annawadi is _____. The author describes people who _____.

Close Reading

Words and Phrases in Context

8. What words or phrases does the author use to support you in determining the meaning of *society* used in **paragraph 6?**

Key Ideas and Details

9. State whom the author is referring to when she writes *some* in the sentence, "Some people called him garbage, and left it at that."

Writing

10. Why does the author choose the term *Mumbai garbage trader* to describe Abdul?

¶6 The airport and hotels spewed waste in the winter, the peak season for tourism, business travel, and society weddings, whose lack of **restraint** in 2008 reflected a stock market at an all-time high. Better still for Abdul, a frenzy of Chinese construction in advance of the summer's Beijing Olympics had inflated the price of scrap metal worldwide. It was a fine time to be a Mumbai garbage trader, not that that was the term passersby used for Abdul. Some called him garbage, and left it at that.

Residents bathe on top of a water pipeline running through Dharavi slum in Mumbai, India. (February 2007)

Words to Know

spewed: *(v.)* caused (something) to flow out in a fast and forceful way

waste: *(n.)* garbage; trash

inflated: *(v.)* made larger or more than it actually should be

¶7 Abdul was now working as fast as he could in order to finish by dusk, when strapping Hindu boys began playing cricket on the maidan, aiming their drives at his sorted piles, and sometimes his head. While the cricketers sorely tested Abdul's policy of non-confrontation, the only physical fight he'd ever had was with two ten-year-olds who had turf-stomped one of his little brothers. And these cricketers had just sent another Muslim kid to the hospital after smashing his head in with their bats.

¶8 At 6 P.M., Abdul stood up, triumphant. He'd beaten the cricketers, and before him were fourteen lumpy sacks of sorted waste. As smoke clouds rose from the surrounding hotels—their evening fumigation against mosquitoes—Abdul and two of his little brothers hauled the sacks to the truckbed of a lime-green, three-wheeled jalopy. This small vehicle, one of the Husains' most important possessions, allowed Abdul to deliver the waste to the recyclers. And now out onto Airport Road and into the city's horn-honk opera.

New Delhi, India

Words to Know

strapping: *(adj.)* tall, strong, and healthy

triumphant: *(adj.)* showing pleasure and pride because of a victory or success

Close Reading

Writing

11. How does Abdul differ from the "strapping Hindu boys"? How does he feel about them?

Key Ideas and Details

12. Describe Abdul's work ethic or dedication to work. What details in **paragraph 8** support your idea about him?

Close Reading

Writing

13. Abdul thinks that wishing for things to be different in India is "a childish pastime." What can you infer about Abdul based on this description?

Academic Vocabulary

14. How does a passerby previously describe Abdul because of his "stigmatized occupation"? How is Abdul nothing like the way he is "stigmatized"?

Words and Phrases in Context

15. Define *close* as it is used in **paragraph 9**. What context clues help you determine its meaning?

¶**9** For all Mirchi's* talk of progress, India still made a person know his place, and wishing things different struck Abdul as a childish pastime, like trying to write your name in a bowl of melted kulfi. He had been working as hard as he could in the **stigmatized** occupation he'd been born to, and it was no longer a profitless position. He intended to return home with both hands and a pocketful of money. His mental estimates of the weight of his goods had been roughly correct. Peak-season recyclables, linked to a flourishing global market, had bestowed on his family an income few residents of Annawadi had ever known. He had made a profit of five hundred rupees, or eleven dollars a day—enough to jump-start the plan that inspired his mother's morning curses, and that even the little Husains knew to keep close.

**Mirchi is Abdul's brother.*

Katherine Boo grew up in and around Washington, DC. She is an award-winning journalist and author. Her writings focus on issues of poverty, opportunity, social and economic policy, and education. In 2012, Boo published her first book, *Behind the Beautiful Forevers*, which won the National Book Award on November 14, 2012.

Words to Know

pastime: *(n.)* a pleasant activity that one does to use up spare time

kulfi: *(n.)* a popular frozen milk-based dessert from India

profitless: *(adj.)* not making money on a business situation

¶**10** With this take, added to savings from the previous year, his parents would now make their first deposit on a twelve-hundred-square-foot plot of land in a quiet community in Vasai, just outside the city, where Muslim recyclers **predominated**. If life and global markets kept going their way, they would soon be landowners, not squatters, in a place where Abdul was sure no one would call him garbage.

Close Reading

Words and Phrases in Context

16. What is the "take"? What do Abdul's parents plan to do with the take?

Academic Vocabulary

17. Explain why is it important to Abdul to move to a community where Muslim recyclers predominate.

Writing

18. Describe the mood and how the author creates it in **paragraph 10**.

Words to Know

previous: *(adj.)* happening before another event

global markets: *(n.)* groups of people and businesses around the world that buy products from around the world

squatters: *(n.)* someone who lives in an empty building or on a piece of land without permission and without paying rent

Identify Evidence | Analyze Individuals, Events, and Ideas

Reread the excerpt from ***Behind the Beautiful Forevers***. How does the author convey the challenges Abdul faces while trying to succeed in a society that "still made a person know his place"? How does Boo use techniques and strategies to elaborate on the events and the individuals they affect?

- As you read, use the Evidence column to record examples from the text that describe Abdul's experiences.
- In the Explanation column, explain how the use of techniques and strategies help to reveal the challenges faced by Abdul.

Evidence	Source	Page	Explanation
1. "Abdul was asleep on the gritty maidan, which for years has passed as his bed."	Boo	207	This detail shows that the Husains have little money and Abdul must sleep outside. The author's choice to include this detail shows that the tone is sympathetic.
2. "the Husains' latest plan of escape from Annawadi"			
3. "And Abdul crouched on the maidan, beginning to sort two weeks' worth of purchased trash, a stained shirt hitching up his knobby spine."			
4. "Abdul rose with minimal whining, since the only whining his mother tolerated was her own."			

Evidence	Source	Page	Explanation
5.			
6.			
7.			

Key Ideas and Details

Determining the Central Idea

1. Use the evidence you collected to summarize the key idea of Boo's text.

2. List three key individuals that Boo introduces in this excerpt. Explain why each individual is important to the central idea.

Individual	Significance

3. List three challenges that Abdul faces that Boo introduces in this excerpt. Explain the significance of each detail.

Event	Significance

Craft and Structure

Structure of the Literary Nonfiction Text

1. Boo repeats the idea that people call Abdul "garbage" in paragraph 6 and 10. How does the repetition used by the author affect the text?

2. What strategy does Boo's use of repetition highlight? Explain.

Author's Purpose

3. How can you summarize the events of the story to form an idea of the author's intentions in writing this piece?

Repetition

Repetition occurs when the same word or phrase is used over and over again. Repetition is used to reinforce an idea and to highlight the tone.

Collaborate and Present

Plan and Deliver a Presentation

Both Doris Pilkington and Katherine Boo describe characters using rich description.

Assignment: Work with a small group to create a character map for one of the people depicted in the texts. Follow the steps below to create your character map and present it to the class.

Analyze the Content

1. Consider the following questions:
- Which characters do you understand best? What do you know about them?
- What information helps you understand these characters?

2. As a group, select one character. Choose at least three actions, descriptions, and relationships that helped you gain a deep understanding of the character. Record your notes in your character map.

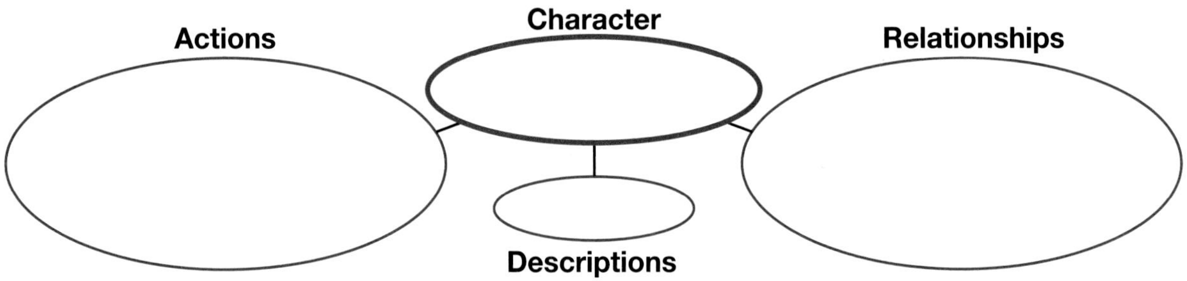

Prepare to Present

3. As a group, decide on the two or three strongest examples each for actions, descriptions, and relationships. Write one sentence summing up your group's understanding of the character. Include this description on your map.
- Decide which members of the group will present each part of the map.

Present

4. Share your one-sentence description with the class, using your map as a visual.

Seeking Clarification

- In other words, you believe that . . .
- If I understand you correctly, you feel that . . .
- So, you think that . . .

Reporting Ideas

- _____ compared
- _____ concluded
- _____ believes

Presentation

- Use formal English.
- Face your audience.
- Stand up straight and speak with confidence.
- Avoid fidgeting.

Presentation Checklist

Use the checklist below to evaluate your collaboration skills, reasoning, and final presentation. Think carefully about your work. If you know you completed an item thoroughly, give yourself a check (✓).

COLLABORATE AND PRESENT CHECKLIST		
Comprehension & Collaboration	**Evidence & Reasoning**	**Presentation of Knowledge & Ideas**
☐ Come to discussions prepared, having read and studied material. ☐ Refer to evidence when contributing to the discussion. ☐ Follow rules for discussions and lead by example. ☐ Ask and answer specific questions. ☐ Make comments that contribute to the topic under discussion and bring the discussion back on topic. ☐ Acknowledge new ideas expressed by others. ☐ Analyze ideas presented in diverse media. ☐ Include visual displays to emphasize key points.	☐ Create a character map. ☐ Focus on one character. ☐ Identify and describe actions, descriptions, and relationships of character. ☐ Cite textual evidence for each category.	☐ Adapt language to a variety of contexts and tasks to demonstrate knowledge of formal English. ☐ Include multimedia components (graphics, images, music, sound) and visual displays. ☐ Use appropriate volume/tone (clear, not too fast, too slow, or too loud) and avoid using "like" or "ummm." ☐ Have strong posture, a confident stance, and make frequent eye contact. ☐ Occasionally move from one spot to another without fidgeting. ☐ Smile and appear to be relaxed.
Number of ✓s in this category: ___	**Number of ✓s in this category: ___**	**Number of ✓s in this category: ___**
Total # of ✓s: __		

Add up the total number of checks (✓) in each category. Then use the scoring guide below to calculate your final score.

Scoring Guide			
16 to 18 ✓s	**13 to 15 ✓s**	**11 to 12 ✓s**	**10 or less ✓s**
④ Exemplary	**③ Meets Standards**	**② Needs Work**	**① Does Not Meet Standards**

Read the Model

Writers use many strategies to craft ideas and persuade readers. The writer of this argumentative essay explains why she feels one author was more successful at conveying the challenges faced by the main characters in the informative texts. Read and discuss the model essay below.

Argumentative Essay

An **argumentative essay** provides a clearly stated claim that is supported with logical reasoning and relevant evidence.

The **introduction** states the title and author of the text that the writer will analyze.

- Identify the claim.

The **two body paragraphs** provide logical reasons in support of the claim.

- Identify two reasons that support the claim.
- Identify examples of text citations.

Transition words or phrases organize and link ideas, sentences, and paragraphs.

- Identify transitions words and explain their function.

The **conclusion** sums up or restates the claim.

- Identify the conclusion.

Bringing Challenges to Life

By Anna Vivaldi

In their writings, author Phillip Hoose and playwrights Frances Goodrich and Albert Hackett describe the stolen childhoods of two girls. "First Day in a Sweatshop" shares Rose Cohen's firsthand account of the daily life of a young girl working in a sweatshop. In the play *The Diary of Anne Frank,* the writers tell the story of a young Jewish girl and her family forced into hiding during the Holocaust. Although both selections capture and convey details of the difficulties each family faced, I believe Hoose is more successful in conveying challenges.

Hoose's writing is more successful because of the narrative structure he uses. As Rose shares the details of her life, the reader is easily able to relate to her. She clearly describes the unfriendly environment, her demanding boss, the long days she is forced to work, and her lonely life. For instance, the reader could easily share Rose's emotions when she says, "'My face felt so burning hot I could scarcely see'" (Hoose 231). In contrast, the play about Anne Frank allows the reader to see the challenges in her life without directly experiencing her thoughts and feelings until the very end of the scene.

Another reason Hoose's writing is more compelling is his descriptive language. Cohen carefully selects each word she uses to paint a picture of the challenges in her life. For example, instead of telling us that she is lonely, Cohen says she "'stood facing the dark, cold silent room'" (232). On the other hand, the play uses straightforward language to describe the intense restrictions Anne's family faces as they go into hiding. Anne's father tells the family that they can never leave the secret annex ". . . not even at nighttime, when everyone is gone" (Goodrich & Hackett 235). The reader learns of the difficult conditions, but because they are listed in straightforward, plain language, the images are not as vivid or clear as they are in Cohen's piece.

In conclusion, I feel that through the narrative structure and excellent descriptive language, Hoose is much more successful than Goodrich and Hackett in conveying the challenges that Rose Cohen and her family face.

Analyze the Model

An argumentative essay states a claim and supports it with logical reasons and evidence from the text.

Claim

Which author most successfully conveys the impact of family challenges on children?

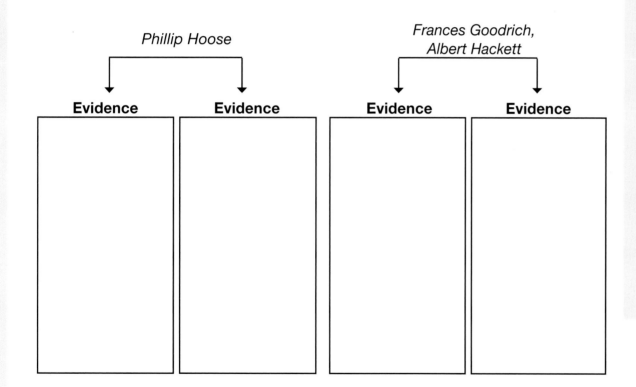

Phillip Hoose

Evidence

Evidence

Frances Goodrich, Albert Hackett

Evidence

Evidence

Text Strategy

In an **argumentative essay**, the writer uses an organizational structure that effectively and logically sequences claims, counterclaims, reasons and evidence.

The claim presents a clear plan for the essay.

- Evaluate the claim.

The topic sentence of each body paragraph clearly states reasons in support of the claim.

- Evaluate whether each topic sentence supports the claim.

Relevant evidence includes logical reasoning, such as direct quotations from the text, that supports the writer's ideas.

- Evaluate whether all sentences in each body paragraph support the topic sentence.

Step 1 | Gather Evidence

Analyze which author conveys the challenges faced by the people or main characters most successfully. Consider the techniques and the strategies that the authors use.

What You Need to Know | Examine the evidence from the excerpts from *Behind the Beautiful Forevers* and *Rabbit-Proof Fence* that show how the authors describe the challenges each family faces and their effects on children.

What You Need to Write | Use a note-taking guide to list evidence that describes and supports each author's description of the challenges each family faced and how those challenges affected the children in the family.

Rabbit-Proof Fence

Point:

Evidence:

Page # _____

Point:

Evidence:

Page # _____

Point:

Evidence:

Page # _____

Behind the Beautiful Forevers

Point:

Evidence:

Page # _____

Point:

Evidence:

Page # _____

Point:

Evidence:

Page # _____

Step 2 | Organize Ideas

What You Need to Know | In order to write a successful argument, you need to support your claim with evidence and details.

To develop your claim:

1. Review the reasons you have listed and be sure you can support each with specific details and evidence from the text.
2. Prepare to present analysis of both sides of the claim.

What You Need to Write | Use a graphic organizer to list and organize text evidence from the note-taking guide to form your argument. Study the evidence you have gathered and determine which author most successfully conveyed the challenges each family faced. Then, select your strongest evidence and present your points one by one.

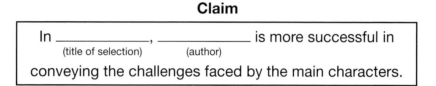

Claim

In ____________ (title of selection), ____________ (author) is more successful in conveying the challenges faced by the main characters.

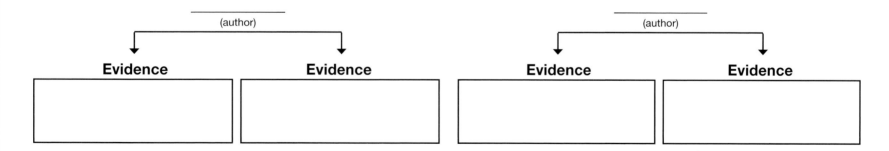

____________ (author)

Evidence	Evidence

____________ (author)

Evidence	Evidence

Step 3 | Draft

Write a draft of your essay on the computer or on paper.

Language Study | Select Strong Supporting Evidence

See It | **Good writers support their claims with convincing reasons and relevant evidence. Examine paragraph 2 of the model essay.**

Try It | **Only four of the eight statements below support the following claim: India is the perfect destination for your next vacation. Read each carefully and then write the four you select. Be prepared to defend your choice of statements.**

1. The food in India is diverse and flavorful.
2. About one-third of India's large population lives in poverty.
3. While in India, you can visit the Taj Mahal, one of the seven modern wonders of the world.
4. New Delhi is the capital of India.
5. The official money of India is the Indian rupee.
6. India's diverse geography allows visitors to see the Himalaya Mountains, beaches, and deserts without leaving the country.
7. Rishikesh, India is often referred to as the yoga capital of the world, and many people travel there to learn to meditate and practice yoga.
8. Most of the land of India forms a peninsula, so the country is surrounded by water on three sides.

India is the perfect destination for your next vacation.

1.

2.

3.

4.

Apply It

Which author do you feel best conveys the challenges faced by the main characters? Use these frames to practice using varied syntax for writing a claim.

1. After reading both selections, I believe ___________.

2. In my opinion, ___________ (author's name) was more successful at ___________.

3. Despite ___________ (counterclaim), ___________ (author's name) was more effective at ___________ (claim).

4. After analyzing the evidence, I maintain that ___________ (author) was more successful in conveying ___________.

5. ___________ (author's name) used ___________ to convey the challenges ___________ (main character's name) faced.

Now revisit your draft and edit your claim.

____

____

____

____

Conventions Study | Clarify Relationships

See It

Writers use transitional words and phrases to create cohesion and clarify the relationships among claims and reasons or evidence.

Comparing	Contrasting
equally, in the same way, similarly, likewise, as with, like, compared with, in the same fashion	*whereas, instead of, alternatively, otherwise, unlike, on the other hand, however, in contrast*

Try It

Find the transition words or phrases that the writer used in the sentence below from the model.

Contrasting	Adding	Illustrating
whereas, instead of, otherwise, alternatively, on the other hand	*adding, additionally, furthermore, moreover, too, as well as*	*for example, such as, for instance, as revealed by, in the case of, as shown by*

She clearly describes the unfriendly environment, her demanding boss, the long days she is forced to work, and her lonely life. In contrast, the play about Anne Frank allows the reader to see the challenges in her life without directly experiencing her thoughts and emotions until the very end of the scene.

What transition words or phrases did the writer use to connect ideas in this paragraph?

Apply It

Now go back to one of your body paragraphs. Edit transition words and phrases to be sure they tie your ideas together and help the reader follow your argument.

Step 4 | Revise and Edit

Revise your draft with a partner.

Organization and Clarity					
State the titles and authors of the texts in the introductory statement. Effectively introduce the claim.	Self	1	2	3	4
	Partner	1	2	3	4
Logically organize and sequence reasons and evidence in the essay. Combine evidence from both texts in order to prove or support the claim.	Self	1	2	3	4
	Partner	1	2	3	4
Summarize and restate a claim in the conclusion.	Self	1	2	3	4
	Partner	1	2	3	4
Evidence and Reasoning					
State the challenges faced by the main character in both texts.	Self	1	2	3	4
	Partner	1	2	3	4
Explain the strategies that make one writer more successful.	Self	1	2	3	4
	Partner	1	2	3	4
Include convincing reasons to support the claim.	Self	1	2	3	4
	Partner	1	2	3	4
Use relevant evidence from the text to support the claim. Cite the author and page number.	Self	1	2	3	4
	Partner	1	2	3	4
Language and Conventions					
Include formal, academic language appropriate to an argumentative essay. Use academic and domain-specific vocabulary from the text.	Self	1	2	3	4
	Partner	1	2	3	4
Use transition words to clarify relationships between evidence and claims.	Self	1	2	3	4
	Partner	1	2	3	4
Spell all words correctly. Use standard capitalization and effective punctuation.	Self	1	2	3	4
	Partner	1	2	3	4

Scoring Guide | ① needs improvement ② average ③ good ④ excellent

Step 5 | Publish

Publish your essay either in print or digital form.

Publish

Publish your argumentative essay either in print or digital form. Use the rubric below to consider the success of your final performance task.

PERFORMANCE TASK RUBRIC

Score Point	Organization and Clarity	Evidence and Reasoning	Language and Conventions
Exemplary ④	• introductory paragraph includes a **thesis statement** that **makes a convincing claim** about why the author conveys challenges most successfully • body paragraphs are **effectively organized** and **present logical reasons and evidence** to support the claim • includes **well-chosen** text evidence, precise language, and words that clarify • concluding statement **restates the thesis statement** and reasons for the claim	• **accurately explains and convincingly persuades** why the writer is most successful conveying challenges • includes **relevant** factual evidence from the informational text to support each reason for the claim	• demonstrates a **strong command** of the conventions of standard English grammar and usage, as well as of standard English capitalization, punctuation, and spelling • vocabulary is **appropriate** to the topic (vocabulary to make a claim and persuade; vocabulary to discuss text structure and technique; vocabulary that clarifies relationships among claims and reasons to create cohesion)
Meets Standards ③	• introductory paragraph **includes an adequate thesis statement that makes a claim** about why the author conveys challenges most successfully • body paragraphs are **logically organized** and **present reasons and evidence** to support the claim • includes **some** text evidence, precise language and words and phrases that clarify • concluding statement **restates the thesis statement**	• **adequately explains and generally persuades** why the writer is most successful conveying challenges • includes **some relevant** factual evidence from the informational text to support each reason for the claim	• demonstrates **a near command** of the conventions of standard English grammar and usage, as well as of standard English capitalization, punctuation, and spelling **with some errors** • vocabulary is **appropriate** to the topic (vocabulary to make a claim and persuade; vocabulary to discuss text structure and technique; vocabulary that clarifies relationships among claims and reasons to create cohesion)

PERFORMANCE TASK RUBRIC			
Score Point	**Organization and Clarity**	**Evidence and Reasoning**	**Language and Conventions**
Needs Work ②	• introductory paragraph **includes a weak thesis statement that attempts to make a claim** about why the author conveys challenges most successfully • **somewhat logically organized** and **partially presents reasons and evidence** to support the claim • includes **a limited amount** of text evidence, precise language and words and phrases that clarify • concluding statement **restates the thesis statement**	• **partially explains and minimally persuades** why the writer is most successful conveying challenges • includes **one or two examples of relevant** factual evidence from the informational text to support each reason for the claim	• demonstrates a **marginal command** of the conventions of English grammar and usage, as well as of standard English capitalization, punctuation, and spelling • there **are many errors; however, the text is still understandable** • includes only **one or two examples** of vocabulary that is appropriate to the topic (vocabulary to make a claim and persuade; vocabulary to discuss text structure and technique; vocabulary that clarifies relationships among claims and reasons to create cohesion)
Does Not Meet Standards ①	• introductory paragraph is **unclear** and does not include a thesis statement • body paragraphs are **not organized logically** and/or **do not present reasons and evidence** to persuade the reader • essay includes **little text evidence** and words and phrases that clarify • concluding statement is **unclear and does not persuade**	• response is **partial or inaccurate explanation** of why the writer is most successful conveying challenges • includes **no factual textual evidence** from the informational text	• demonstrates **almost no command** of the conventions of standard English grammar and usage, as well as of standard English capitalization, punctuation, and spelling • there **are many errors that disrupt** the reader's understanding of the text • **does not include** vocabulary that is appropriate to the topic (vocabulary to make a claim and persuade; vocabulary to discuss text structure and technique; vocabulary that clarifies relationships among claims and reasons to create cohesion)

Questions

Text Structure

1. What is the function of this italicized first paragraph of the text? How does it relate to the rest of the text?

Words and Phrases in Context

2. What is an immigrant? Identify context clues that indicate its meaning.

from *We Were There Too! Young People in U.S. History*

by Phillip Hoose

First Day in a Sweatshop

Russia and New York City, 1892

¶1 *Rose Cohen grew up in a tiny Russian village where Jewish life was brutally controlled by the army of the czar. Jews were forced to live within a barren region that stretched from the Baltic Sea to the Black Sea. Rose's father fled to America, bribing troops at the border to let him pass. Rose heard nothing more from him until the day in 1892 when she received a package covered with mysterious stamps. Inside were two steamship tickets to America—one for Rose, then twelve, and one for her aunt, a few years older. Her father sent for Rose first because he had taught her to sew. She could help him make enough money in New York to send for the others. Rose's father met her ship in New York City and then led her to their new home—a grimy tenement in the Lower East Side. Like many immigrants before and after them, father and daughter vowed that they would work hard so that next year at that time the family would all be together. Rose Cohen wrote of her first two days in a New York sweatshop.*

Words to Know

brutally: *(adv.)* cruelly or harshly

czar: *(n.)* the title of the ruler of Russia 1917

tenement: *(n.)* a large building divided into apartments, especially in the poorer areas of a city

sweatshop: *(n.)* a place where people work long hours for low pay in poor conditions

¶2 "About the same time that the bitter cold came, father told me one night that he had found work for me in a shop where he knew the presser. I lay awake long that night. I was eager to begin life on my own responsibility but was also afraid. We rose earlier than usual that morning for father had to take me to the shop and not be late for his own work. I wrapped my thimble and scissors, with a piece of bread for breakfast, in a bit of newspaper, carefully stuck two needles into the lapel of my coat and we started.

¶3 The shop was on Pelem Street, a shop district one block long and just wide enough for two ordinary sized wagons to pass each other . . . Father said, 'good-bye' over his shoulder and went away quickly. I watched him until he turned onto Monroe Street.

¶4 "I found a door, and pushed it open and went in. A tall, dark, beardless man stood folding coats at a table . . . 'Yes,' he said crossly. 'What do you want?'

¶5 "I said, 'I am the new feller hand.' He looked at me from head to foot. My face felt so burning hot I could scarcely see. 'It is more likely,' he said, 'that you can pull bastings than fell sleeve lining.' Then turning from me he shouted over the noise of the machine: 'Presser, is this the girl?' The presser put down the iron and looked at me. 'I suppose so,' he said. 'I only know the father.'

¶6 "The cross man said, 'Let's see what you can do.' He kicked a chair, threw a coat upon it and said, 'Make room for the new feller hand.' One girl tittered, two men glanced at me over their shoulders and pushed their chairs apart a little...All at once the thought came, 'If I don't [sew] this coat quickly and well he will send me away at once.' I picked up the coat, threaded my needle and began hastily, repeating the lesson father impressed upon me: 'Be careful not to twist the sleeve lining, take small false stitches.'"

¶7 The man inspected the sleeve and then silently tossed Rose two other coats to sew. She reached her apartment well after dark. She went back out the next day before the light of dawn. Everyone was already at their stations. The boss bawled her out for being late. This is not an office, he told her. She bent down low and began to work.

Words to Know

presser: *(n.)* someone who presses or irons clothes

tittered: *(v.)* laughed quietly in a high voice, especially because you were nervous

bawled: *(v.)* shouted in a loud voice, yelled

Questions

Text Structure

3. Who is speaking in this paragraph? What are the words in quotation marks?

Key Ideas and Details

4. What is a *feller hand*? About how many hours a day does Rose work? What does her boss mean when he tells her "this is not an office"?

Questions

Key Ideas and Details

5. How does Rose illustrate the claim that "from this hour a hard life began for me"?

Words and Phrase in Context

6. What does Rose mean when she says, "More tears fell on the sleeve lining than there were stitches in it"?

Key Ideas and Details

7. Explain how Rose's boss takes advantage of her financially.

Key Ideas and Details

8. What motivates Rose to work so hard and keeps her from finding a new job? Find details in the text that explain.

¶**8** "From this hour a hard life began for me. [The boss] refused to employ me except by the week. He paid me three dollars and for this he hurried me from early until late . . . He was never satisfied. By looks and manner he made me feel that I was not doing enough. Late at night when the people would stand up and begin to fold their work away . . . he would come over with still another coat. 'I need it first thing in the morning,' he would give as an excuse. I understood that he was taking advantage of me because I was a child. And now that it was dark in the shop except for the low single gas jet over my table and the one over his at the other end of the room, and there was no one to see, more tears fell on the sleeve lining than there were stitches in it.

¶**9** "[When I got home] my father explained, 'It pays him better to employ you by the week. Don't you see if you did piece work [and got paid for each coat] he would have to pay you as much as he pays a woman piece worker? But this way he gets almost as much work out of you for half the amount a woman is paid.'

¶**10** "I myself did not want to leave the shop for fear of losing a day or even more perhaps in finding other work. To lose half a dollar meant that it would take so much longer before mother and the children would come . . . Often as the hour for going home drew near I would make believe they were home waiting. On leaving the shop I would hasten along through the street keeping my eyes on the ground so as to shut out everything but what I wanted to see. I pictured myself walking into the house. There was a delicious warm smell of cooked food. Mother greeted me near the door and the children gathered about me shouting and trying to pull me down. Mother scolded them saying, 'Let her take her coat off, see how cold her hands are!' I used to keep this up until I turned the key in the door and opened it and stood facing the dark, cold silent room."

Words to Know

drew: *(v.)* to move gradually or steadily in time or space

hasten: *(v.)* to move or act quickly

scolded: *(v.)* to angrily criticize someone, especially a child about something they have done

WHAT HAPPENED TO ROSE COHEN?

¶**11** She kept working in shops and helped make enough money to send for the rest of her family. She became a union leader and organizer. She refused to marry a man her father had picked for her and later married Joseph Cohen. When their daughter Evelyn was born, Rose stopped working in sweatshops. She took writing classes and followed her passion, writing. She wrote five short articles and a book about her life. All were praised. She died in 1925.

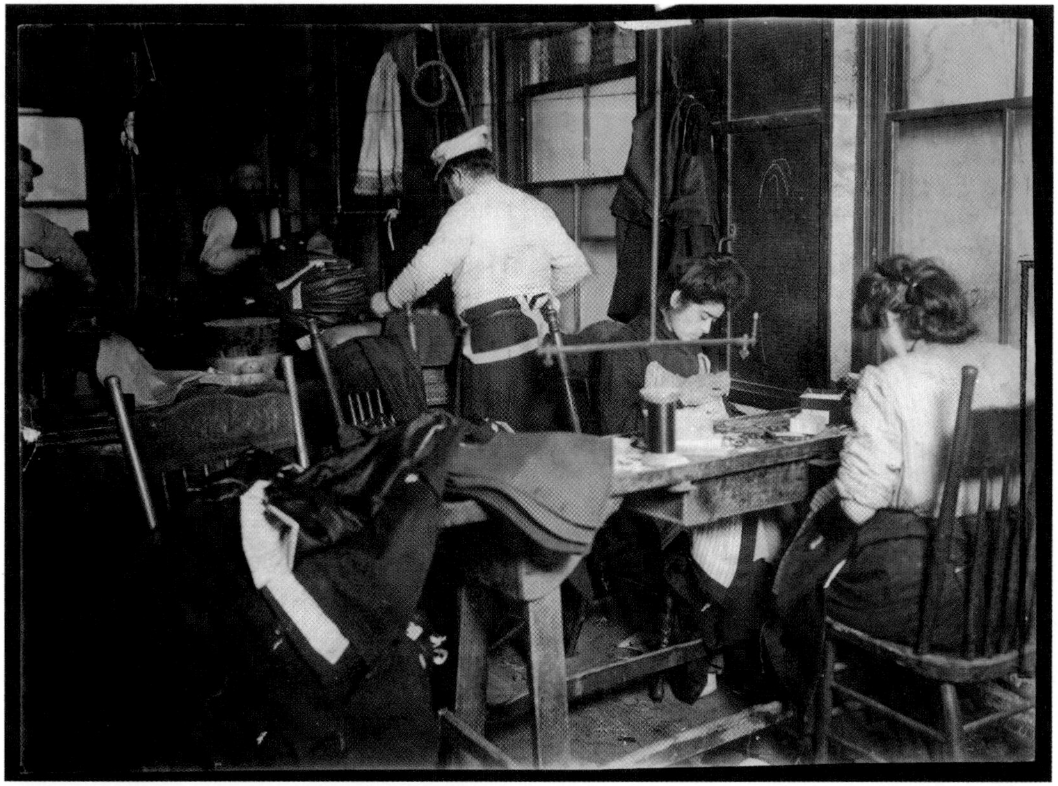

A group of sweatshop workers, New York, NY, 1908

Words to Know

union: *(n.)* an organization of workers formed to protect the rights and interests of its members

praised: *(v.)* admired and approved of someone or something

Questions

Key Ideas and Details

9. How is Rose Cohen's story an example of a stolen childhood? Based on **paragraph 11**, how do you think her childhood experiences affected her adult life?

Questions

Key Ideas and Details

1. Why are the Franks in hiding?

Text Structure

2. What type of text is this? Which elements of the text structure help you identify the text type?

Key Ideas and Details

3. Who are Anne's "movie stars"? What does her dialogue here reveal about her personality?

from *The Diary of Anne Frank*

by Frances Goodrich and Albert Hackett

It's July 1942. World War II is raging. German dictator Adolf Hitler and his Nazi Army have taken over several European countries, and they are rounding up Jewish families and sending them to concentration camps.

In Amsterdam, Holland, a Jewish couple, Otto and Edith Frank, and their daughters, Margot and Anne, have just gone into hiding in a secret annex above Mr. Frank's office space. Joining them are their friends, Mr. and Mrs. van Daan and son Peter. The group must share three rooms and a small attic space. Shortly after they move in, Anne Frank, then 13, begins documenting their experiences in a diary that will become world famous.

Mr. Frank Anneke, there's a box there. Will you open it?

[He indicates a carton on the couch. ANNE brings it to the center table. In the street below, there is the sound of children playing.]

Anne *(as she opens the carton).* You know the way I'm going to think of it here? I'm going to think of it as a boardinghouse. A very peculiar summer boardinghouse, like the one that we—*(She breaks off as she pulls out some photographs.)* Father! My movie stars! I was wondering where they were! I was looking for them this morning . . . and Queen Wilhelmina! How wonderful!

Mr. Frank There's something more. Go on. Look further. *(He goes over to the sink, pouring a glass of milk from a thermos bottle.)*

Words to Know

dictator: *(n.)* a person who rules a country with total authority and often in a cruel or brutal way

concentration camps: *(n.)* type of prisons where large numbers of people who are not soldiers are kept during a war and are usually forced to live in very bad conditions

annex: *(n.)* a building that is attached to or near a larger building and usually used as part of it

Anne *(pulling out a pasteboard-bound book)*. A diary! *(She throws her arms around her father.)* I've never had a diary. And I've always longed for one. *(She looks around the room.)* Pencil, pencil, pencil, pencil. *(She starts down the stairs.)* I'm going down to the office to get a pencil.

Mr. Frank Anne! No! *(He goes after her, catching her by the arm and pulling her back.)*

Anne *(startled)*. But there's no one in the building now.

Mr. Frank It doesn't matter. I don't want you ever to go beyond that door.

Anne *(sobered)*. Never . . . ? Not even at nighttime, when everyone is gone? Or on Sundays? Can't I go down to listen to the radio?

Mr. Frank Never. I am sorry, Anneke. It isn't safe. No, you must never go beyond that door.

[For the first time ANNE realizes what "going into hiding" means.]

Anne I see.

Mr. Frank It'll be hard, I know. But always remember this, Anneke. There are no walls, there are no bolts, no locks that anyone can put on your mind. Miep will bring us books. We will read history, poetry, mythology. (*He gives her the glass of milk.*) Here's your milk. (*With his arm about her, they go over to the couch, sitting down side by side.*) As a matter of fact, between us, Anne, being here has certain advantages for you. For instance, you remember the battle you had with your mother the other day on the subject of overshoes? You said you'd rather die than wear overshoes? But in the end you had to wear them? Well now, you see, for as long as we are here, you will never have

---

Words to Know

sobered: *(v.)* having to become more serious in behavior or attitude

bolts: *(n.)* a wood or metal rod used to fasten a door

inherited: *(v.)* received money, property etc. from someone after they died

Questions

Key Ideas and Details

4. Why does Mr. Frank tell Anne she "must never go beyond that door"? Explain what Anne has just realized "for the first time."

Words and Phrases in Context

5. What does Mr. Frank mean when he says, "There are no walls, there are no bolts, no locks that anyone can put on your mind"?

Questions

Key Ideas and Details

6. Does Mr. Frank really believe Anne will have "a fine life" in hiding? Explain.

Key Ideas and Details

7. Why is it too late for Peter to run water for his cat? Why are Peter, Anne, and Mr. Frank "frozen for a minute in fear" as Peter "starts back for his room"? Explain what you can infer about life in hiding from this scene.

Key Ideas and Details

8. As described in the stage directions, what do Anne's actions in this scene reveal about her character?

to wear overshoes! Isn't that good? And the coat that you inherited from Margot, you won't have to wear that anymore. And the piano! You won't have to practice on the piano. I tell you, this is going to be a fine life for you!

[ANNE's panic is gone. PETER appears in the doorway of his room, with a saucer in his hand. He is carrying his cat.]

Peter I . . . I . . . I thought I'd better get some water for Mouschi before . . .

Mr. Frank Of course.

[As he starts toward the sink, the carillon begins to chime the hour of eight. He tiptoes to the window at the back and looks down at the street below. He turns to PETER, indicating in pantomime that it is too late. PETER starts back for his room. He steps on a creaking board. The three of them are frozen for a minute in fear. As PETER starts away again, ANNE tiptoes over to him and pours some of the milk from her glass into the saucer for the cat. PETER squats on the floor, putting the milk before the cat. MR. FRANK gives ANNE his fountain pen and then goes into the room at the right. For a second ANNE watches the cat; then she goes over to the center table and opens her diary.

In the room at the right, MRS. FRANK has sat up quickly at the sound of the carillon. MR. FRANK comes in and sits down beside her on the settee, his arm comfortingly around her.

Upstairs, in the attic room, MR. and MRS. VAN DAAN have hung their clothes in the closet and are now seated on the iron bed. MRS. VAN DAAN leans back, exhausted. MR. VAN DAAN fans her with a newspaper.

ANNE starts to write in her diary. The lights dim out; the curtain falls.

In the darkness ANNE's voice comes to us again, faintly at first and then with growing strength.]

Words to Know

pantomime: *(n.)* a method of performing using only actions and not words

creaking: *(v.)* making a long, high sound

Anne's Voice I expect I should be describing what it feels like to go into hiding. But I really don't know yet myself. I only know it's funny never to be able to go outdoors . . . never to breathe fresh air . . . never to run and shout and jump. It's the silence in the nights that frightens me most. Every time I hear a creak in the house or a step on the street outside, I'm sure they're coming for us. The days aren't so bad. At least we know that Miep and Mr. Kraler are down there below us in the office. Our <u>protectors</u>, we call them. I asked Father what would happen to them if the Nazis found out they were hiding us. Pim said that they would suffer the same <u>fate</u> that we would. . . . Imagine! They know this, and yet when they come up here, they're always cheerful and gay, as if there were nothing in the world to bother them. . . . Friday, the twenty-first of August, nineteen forty-two. Today I'm going to tell you our general news. Mother is <u>unbearable</u>. She insists on treating me like a baby, which I <u>loathe.</u> Otherwise things are going better. The weather is . . .

[As ANNE's voice is fading out, the curtain rises on the scene.]

On August 4, 1944, Anne and the others in the Secret Annex were arrested and sent to concentration camps after someone betrayed their hiding place. In March 1945, Anne died of disease in the Bergen-Belsen camp in Germany. She was 15 years old.

Questions

Key Ideas and Details

9. Who are Miep and Mr. Kraler? Why does Anne find it remarkable that they are "always cheerful and gay, as if there were nothing in the world to bother them"?

Words to Know

<u>protectors</u>: *(n.)* a person or thing that prevents harm on someone or something

<u>fate</u>: *(n.)* the things that will happen to a person or thing

<u>unbearable</u>: *(adj.)* too unpleasant, painful, or annoying to deal with

<u>loathe</u>: *(v.)* to hate someone or something very much

Literature Circle Leveled Novels

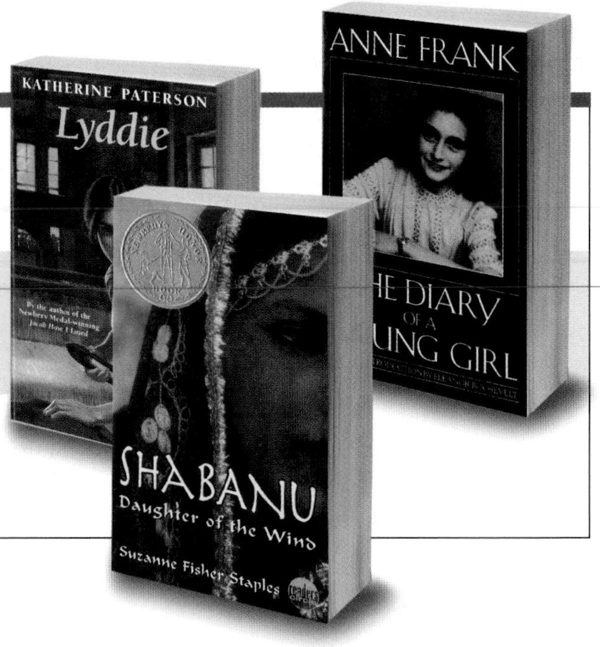

Lyddie *by Katherine Paterson*
Determined to earn the money to save her family's farm, Lyddie faces unsafe working conditions in a factory in 19th century Lowell, Massachusetts. **Lexile**® measure: 820L

Shabanu: Daughter of the Wind *by Suzanne Fisher Staples*
Shabanu, a young nomad of the Cholistan Desert in Pakistan, must submit to the marriage her father arranges for her or go against centuries of tradition by defying him. **Lexile**® measure: 970L

Diary of a Young Girl *by Anne Frank*
This groundbreaking account tells of Anne Frank's two harrowing years spent hiding from the Nazis in a secret annex in the Netherlands during WWII. **Lexile**® measure: 1080L

Fiction, Nonfiction, and Novels

When My Name Was Keoko *by Linda Sue Park.* Ten-year-old Sun-hee and her older brother Tae-yul struggle to maintain their identity and dignity during the Japanese occupation of Korea, when suddenly their customs, their language, and even their names are forbidden. **Lexile**® measure: 610L

Number the Stars *by Lois Lowry.* 10-year-old Annemarie helps smuggle her best friend out of Nazi-controlled Denmark under extreme danger and hardship. **Lexile**® measure: 670L

The Road to Paris *by Nikki Grimes.* When Paris and her brother Malcolm are placed in two separate foster homes, Paris must navigate a new family all on her own, while trying to fit in as the only biracial kid in an all-white neighborhood. **Lexile**® measure: 700L

The Boy in the Striped Pajamas *by John Boyne* When Bruno makes friends with a boy named Shmuel on the other side of the mysterious fence separating his home from a large camp, the resulting lesson is devastating. **Lexile**® measure: 1080L

Out of the Dust *by Karen Hesse.* Billie Jo's childhood is shattered when a household accident injures her and kills her mother, in the harsh setting of the Oklahoma Dust Bowl. **Lexile**® measure: NP

Free the Children: A Young Man Fights Against Child Labor and Proves That Children Can Change the World *by Craig Kielburger* Read the true story of one child's transformation from a normal, middle-class kid from the suburbs to an activist fighting against child labor.

Films and TV

Stolen Childhoods (Galen Films, 2004) Learn the stories of child laborers around the world, told in their own words. (85 min.)

Ken Burns: The Dust Bowl (PBS, 2012) Learn about the worst man-made ecological disaster in American history. Menacing black blizzards killed farmers' crops and livestock, threatened the lives of their children, and forced thousands of desperate families to pick up and move somewhere else. (240 min.)

S21: The Khmer Rouge Killing Machine (First Run Features, 2002) Learn about the history of the Khmer Rouge genocidal campaign in Cambodia. The notorious detention center code-named "S21" was the schoolhouse-turned-prison where 17,000 men, women and children were tortured, interrogated, and executed, their "crimes" meticulously documented to justify their execution. (101 min.)

The Diary of Anne Frank (20th Century Fox, 1959) Following the Nazi invasion of Amsterdam, 13-year-old Anne and her family go into hiding in the confines of an attic. Learn about Anne's remarkable account of their lives. (180 min.)

Websites

The Holocaust: A Learning Site for Students Explore historical photographs, maps, images and artifacts from the Holocaust.

PBS Search for "Dust Bowl" to find features, biographies, photos, and videos about the Dust Bowl.

The Anne Frank Center USA Explore pages of the diary of Anne Frank and find out more about her life and the Holocaust.

Magazines

Time Search for "child labor laws" to find out more about child labor laws in the United States.

National Geographic World Look for articles about child soldiers and refugee children.

The New York Times Upfront Students can search for "Armed and Underage" to read about child soldiers in northeastern Congo.

Life Search for "Dust Bowl" to find historical photographs of Dust Bowl survivors.

UNIT 6

AMERICA SPEAKS

What does it mean to be an American?

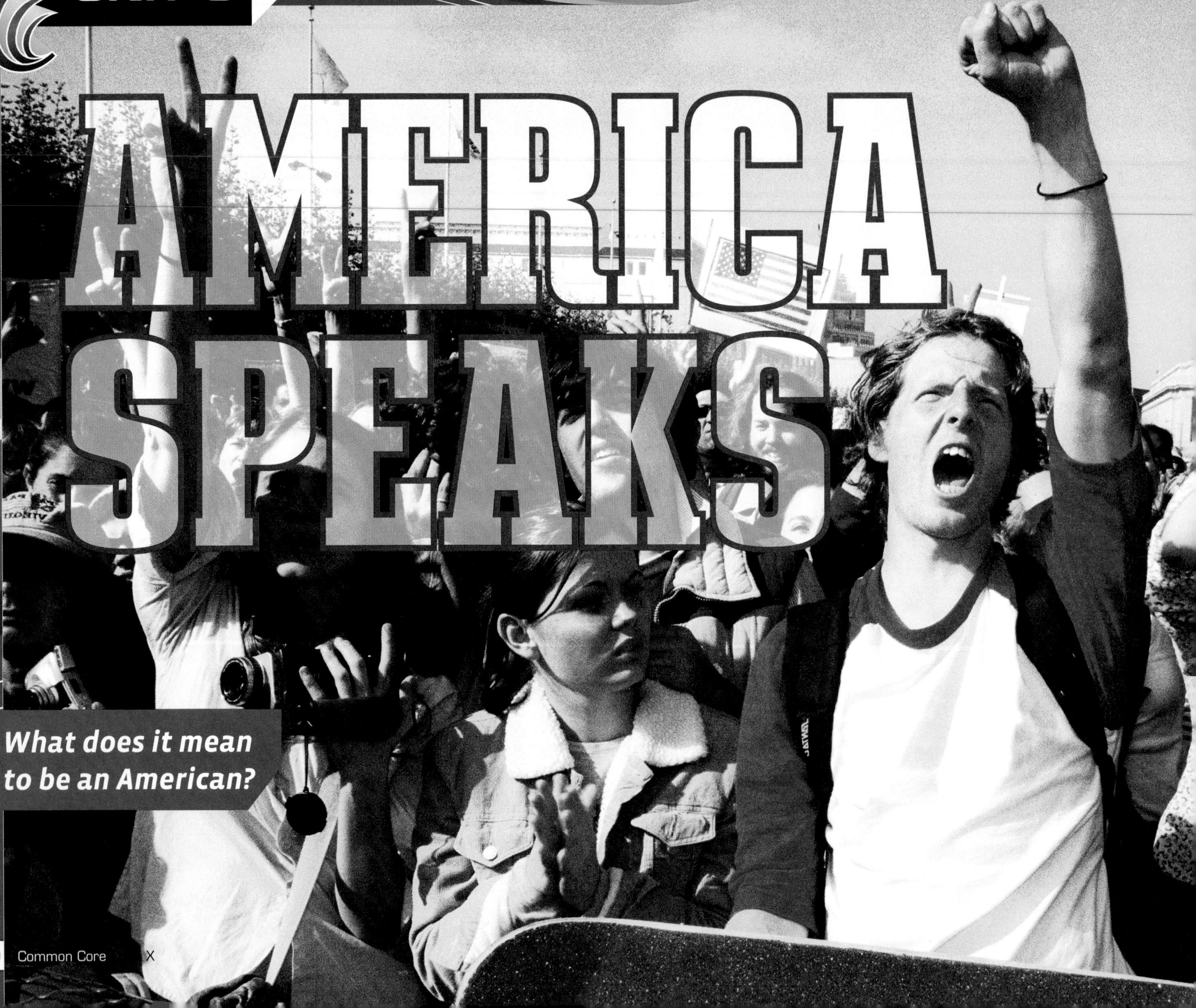

Unit Introduction

Discover three poets' and an author's views of what it means to be an American.

In "I Hear America Singing," Walt Whitman celebrates the variety of American workers' voices. In "I, Too," Langston Hughes speaks up for African Americans rights. In "I, Too, Sing America," Julia Alvarez makes sure the Latin voice is heard celebrating the diversity and unity in America.

In *Kira-Kira*, Cynthia Kadohata discusses a Japanese family's experience with racial discrimination in America.

WRITING PERFORMANCE TASK

These writers claim a specific vision of what it means to be an American. Compare and contrast their perspectives, referencing their literary devices and figurative language.

POETRY/NOVEL EXCERPT

"I Hear America Singing" by Walt Whitman;
"I, Too" by Langston Hughes;
"I, Too, Sing America" by Julia Alvarez

Language
- Academic Vocabulary
- Word Study: Dictionary

Reading Poetry
- Identify Evidence
- Key Ideas and Details
- Craft and Structure

from ***Kira-Kira*** by Cynthia Kadohata

Language
- Academic Vocabulary
- Word Study: Context Clues

Reading a Novel Excerpt
- Identify Evidence
- Key Ideas and Details
- Craft and Structure

SPEAKING AND LISTENING

Present a Poem
- Collaborate and Present

Checklist: Presentation
- Scoring Guide

WRITING

Writing: Informative/Literary Analysis
- Read the Model
- Analyze the Model
- Gather Evidence
- Organize Ideas
- Performance Task Rubric
- Language Study: Compare and Contrast Statements
- Conventions Study: Domain-Specific Vocabulary
- Revise, Edit, and Publish

EXTENDED READINGS

Poem
"One Today" by Richard Blanco

Academic Vocabulary

"I Hear America Singing" by Walt Whitman; "I, Too" by Langston Hughes; "I, Too, Sing America" by Julia Alvarez

Rate your understanding of each word. Then read its meaning and write a sample sentence.

Word	Meaning	Example
bilingually *(adv.)* p. 249 ① ② ③ ④		
blithe *(adj.)* p. 243 ① ② ③ ④	happy and without worry, carefree	
heartland *(n.)* p. 248 ① ② ③ ④	the central part of a country or area of land	
hemisphere *(n.)* p. 248 ① ② ③ ④		The United States is in the northern part of the Western Hemisphere.
maestro *(n.)* p. 249 ① ② ③ ④		The maestro tapped his baton and the orchestra snapped to attention.
robust *(adj.)* p. 244 ① ② ③ ④	strong and healthy, sturdy	

Rating Scale ① I don't know the word. ② I've seen it or heard it. ③ I know its meaning. ④ I know it and use it.

Word Study

Dictionary

A **dictionary** is a reference book that contains words listed in alphabetical order and that gives information about the words' meanings, forms, and pronunciations.

Use the dictionary entry for the word *melodious* to answer the questions below:

melodious (me•**lo**•de•es) *adjective.* musical. having or making a pleasant musical sound. *Jane's melodious voice put the children to sleep during story time.*

1. Is the *l* in *melodious* pronounced in the first or second syllable?
2. What part of speech is the word *melodious*?
3. What is the adverb form of the word *melodious*?

I Hear America Singing

By Walt Whitman

I hear America singing, the varied carols I hear,
Those of mechanics, each one singing his as it should be **blithe** and strong.
The carpenter singing his as he measures his plank or beam,
The mason singing his as he makes ready for work, or leaves off work,
The boatman singing what belongs to him in his boat,
The deckhand singing on the steamboat deck,

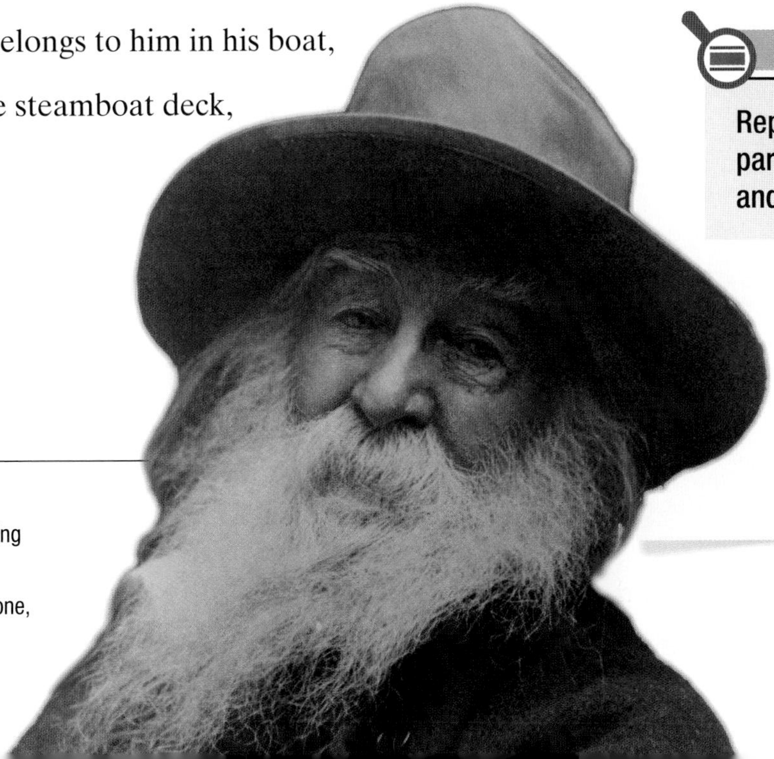

Words to Know

carpenter: *(n.)* someone whose job is making and repairing wooden objects

mason: *(n.)* a skilled worker who builds or works with stone, brick, or concrete

Close Reading

Words and Phrases In Context

1. Distinguish between the denotative and connotative meaning of *carols* as used in **line 1**.

Denotation and Connotation

Denotation is the exact meaning or dictionary definition of a word.

Connotation is the feeling or emotion associated with a word.

Text Structure

2. Explain why you think the author repeats the word *singing*.

Repetition

Repetition is the use of a particular word or phrase over and over.

Close Reading

Assonance and Alliteration

Assonance is the repeated use of words that share the same vowel sound.

Alliteration is the repeated use of words that share the same beginning sound.

Text Structure

3. Explain the effects of assonance (repeated "ing" sounds) and alliteration ("mason," "makes").

Writing

4. What words or phrases support the idea that Whitman celebrates Americans doing their various jobs?

The shoemaker singing as he sits on his bench, the hatter singing as he stands,
The wood-cutter's song, the <u>ploughboy</u>'s on his way in the morning, or at noon <u>intermission</u> or at sundown,
The delicious singing of the mother, or of the young wife at work, or of the girl sewing or washing,
Each singing what belongs to him or her and to none else,
The day what belongs to the day—at night the party of young fellows, **robust**, friendly,
Singing with open mouths their strong melodious songs.

Words to Know

<u>ploughboy</u>: *(n.)* a boy who leads the animal that pulls a plow

<u>intermission</u>: *(n.)* a short break between the parts of a performance (such as a play, movie, or concert)

I, Too

by Langston Hughes

I, too, sing America.

I am the darker brother.
They send me to eat in the kitchen
When <u>company</u> comes,
But I laugh,
And eat well,
And grow strong.

Words to Know

company: *(n.)* people who are visiting you in your home

Close Reading

Tone

Tone is the writer's attitude toward the writing and the readers.

Literary Analysis

5. Describe Hughes's tone in **stanza 1** and **stanza 2.**

Words and Phrases In Context

6. Explain who Hughes refers to when he says *darker* in **line 2** and *they* in **line 3**.

Close Reading

Writing

7. Describe the character traits of the speaker, based on his thoughts "Nobody'll dare say to me" and "They'll see how beautiful I am."

Literary Analysis

8. Who should "be ashamed" and why?

Literary Analysis

9. What does Hughes mean when he says while now they "send me to eat in the kitchen," but "Tomorrow, I'll be at the table"?

Tomorrow,
I'll be at the table
When company comes.
Nobody'll dare
Say to me,
"Eat in the kitchen,"
Then.
Besides,
They'll see how beautiful I am
And be ashamed—
I, too, am America.

I, Too, Sing America

By Julia Alvarez

I know it's been said before
but not in this voice
of the *plátano*
and the mango,
marimba y bongó,
not in this *sancocho*
of *inglés*
con español.

Ay sí,
it's my turn
to oh say
what I see,
I'm going to sing America!

Glossary	
plátano	banana
y	and
marimba y bongó	musical instruments
sancocho	a rich stew made with vegetables and meat
inglés con español	English with Spanish
Ay sí	Oh, yes

Close Reading

Literary Analysis

10. Identify whose voice Alvarez is referring to in **line 2**. What voices have said it before?

Text Structure

11. Explain why the author writes in Spanish and English.

Words and Phrases In Context

12. Explain the meaning of "not in this sancocho of inglés con español" in **stanza 1**.

Text Structure

13. Identify the song that Alvarez references in **lines 11–12** "to oh say what I see."

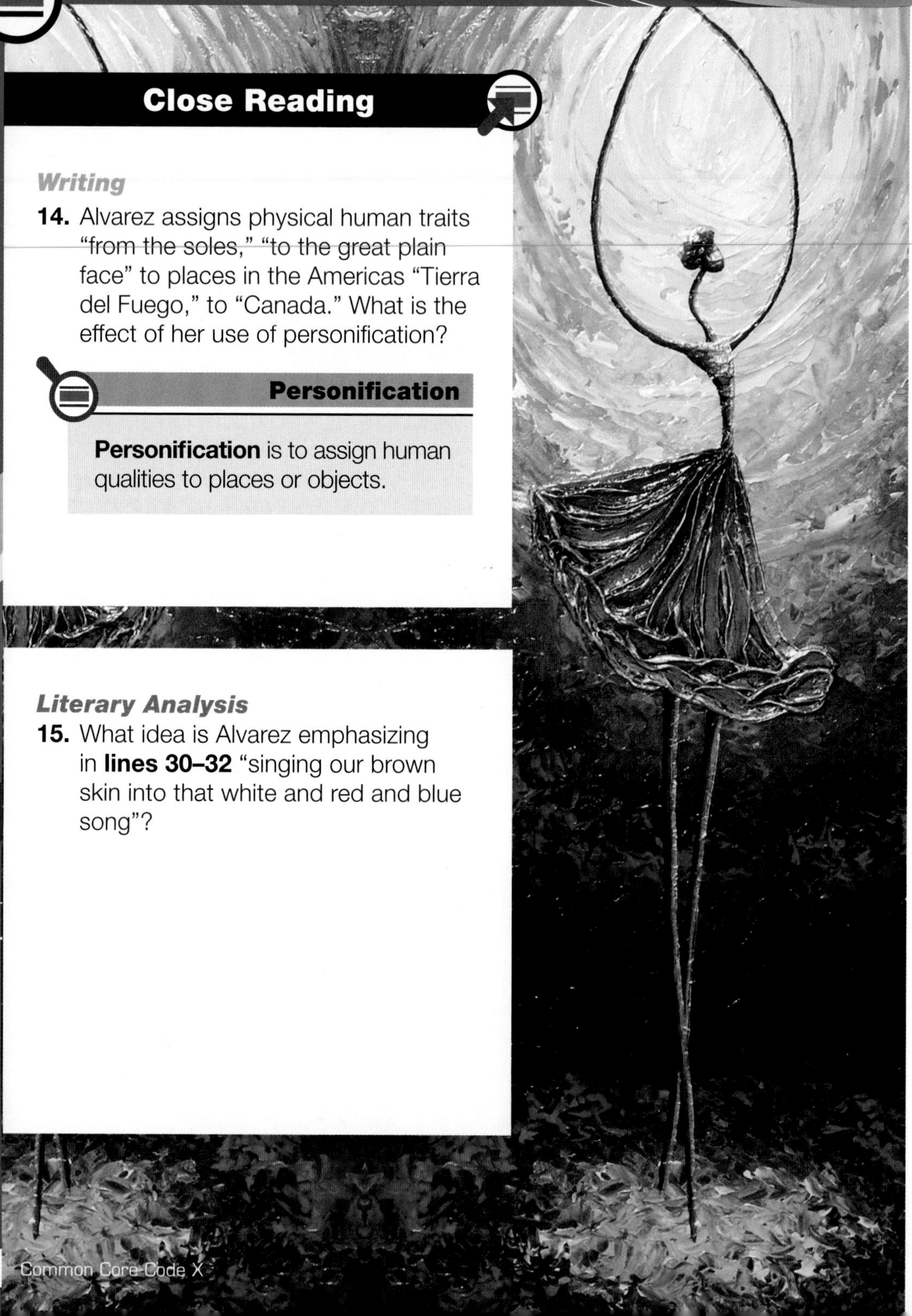

Close Reading

Writing

14. Alvarez assigns physical human traits "from the soles," "to the great plain face" to places in the Americas "Tierra del Fuego," to "Canada." What is the effect of her use of personification?

Personification

Personification is to assign human qualities to places or objects.

Literary Analysis

15. What idea is Alvarez emphasizing in **lines 30–32** "singing our brown skin into that white and red and blue song"?

with all *América*
inside me:
from the <u>soles</u>
of *Tierra del Fuego*
to the thin waist
of *Chiriquí*
up the spine of the
Mississippi
through the **heartland**
of the *Yanquis*
to the great plain face of Canada—
all of us
singing America,
the whole **hemispheric**
familia
belting our *canción*,
singing our brown skin
into that white
and red and blue song—
the big song
that sings
all America,
el canto
que cuenta
con toda América:

un new song!
Ya llegó el momento,

Words to Know

<u>soles</u>: *(n.)* bottom parts of the feet

our moment
under the sun—
ese sol that shines

on everyone.

So, hit it **maestro**!
give us that Latin beat,
¡Uno-dos-tres!
One-two-three!
Ay sí,
(y **bilingually**):
Yo también soy América
I, too, am America

Glossary	
Tierra del Fuego	an island off the southernmost tip of South America
familia	family
Chiriquí	a province in Panama
canción	song
Yanquis	Yankees; U.S. citizens
el canto que cuenta con toda América	the song that includes all of America
un	a
Ya llegó el momento	the moment has arrived
ese sol	that sun
y	and
Yo también soy América	I, too, am America

Close Reading

Text Structure

16. What is the effect of Alvarez's reference to music in **lines 46-49** "give us that Latin Beat"?

Literary Analysis

17. Explain what Alvarez means when she says "I, too, am America."

Identify Evidence | Analyze Individuals, Events, and Ideas

What details does each poet use to describe the American experience?

- In the Evidence column, record details from the text that describe aspects of the American experience from each poet's point of view.
- In the Explanation column, explain how the evidence introduces, illustrates, or elaborates upon the central idea.

Evidence	Source	Page	Explanation
1. "I hear America singing, the varied carols I hear . . ."	Whitman	243	Whitman's America is a joyful one where hardworking individuals sing "carols," meaning joyful songs.
2.			
3. "They send me to eat in the kitchen When company comes"	Hughes	245	Hughes's America is filled with inequality; i.e., the speaker is sent away when company comes.
4.			

Evidence	Source	Page	Explanation
5. "I know it's been said before but not in this voice of the *plátano* and the mango,"	Alvarez	247	Alvarez introduces her "voice" or point of view as a Latina, in comparison to Whitman and Hughes.
6.			

Key Ideas and Details

Determining the Central Idea

1. Use the evidence you collected to summarize the key ideas about the American experience as seen through the eyes of these three poets.

2. List two ideas from each poet. Explain why each is important to the central idea.

Poet	Text	Significance

Craft and Structure

Structure of the Poem

1. Make a list of literary devices and figurative language that each poet uses.

Whitman	Hughes	Alvarez
• imagery: harmonious chorus of proud American workers		

Point of View and Perspective

2. What is the point of view (first, second, or third) and the subject of each poem?

Whitman	Hughes	Alvarez

3. Describe each poet's perspective about what it means to be American.

Whitman	Hughes	Alvarez

Academic Vocabulary

from *Kira-Kira* by Cynthia Kadohata

Rate your understanding of each word. Then read its meaning and write a sentence in the sample box. If an example is given, write the meaning.

Word	Meaning	Example
dismayed (*adj.*) p. 256 ① ② ③ ④		The organizers were very dismayed at the poor volunteer turnout.
genius (*n.*) p. 256 ① ② ③ ④	a very high level of intelligence, mental skill, or ability	
expectantly (*adv.*) p. 256 ① ② ③ ④		The audience expectantly stomped their feet for the star to appear.
meld (*v.*) p. 259 ① ② ③ ④		They hoped to meld their talents to make a unique piece of art.
solemnly (*adv.*) p. 259 ① ② ③ ④	very serious or formal in manner, behavior, or expression	

Rating Scale ① I don't know the word. ② I've seen it or heard it. ③ I know its meaning. ④ I know it and use it.

Word Study

Context Clues

Context Clues are words in a text that help you figure out the meaning of an unfamiliar word. Sometimes words are defined in the text or meaning is suggested.

Circle the context clues to find the meaning of the bold words in the sentences below.

1. She reached under the refrigerator and pulled out a tray. A **worn** envelope sat inside. She opened the envelope up and showed me what was inside: cash . . . She handed me the envelope, and I took the money in my hands. It felt damp and cool . . . She put the money back . . . "They think it's hidden, but I saw Mom take it out."

2. An antebellum **mansion** was not as beautiful as, say, a mountain or the sky, but for a house it was pretty darn nice. Before the Civil War, really rich white people lived in the mansions and owned slaves.

from
Kira-Kira
by Cynthia Kadohata

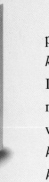

¶**1** My sister, Lynn, taught me my first word: *kira-kira*. I pronounced it ka-a-ahhh, but she knew what I meant. *Kira-kira* means "glittering" in Japanese. Lynn told me that when I was a baby, she used to take me onto our empty road at night, where we would lie on our backs and look at the stars while she said over and over, "Katie, say '*kira-kira, kira-kira*.'" I loved that word! When I grew older, I used *kira-kira* to describe everything I liked: the beautiful blue sky, puppies, kittens, butterflies, colored Kleenex.

Close Reading

Text Structure

1. Identify the point of view.

Literary Analysis

2. Katie "used *kira-kira* to describe everything [she] liked." What does the list of things she liked say about how she views the world?

Point of View

Point of view is the position from which a narrative is told.

- first person = the narrator is part of the story (***I, me, my, mine, we, ours***)
- second person = the narrator gives information or addresses someone (***you, yours***)
- third person = the narrator tells another person's story (***he, she, her, they, them***)

Words to Know

glittering: *(adj.)* bright and shining with quick flashes of light

Close Reading

Literary Analysis

3. Katie's mother "vowed to send us to Japan one day," and Katie doesn't care "so long as Lynn came along." Compare and contrast what Katie and her mother value.

Literary Analysis

4. Katie thinks that "Lynn was the bravest girl in the world. She was also a genius." Explain how the author's use of hyperbole reveals how Katie views her sister, Lynn.

Hyperbole

Hyperbole is an obvious exaggeration or overstatement.

Text Structure

5. Explain the effect of italicizing the word *love* in **paragraph 7**.

My mother said we were misusing the word; you could not call a Kleenex *kira-kira.* She was **dismayed** over how un-Japanese we were and vowed to send us to Japan one day. I didn't care where she sent me, so long as Lynn came along.

¶**3** Lynn was the bravest girl in the world. She was also a **genius**. I knew this because one day I asked her, "Are you a genius?" And she said, "Yes." I believed her because the day my father taught her how to play chess, she won her first game. She said she would teach me how to play if I wanted. She always said she would teach me everything in the world I needed to know. She said we would be rich someday and buy our parents seven houses. But first they would buy a house for all of us. That wonderful day was not far off. I found this out one afternoon when Lynn pulled me into the kitchen, her eyes shining. "I have to show you something," she said.

She reached under the refrigerator and pulled out a tray. A worn envelope sat inside. She opened the envelope up and showed me what was inside: cash.

¶**5** "Is that real?" I said.

"Uh-huh. It belongs to Mom and Dad. It's for our house we're going to buy."

¶**7** We lived in a little rented house in Iowa. I liked our little rented house, but Lynn always told me I would *love* our very own house. Then we could get a dog, a cat, and a parakeet.

Lynn looked at me **expectantly**. I said, "Doesn't money belong in a bank?"

Words to Know

vowed: *(v.)* made a serious promise to yourself or someone else

parakeet: *(n.)* a small, brightly colored bird; a popular pet bird

¶9 "They don't trust the bank. Do you want to count it?"

She handed me the envelope, and I took the money in my hands. It felt damp and cool. "One, two, three…" I counted to eleven. Eleven hundred-dollar bills. I wasn't sure what to think. I found a dollar once in a parking lot. I bought a lot of stuff with that. With eleven hundred dollars, it seemed you could buy anything. "I hope our house is painted sky blue," I said.

¶11 "It will be." She put the money back. "They think it's hidden, but I saw Mom take it out."

Our parents owned a small Oriental foods grocery store. Unfortunately, there were hardly any Oriental people in Iowa, and the store went out of business shortly after Lynn and I first counted the money under the refrigerator. My father's brother, my uncle Katsuhisa, worked in a poultry hatchery in Georgia. He said he could get my father a job at the hatchery. And, he said, he could get my mother a job working in a poultry processing factory. A few weeks after the store went out of business, my father decided to take us down to Georgia to join the poultry industry.

¶13 From the car, Georgia didn't seem so different from anyplace else. But when we got out of the car and talked to people, we couldn't understand them because of their southern accents. They talked like their mouths were full of rubber bands!

Words to Know

damp: *(adj.)* somewhat or slightly wet

Oriental: *(adj.)* an antiquated term for something relating to or situated in eastern Asia

poultry: *(n)* domesticated fowl: chicken, ducks, turkeys, geese

hatchery: *(n.)* a place where fish or chicken eggs hatch in a controlled environment

Close Reading

Literary Analysis

6. Describe Lynn and Katie's parents' view of American institutions, specifically "the bank."

7. The family moves from Iowa to Georgia. Discuss a difference the girl's encounter, revealed through the author's use of simile: "They talked like their mouths were full of rubber bands" in **paragraph 13**.

Simile

Simile is a comparison of two things using the word *like* or *as.*

Writing

8. Explain the causes and effects of the family business failing. ("The store went out of business.") What does the family's response to this event reveal about them? Provide textual evidence.

Close Reading

Literary Analysis

9. Describe the family's experience and their reaction to segregation in America: "COLORED IN BACK."

Text Structure

10. Explain the effect of capitalization used in **paragraph 14**.

Writing

11. Review what you learn about Lynn's future dream to own her "very own house" in **paragraph 7**. What do her actions in **paragraph 15** reveal about how she will make those dreams come true?

People stared at us when we went into their restaurants. The restaurant signs said things like COLORED IN BACK. The white people sat at the front. We didn't know where to sit, so we always ordered to-go. We didn't see another Japanese person anywhere. We got stared at quite a bit. Sometimes a white lady would lean over us and exclaim, "How cute!" Some of them touched our faces, as if they weren't sure we were real.

¶**14** Georgia had many claims to fame. During our driving, Lynn read me all the signs: GORDON, CHICKEN CAPITAL OF THE WORLD; VIDALIA, HOME OF THE SWEETEST ONIONS IN THE WORLD; CORDELE, WATERMELON CAPITAL OF THE WORLD; MILTON, THE WORLD'S BEST PEACHES; and TEMPLETON, WHERE PEANUTS ARE KING. We also saw seven different restaurants that claimed to have the world's best BBQ.

¶**15** Several times we drove by an antebellum mansion. "Antebellum" means "before the Civil War." Lynn taught me that. She had tried to read the whole dictionary once, so she knew the definitions of a lot of words that started with "a." An antebellum mansion was not as beautiful as, say, a mountain or the sky, but for a house it was pretty darn nice. Before the Civil War, really rich white people lived in the mansions and owned slaves. I didn't know who lived in them now.

Words to Know

stared *(v.)* looked at someone or something for a long time, often with your eyes wide open

fame *(n.)* the state of being known about by a lot of people because of your achievements

¶**16** Our new town was called Chesterfield. Uncle told us the population was 4,001. Six other Japanese families lived in Chesterfield. Including us, that made a grand total of thirty-one Japanese people. All of the fathers worked at the hatchery in a nearby town.

¶**17** The day before I started first grade, Lynn sat me down for a talk. She gave me talks only when something very, very serious was happening. She always told me the truth and didn't treat me like a baby. It was she and not my parents who'd first told me we were leaving Iowa.

¶**18** We sat cross-legged on the floor in our room and held hands and closed our eyes while she chanted, "Mind **meld**, mind meld, mind meld." That was our friendship chant.

¶**19** She gazed at me **solemnly**. "No matter what happens, someday when we're each married, we'll own houses down the block from each other. We'll live by the sea in California."

¶**20** That sounded okay with me. "If y'all are going to live by the sea, I will too," I said. I had never seen the California sea, but I imagined it was very pretty. She leaned forward then, and I knew she was going to get to the point of this talk.

Words to Know

chanted: *(v.)* repeated a word or phrase again and again

gazed: *(v.)* looked at someone for a long time, giving him or her all your attention

leaned: *(v.)* moved or bent your body in a particular direction

Close Reading

Words and Phrases In Context

12. Define *grand* as used in **paragraph 16**. What is the author's purpose in using the word ironically?

Literary Analysis

13. Describe Lynn and Katie's relationship. Provide textual evidence.

Academic Vocabulary

14. Explain what the sisters "meld." How does this add to the seriousness of the moment? How does the use of alliteration effect the phrase?

Close Reading

Writing

15. Identify evidence to elaborate on the idea of isolation weaved throughout this section.

Text Structure

16. Label the speaker of each line of dialogue throughout this section.

Literary Analysis

17. Explain the effect of hyperbole "quite amazing" and "even perfect" in **paragraph 26**.

¶**21** "Have you noticed that sometimes people won't say hello to Mom when we're out shopping?"

"Uh-huh."

¶**23** "Well, some of the kids at school may not say hello to you, either."

"You mean because they don't know me?"

¶**25** "No, I mean because they don't want to know you."

"Why wouldn't they want to know me?" Who wouldn't want to know me? This was a new idea for me. Our father had always thought we were quite amazing, and Lynn, of course, had always thought I was perfect, so I thought of myself as rather amazing and maybe even perfect.

¶**27** "Because, there's only thirty-one Japanese people in the whole town, and there's more than four thousand people in the town, and four thousand divided by thirty-one is…a lot more of them than of us. Do you understand?"

"No."

Words to Know

quite: *(adv.)* very, but not extremely

¶**29** Lynn's face darkened. That was kind of unusual. "Haven't you noticed that Mom and Dad's only friends are Japanese?"

"I guess so."

¶**31** "That's because the rest of the people are ignoring them. They think we're like doormats—or ants or something!" Now she was really angry.

"Ants?"

¶**33** She suddenly reached out and hugged me to her. "You tell me if anybody treats you like that, and I'll take care of it!"

¶**34** "Okay." Sometimes Lynn didn't seem to make sense. That was because I was so young and she was such a genius.

¶**35** Then she kissed my face and said, "You're the most wonderful girl in the world!"

Words to Know

unusual: *(adj.)* different from what is usual or normal

sense: *(n.)* to have a clear meaning and be easy to understand

Close Reading

Words and Phrases In Context

18. Define "darkened" as used in **paragraph 29**. Identify context clues that help you determine the meaning.

Literary Analysis

19. Compare and contrast the mood created by the author's use of figurative language in **paragraph 31** ("they think we're like doormats—or ants") and **paragraph 35** ("You're the most wonderful girl in the world").

Literary Analysis

20. Discuss whether or not you think Katie will be okay. Provide textual evidence.

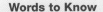

Identify Evidence | Analyze Individuals, Events, and Ideas

What details and events does Kadohata use to describe Katie and Lynn's family's American experience?

- In the Evidence column, record details from the text that describe aspects of life in America as experienced by the Japanese family.
- In the Explanation column, explain how the evidence introduces, illustrates, or elaborates on that experience.

Evidence	Source	Page	Explanation
1. "Kira-kira means 'glittering' in Japanese."	Katie/ Narrator	255	The author introduces the fact that the family is Japanese.
2.			
3.			
4.			

Evidence	Source	Page	Explanation
5.			
6.			
7.			
8.			

Key Ideas and Details

Determining the Central Idea

1. Use the evidence you collected to summarize the key idea of this excerpt from *Kira-Kira*.

2. List three key individuals. Explain how each is important to the story.

Individuals	Significance

3. List three events in the story and the significance of each.

Events	Significance

Craft and Structure

Structure of the Narrative

1. Make a list of the significant events in the lives of the Japanese sisters in chronological order.

First	
Second	
Third	
Fourth	
Fifth	

Perspective

2. Make a list of literary devices and figurative language that the author uses to help convey her perspective.

Figurative Language/Literary Device	Significance

3. Describe Kadohata's perspective about what it means to be an American.

Collaborate and Present

Plan and Deliver a Presentation

Assignment: Choose one poem to memorize and present to the class. Discuss how hearing and seeing the poem contributes to its meaning or changes its effect.

Analyze the Content

1. Consider the following questions:
   - Which poem would you like to present? Why?
   - What multimedia component and/or visual display can you add to your presentation?

2. Choose one poem. Brainstorm ways to enhance your presentation through tone, multimedia components, visual displays, or acting.

Poem	Presentation Ideas

Collaborate

3. Work with a partner to brainstorm ways to enhance your presentation. Practice reciting your poem and start to memorize lines.

Present

4. Deliver your presentation.

Seeking Clarification

- In other words, you think that . . .
- If I understand you correctly, you would like to . . .
- So you would prefer to . . .

Reporting Ideas

- _____ noticed
- _____ suggested
- _____ agreed

Presentation

- Use formal English.
- Face your audience.
- Stand up straight and speak with confidence.
- Avoid fidgeting.

Presentation Checklist

Use the checklist below to evaluate your collaboration skills, reasoning, and final presentation. Think carefully about your work. If you know you completed an item thoroughly, give yourself a check (✓).

COLLABORATE AND PRESENT CHECKLIST		
Comprehension & Collaboration	**Evidence & Reasoning**	**Presentation of Knowledge & Ideas**
☐ Come to discussions prepared, having read and studied material. ☐ Refer to evidence when contributing to the discussion. ☐ Follow rules for discussions and lead by example. ☐ Ask and answer specific questions. ☐ Make comments that contribute to the topic under discussion. ☐ Review the key ideas under discussion and demonstrate understanding of multiple perspectives through reflection and paraphrasing.	☐ State the title and author of the poem. ☐ Present information relevant to the task. ☐ Explain how hearing and seeing the poem contributes to its meaning or changes its effects. ☐ Synthesize the key ideas from your poem with a conclusion.	☐ Adapt language to a variety of contexts and tasks to demonstrate knowledge of formal English. ☐ Include multimedia components (e.g., graphics, images, music, sound) and visual displays. ☐ Use appropriate volume/tone (clear, not too fast, too slow, or too loud) and avoid using "like" or "ummm." ☐ Have strong posture and a confident stance, and make frequent eye contact. ☐ Occasionally move from one spot to another without fidgeting. ☐ Smile and appear to be relaxed.
Number of ✓s in this category: ___	**Number of ✓s in this category: ___**	**Number of ✓s in this category: ___**
Total # of ✓s: __		

Add up the total number of checks (✓) in each category. Then use the scoring guide below to calculate your final score.

Scoring Guide			
14 to 16 ✓s	**11 to 13 ✓s**	**9 to 10 ✓s**	**7 or less ✓s**
④ Exemplary	**③ Meets Standards**	**② Needs Work**	**① Does Not Meet Standards**

Read the Model

Writers use many strategies to craft ideas and share information. The writer of this informative essay compares and contrasts the perspectives of two authors and how they use figurative language and literary devices to express their vision of the same topic. Read and discuss the model essay below.

Literary Analysis

In a **literary analysis**, the writer interprets how elements of a literary text contribute to the meaning.

The **introduction** states the title and author of the text that the writer will analyze, and includes the thesis statement.

- Describe how the writer introduces the topic.

The two **body paragraphs** express the writer's main points about the text.

- Find two examples of text citations.
- Find two examples of the writer's use of transition words.

The **conclusion** sums up or restates the thesis.

- Identify the conclusion.

Every One an American

By Gloria Woon

Poets Richard Blanco and Julia Alvarez both express in their poems that they are truly Americans, but their perspectives are different. In "One Today," Richard Blanco's vision is that he is one American among many in one country. In "I, Too, Sing America," Julia Alvarez sings a rhythmic response to Walt Whitman's poem "I Hear America Singing" to portray her vision of Latinos as wanting to be heard as American. Both poems convey these visions through literary devices and figurative language to develop the concept of what it means to be an American.

The literary devices the authors choose to express their perspectives are similar in some ways. Both authors use repetition. In Blanco's poem, the word *one* is often repeated, such as in "one sun, one light, one ground, one wind, one sky, one moon," to emphasize his vision that all people in this land are Americans (278). In her poem, Alvarez repeats the word *song* as in "the big song, a new song," "white and red and blue song" to focus on herself and all Latinos as outsiders who want a voice as insiders in America (248). In addition, both authors use figurative language to make meaningful connections for readers. In "One Today," Blanco uses similes, such as "one moon like a silent drum tapping on every rooftop . . . of one country" to depict the variety and unity of America (281). Alvarez uses personification to compare the Americas to a person whose soles are at the tip of Argentina, whose waist is Panama, whose spine is the Mississippi, and whose face is Canada. To her, the whole western hemisphere is one body, her American family.

Blanco and Alvarez make different kinds of language choices to clarify their perspectives. Blanco effectively uses sensory details to create images of the energetic, jubilant mood of Americans moving together through a new day. For example, he taps into the senses of sound and sight with vivid adjectives as in "pencil-yellow school buses" (278), the "plum blush of dusk" (281), and "honking cabs" (279), and with strings of action verbs, such as *charging, teeming, gleaning, launching, screeching, whistling, whispers* (278–280). In contrast, Alvarez weaves her poem with Spanish phrases like *el canto que cuenta con toda América* that emphasize the Latin voice and beat she desires people to hear (248). Instead of painting images as Blanco does, Alvarez creates a tone that demands attention.

In conclusion, both poets use literary devices and figurative language to portray their view of being American, but Blanco sees himself and his family as part of the one America, while Alvarez sees her people as still trying to find their voice so that they too can sing "the big song that sings all America" (248).

Analyze the Model

A compare/contrast essay points out similarities and differences between two texts.

Introduction	
Thesis Statement	
Body: Similarities	
Author Point Evidence	Author Point Evidence
Author Point Evidence	Author Point Evidence
Body: Differences	
Author Point Evidence	Author Point Evidence
Conclusion	
Restate and why it matters	

Text Strategy

In a **point-by-point comparison,** the writer discusses the relevant characteristics of each text to cover the points of similarity and then the differences.

The thesis statement presents a clear plan for the essay.

- Identify the thesis statement.

The topic sentence of each body paragraph clearly states the similarities or differences of the authors.

- Identify the points of similarity and differences.
- Evaluate whether each topic sentence supports the thesis.

Relevant evidence includes direct quotations from the text that support the writer's points.

- Evaluate whether all sentences in each body paragraph support the topic sentence.

The conclusion sums up or restates the thesis and why it matters.

- Describe how the writer concluded her essay.

Step 1 | Gather Evidence

These writers all claim a specific vision of what it means to be an American. Compare and contrast their perspectives referencing their literary devices and figurative language.

What You Need to Know | Examine the evidence you have collected from both texts that compares or contrasts the authors' visions of what it means to be an American.

What You Need to Know | Use a note-taking guide to list evidence from each text that describes each author's perspective and the literary devices and figurative language used to express those perspectives.

Text: ____________________

Author's Perspective:

Literary device/figurative language

Evidence:

Page # ______

Author's Perspective:

Literary device/figurative language

Evidence:

Page # ______

Author's Perspective:

Literary device/figurative language

Evidence:

Page # ______

Text: ____________________

Author's Perspective:

Literary device/figurative language

Evidence:

Page # ______

Author's Perspective:

Literary device/figurative language

Evidence:

Page # ______

Author's Perspective:

Literary device/figurative language

Evidence:

Page # ______

Step 2 | Organize Ideas

What You Need to Know | Use relevant, well-chosen examples from the text to show the authors' visions and points of view.

To develop your topic:

1. Select two to three examples that show each author's vision about what it means to be an American.
2. Choose examples from each text that you can use to compare and contrast the authors' points of view.

What You Need to Write | Use the note-taking guide and the graphic organizer to describe the authors' visions, and list examples of literary devices and figurative language in the text that the authors used to express their visions.

Introduction	
Thesis Statement	
Body: Similarities	
Author **Point** **Evidence**	**Author** **Point** **Evidence**
Body: Differences	
Author **Point** **Evidence**	**Author** **Point** **Evidence**
Conclusion	
Restate thesis and why it matters	

Step 3 | Draft

Write a draft of your essay on the computer or on paper.

Language Study | Compare and Contrast Statements

See It

Statements that compare and contrast give details about how two subjects are similar and how they are different.

When writing statements that compare and contrast:

- identify the subjects being compared or contrasted
- tell how the subjects are similar and different

Comparing	Contrasting
equally, in the same way, similarly, likewise, as with, like, compared with, same as	*whereas, instead of, alternatively, otherwise, unlike, on the other hand, however, in contrast, while, but, different from, although*

- Go back to the model essay and identify the signal words the writer used to show comparison and contrast.

Try It

Put an S **by the sentences that compare or highlight similarities. Put a** D **next to the sentences that contrast or highlight differences. Then underline how the subjects are similar or different.**

☐ 1 Both Abraham Lincoln in his Gettysburg Address and Martin Luther King, Jr., in his "I Have a Dream" speech seek to inspire and give hope to their audiences though repetition of vivid verbs. Lincoln uses the verbs *consecrate*, *dedicate*, and *resolve*, and King uses the verbs *crippled, dramatize,* and *refuse*.

☐ 2 The lyrics of the songs "The Star-Spangled Banner" and "American Pie" offer contrasting views of America; one song describes a new, hopeful nation rising and the other expresses despair.

☐ 3 Both Celia Thaxter and William Wordsworth use similes to describe the spring in their poems, Thaxter describes the daffodils "like beautiful bubbles of amethyst" and Wordsworth says the snow is gone "like an army defeated."

Apply It | Use the sentence frames to help you write compare and contrast statements.

1. The differences/similarities between ________ (author 1) and ________ (author 2) are ________ (point of comparison or contrast).

2. ________ (Although, while) both authors use ________ (feature or quality), ________ (author 1) uses ________ (example) and ________ (author 2) uses ________ (example) to portray ________ (vision or point of view).

3. Both ________ (author 1) and ________ (author 2) present ________ (point of view or vision) on ________ (topic). Each author chooses ________ (similar/different) ways to develop the concept.

4. Two ________ (text type) offer a ________ (similar/different) point of view on ________ (topic) by using ________ (feature or quality).

5. ________ (author 1) vision of ________ (topic) is developed though ________ (feature or quality). In contrast, ________ (author 2) uses ________ (feature or quality) to develop a point of view.

Now, **go back to your draft** and revise any compare and contrast sentences.

____

____

Conventions Study | Domain-Specific Vocabulary

See It

Domain-specific vocabulary words relate to a specific subject. For example, *labor, career,* and *employment* tell about the world of workers.

Try It

Find domain-specific vocabulary that the writer uses in the sentences below from the model. Then look for domain-specific vocabulary that the writer uses as part of this literary analysis.

Blanco effectively uses sensory details to create images of the energetic, jubilant mood of Americans moving together through a new day. For example, he taps into the senses of sound and sight with vivid adjectives, as in "pencil-yellow school buses," the "plum blush of dusk," and "honking cabs," and with strings of action verbs, such as *charging, teeming, gleaning, launching, screeching, whistling, whispers.*

Apply It

Make a list of the domain-specific vocabulary that you used in your essay.

Step 4 | Revise and Edit

Revise your draft with a partner.

Organization and Clarity					
State the authors and titles of the texts in the introduction.	Self	1	2	3	4
	Partner	1	2	3	4
Introduce ideas about the author/poets' perspectives about what it means to be American.	Self	1	2	3	4
	Partner	1	2	3	4
The topic sentence of each body paragraph clearly states the similarities or differences of the author/poets.	Self	1	2	3	4
	Partner	1	2	3	4
The conclusion paragraph restates how the author/poet uses figurative language and literary techniques to describe their vision of what it means to be an American.	Self	1	2	3	4
	Partner	1	2	3	4
Evidence and Reasoning					
Include three or more examples of specific and relevant text evidence highlighting the author/poet's use of literary devices and figurative language.	Self	1	2	3	4
	Partner	1	2	3	4
Language and Conventions					
Use appropriate transitions to link compare and contrast statements.	Self	1	2	3	4
	Partner	1	2	3	4
Use academic and domain-specific vocabulary as appropriate.	Self	1	2	3	4
	Partner	1	2	3	4
Establish and maintain a formal style and objective tone throughout the essay.	Self	1	2	3	4
	Partner	1	2	3	4

Scoring Guide | ① needs improvement ② average ③ good ④ excellent

Step 5 | Publish

Publish your essay either in print or digital form.

Publish

Publish your essay either in print or digital form. Use the rubric below to assess your final performance task.

PERFORMANCE TASK RUBRIC			
Score Point	**Organization and Clarity**	**Evidence and Reasoning**	**Language and Conventions**
Exemplary ④	• introductory paragraph introduces the **topic clearly** and previews the comparison and contrast the writer will make • body paragraphs are **logically organized by similarities and differences** and **analyze** the techniques the authors use • includes **well-chosen** text evidence, precise language, and domain-specific vocabulary • concluding statement **wraps up the ideas** in the essay and compares and contrasts the authors' points of view and techniques	• **accurately compares and contrasts** the authors' points of view **and convincingly analyzes** how they use figurative language and literary devices to convey it • includes **several examples of relevant** textual evidence from the poems to illustrate the authors' points of view and the techniques they use	• demonstrates a **strong command** of the conventions of standard English grammar and usage, as well as of standard English capitalization, punctuation, and spelling • vocabulary is **appropriate** to the topic (vocabulary about being an American; accurate terms for referring to figurative language and literary devices; vocabulary for making point-by-point comparisons and contrasts)
Meets Standards ③	• introductory paragraph introduces the **topic clearly** and **previews** what the essay will be about • body paragraphs are **logically organized by similarities and differences** and include **some analysis** of the techniques • includes **some** text evidence, precise language and domain-specific vocabulary • concluding statement **wraps up the ideas** in the essay and contrasts the authors' points of view	• **adequately compares and contrasts** the authors' points of view and **analyzes** how they use figurative language and literary devices to convey it • includes **relevant** textual evidence from the poems to illustrate the authors' points of view and the techniques they use	• demonstrates **a near command** of the conventions of standard English grammar and usage, as well as of standard English capitalization, punctuation, and spelling **with some errors** • vocabulary is **appropriate** to the topic (vocabulary about being an American; accurate terms for referring to figurative language and literary devices; vocabulary for making point-by-point comparisons and contrasts)

PERFORMANCE TASK RUBRIC			
Score Point	Organization and Clarity	Evidence and Reasoning	Language and Conventions
Needs Work ②	• introductory paragraph introduces the **topic** • body paragraphs are **somewhat logically organized by similarities and differences**, though some ideas developed stray from a comparison of the points of view of the two authors and the techniques they use • includes **a limited amount** of text evidence, precise language and domain-specific vocabulary • **partial** concluding statement **refers to some of the ideas** in the essay	• **compares and contrasts** the authors' points of view and includes a **limited analysis** of the techniques they use to convey it • includes **some textual evidence** from each poem to support analysis	• demonstrates a **marginal command** of the conventions of English grammar and usage, as well as of standard English capitalization, punctuation, and spelling • there **are many errors; however, the text is still understandable** • includes only **one or two examples** of vocabulary that is appropriate to the topic (vocabulary about being an American; accurate terms for referring to figurative language and literary devices; vocabulary for making point-by-point comparisons and contrasts)
Does Not Meet Standards ①	• introductory paragraph is **unclear** • body paragraphs are **not organized logically** and/or **do not compare and contrast** the points of view of the two authors • essay includes **little text evidence** and little precise language • concluding statement is **unclear or does not wrap up** the ideas in the essay.	• response is **partial or inaccurate comparison** of the two authors' points of view and the techniques they use to convey it • includes **no analyses of textual evidence** from each poem	• demonstrates **almost no command** of the conventions of standard English grammar and usage, as well as of standard English capitalization, punctuation, and spelling; there **are many errors that disrupt** the reader's understanding of the text • **does not include** vocabulary that is appropriate to the topic (vocabulary about being an American; accurate terms for referring to figurative language and literary devices; vocabulary for making point-by-point comparisons and contrasts).

Questions

Writing

1. What key idea is Blanco emphasizing by repeating the word *one:* "One Today"; "One sun"; "One ground"; "One sky"; and "one moon"? Who is the "us" the sun rose on?

Literary Analysis

2. What larger idea about work does Blanco introduce in **lines 14–15** "ring up groceries as my mother did for twenty years, so I could write this poem"?

"One Today"

by Richard Blanco

Inaugural poet Richard Blanco read his poem "One Today" at the swearing-in ceremony for President Barack Obama on January 21, 2013.

One sun rose on us today, kindled over our shores,
peeking over the Smokies, greeting the faces
of the Great Lakes, spreading a simple truth
across the Great Plains, then charging across the Rockies.
One light, waking up rooftops, under each one, a story
told by our silent gestures moving behind windows.

My face, your face, millions of faces in morning's mirrors,
each one yawning to life, crescendoing into our day:
pencil-yellow school buses, the rhythm of traffic lights,
fruit stands: apples, limes, and oranges arrayed like rainbows
begging our praise. Silver trucks heavy with oil or paper—
bricks or milk, teeming over highways alongside us,
on our way to clean tables, read ledgers, or save lives—
to teach geometry, or ring-up groceries as my mother did
for twenty years, so I could write this poem.

Words to Know

gestures: *(n.)* a movement of part of your body, especially your hands or head, to show what you mean or how you feel.
ledgers: *(n.)* a book that a company uses to record information about the money it has paid and received.

All of us as vital as the one light we move through,
the same light on blackboards with lessons for the day:
equations to solve, history to question, or atoms imagined,
the "I have a dream" we keep dreaming,
or the impossible vocabulary of sorrow that won't explain
the empty desks of twenty children marked absent today, and forever.
Many prayers, but one light breathing color into stained glass windows,
life into the faces of bronze statues, warmth
onto the steps of our museums and park benches
as mothers watch children slide into the day.

One ground. Our ground, rooting us to every stalk
of corn, every head of wheat sown by sweat
and hands, hands gleaning coal or planting windmills
in deserts and hilltops that keep us warm, hands
digging trenches, routing pipes and cables, hands
as worn as my father's cutting sugarcane
so my brother and I could have books and shoes.

The dust of farms and deserts, cities and plains
mingled by one wind—our breath. Breathe. Hear it
through the day's gorgeous din of honking cabs,
buses launching down avenues, the symphony
of footsteps, guitars, and screeching subways,
the unexpected song bird on your clothes line.

Words to Know

vital: *(adj.)* extremely important.

trenches: *(n.)* a long, narrow hole that is dug in the ground, ditch.

din: *(n.)* a loud, confusing mixture of notes that lasts for a long time.

Questions

Text Structure

3. Explain the effect of the juxtaposition of **line 19** "'I have a dream' we keep dreaming" and **line 21** "the empty desks of twenty children marked absent today, and forever."

Literary Analysis

4. What effect does the poet create by referring to the sounds of "honking cabs" and "screeching subways" as a "gorgeous din"?

Questions

Literary Analysis

5. What is the effect of the poet's use of the words and phrases "hello, shalom, buon giorno, howdy, namaste, or buenos días" in this stanza?

Literary Analysis

6. Why does the poet describe the "Freedom Tower" as "jutting into a sky that yields to our resilience"?

Hear: squeaky playground swings, trains whistling,
or whispers across café tables, Hear: the doors we open
for each other all day, saying: hello, shalom,
buon giorno, howdy, namaste, or buenos días
in the language my mother taught me—in every language
spoken into one wind carrying our lives
without prejudice, as these words break from my lips.

One sky: since the Appalachians and Sierras claimed
their majesty, and the Mississippi and Colorado worked
their way to the sea. Thank the work of our hands:
weaving steel into bridges, finishing one more report
for the boss on time, stitching another wound
or uniform, the first brush stroke on a portrait,
or the last floor on the Freedom Tower
jutting into a sky that yields to our resilience.

Words to Know

prejudice: *(n.)* an unreasonable dislike and distrust of people who are different from you in some way.

resilience: *(n.)* the ability to become strong, happy, or successful again after a difficult situation or event.

One sky, toward which we sometimes lift our eyes
tired from work: some days guessing at the weather
of our lives, some days giving thanks for a love
that loves you back, sometimes praising a mother
who knew how to give, or forgiving a father
who couldn't give what you wanted.

We head home: through the gloss of rain or weight
of snow, or the plum blush of dusk, but always—home,
always under one sky, our sky. And always one moon
like a silent drum tapping on every rooftop
and every window, of one country—all of us—
facing the stars
hope—a new constellation
waiting for us to map it,
waiting for us to name it—together.

Questions

Writing

7. What is the poet's perspective on America and Americans, as conveyed throughout this poem?

Words to Know

constellation: *(n.)* a group of stars that forms a particular shape in the sky and has been given a name..

Literature Circle Leveled Novels

Cuba 15 *by Nancy Osa*
As fifteen-year-old Violet Paz prepares for her *quinceañera*—the traditional celebration marking the transition between girlhood and womanhood—she struggles to answer questions about her Cuban roots and to forge her own identity in her family and with her friends. **Lexile**® measure: 750L

American Born Chinese *by Gene Luen Yang*
A Chinese American boy named Jin-Wang struggles with his identity as he enters middle school and encounters cultural stereotypes that make it hard to achieve his goal of fitting in. **Lexile**® measure: GN530L

Roll of Thunder, Hear My Cry *by Mildred D. Taylor*
An African American family makes sacrifices and fights prejudice to keep their land in the deep South during the 1930s. **Lexile**® measure: 920L

Fiction, Nonfiction, Poetry, and Novels

The Colors of Freedom: Immigrant Stories *by Janet Bode.* Young immigrants to the United States discuss their experiences, challenges, and goals in their own words. **Lexile**® measure: 770L

The House on Mango Street *by Sandra Cisneros.* Read the stories and poems of Ezperanza, a girl growing up in a Latino neighborhood in Chicago. **Lexile**® measure: 870L

Dragonwings *by Laurence Yep.* A young Chinese boy travels to join his father, whom he has never met, in America. They begin to bond as they struggle with poverty and prejudice. **Lexile**® measure: 870L

The Circuit *by Francisco Jiménez.* Follow a young Mexican boy and his family as they move from place to place in pursuit of farm work and the American dream. **Lexile**® measure: 880L

A Home on the Field: How One Championship Soccer Team Inspires Hope for the Revival of Small Town America *by Paul Cuadros.* Read the inspiring story of a team of Latino immigrants who overcame the odds to win the North Carolina state championship. **Lexile**® measure: 940L

Leaves of Grass *by Walt Whitman.* Read poems that celebrate America and its people from the collection that includes "I Hear America Singing." **Lexile**® measure: NP

America Street: A Multicultural Anthology of Stories *edited by Ann Mazer.* Read 14 stories featuring teens who come from diverse cultural backgrounds but share common goals, dreams, and challenges.

Of Beetles and Angels: A Boy's Remarkable Journey From a Refugee Camp to Harvard *by Mawi Asgedom.* Follow the journey of a refugee to America.

Films and TV

American Dreams (Universal Studios, 2002) Throughout this TV series, follow the members of several American families as they experience change in American music, culture, and politics. (1,094 min.)

Becoming American: The Chinese Experience (PBS, 2003) Learn about the history of Chinese immigration to America and listen to Chinese Americans recall their experiences. (180 min.)

Destination America: The People and Cultures That Created a Nation (PBS Paramount, 2006) Follow the history of migration to the U.S. and experience the diversity of cultures and traditions that immigrants have brought with them. (60 min.)

Harlem Renaissance: The Music and Rhythms That Started a Cultural Revolution (Kultur Video, 2004) Learn how the musical and cultural contributions of African Americans shaped American culture. (75 min.)

The New Americans (Kartemquin Educational Films, Inc., 2004) Follow a diverse group of immigrants and refugees as they discover what it means to be Americans in the 21st century. (411 min.)

Remembering Ellis Island (Total Content, 2006) Go behind the scenes at Ellis Island, where more than 10 million people arrived in the hope of starting a new life in America. (60 min.)

Teen Immigrants: Five American Stories (In the Mix; Castle Works, Inc., 1999) Hear the stories of five young immigrants in this compelling documentary film. (30 min.)

West Side Story (MGM, 1961) Ethnic rivalry causes tension and heartbreak in a neighborhood where many immigrants are trying to realize the American dream. (152 min.)

Websites

The Authentic History Center View primary sources and artifacts that demonstrate how ideas about American identity have changed over time.

The New Americans Explore the immigrant experience interactively by viewing the time lines, maps, and personal narratives on this website.

Strangers in the Land of Strangers Experience this online exhibit from the Historical Society of Pennsylvania to learn more about the different groups of immigrants who have challenged what it means to be American.

Magazines

American Heritage Read articles about the development of American culture and history, including the contributions and influence of different immigrant groups.

The Immigrant Magazine Learn more about the lifestyles and cultures of immigrants living in the United States, and the contributions they make to their communities.

National Geographic World Look for articles about the cultures and societies that influence American culture.

U.S. News and World Report Stay up-to-date on such topics as immigration, politics, and culture.

UNIT 7

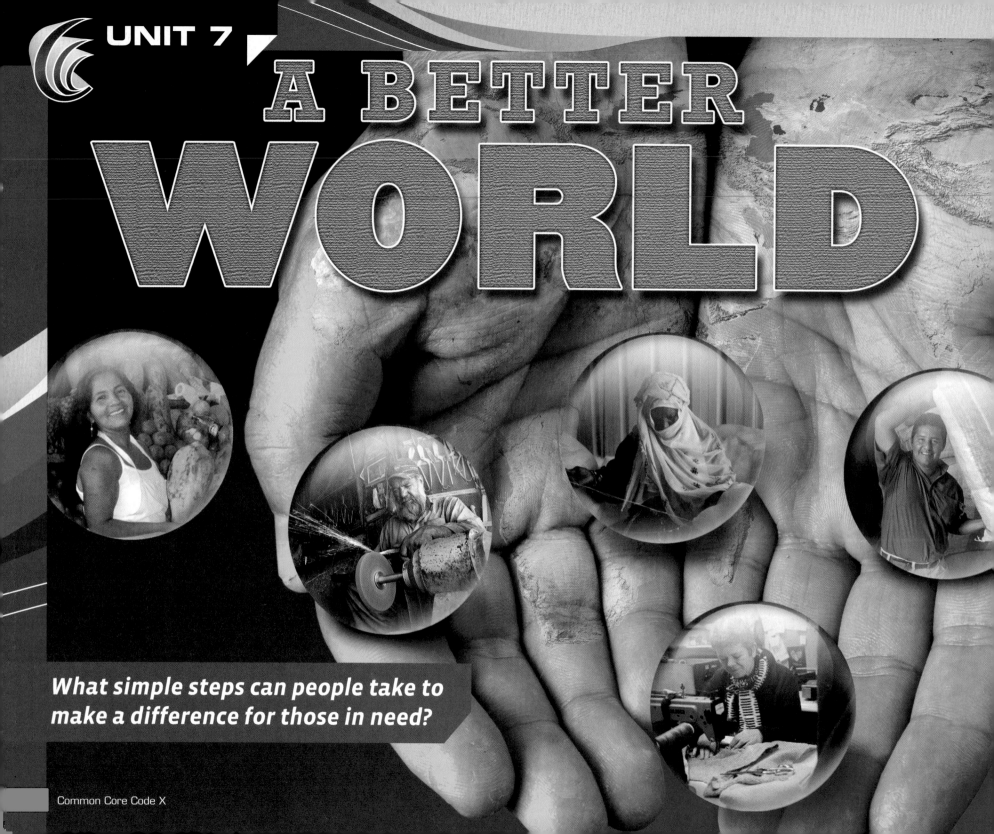

A BETTER WORLD

What simple steps can people take to make a difference for those in need?

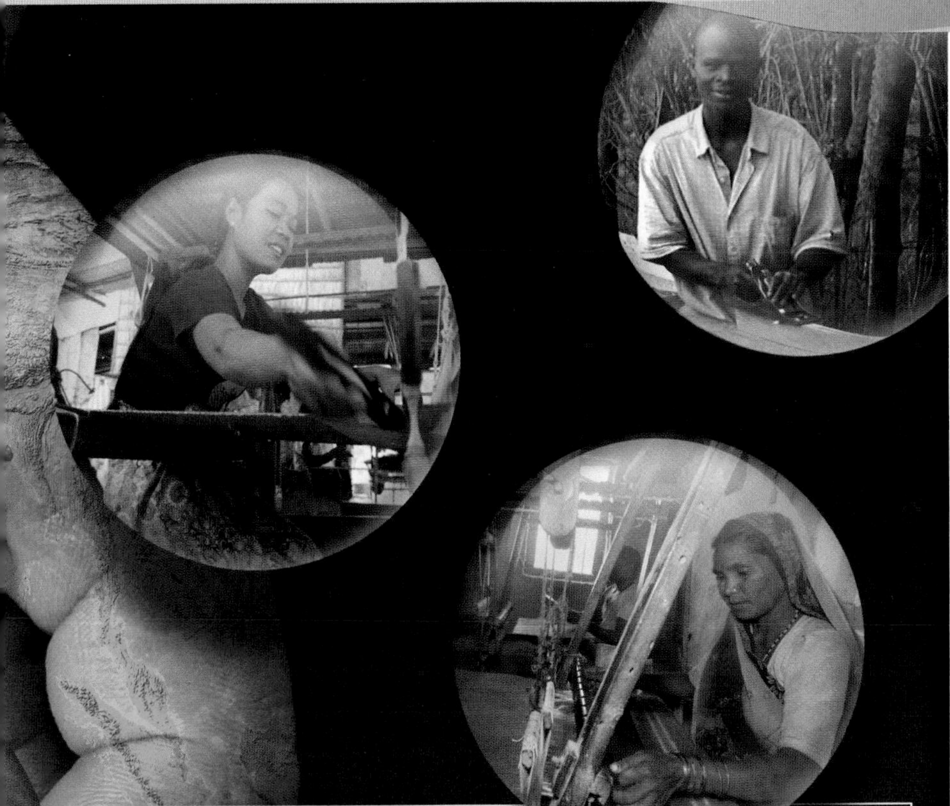

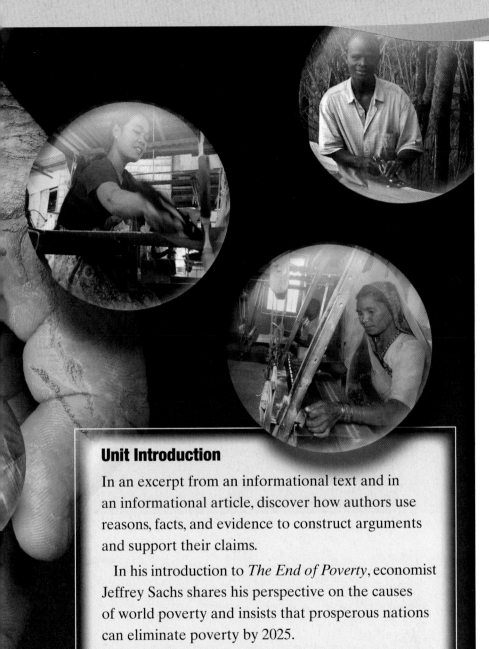

Unit Introduction

In an excerpt from an informational text and in an informational article, discover how authors use reasons, facts, and evidence to construct arguments and support their claims.

In his introduction to *The End of Poverty*, economist Jeffrey Sachs shares his perspective on the causes of world poverty and insists that prosperous nations can eliminate poverty by 2025.

In "Saving the World One Click at a Time," Renée Carver argues that the Internet makes it easy for people—even those who don't have a lot of time or money to spare—to make charitable donations that improve the lives of people in need.

WRITING PERFORMANCE TASK

Trace the authors' lines of argument regarding effective ways to fight poverty. Evaluate the specific claims, distinguishing which claims are supported by reasons, facts, and evidence, and which are not.

INFORMATIONAL EXCERPT/ INFORMATIONAL ARTICLE

from ***The End of Poverty*** by Jeffrey Sachs

Language
- Academic Vocabulary
- Word Study: Base Words and Suffixes

Reading Informational Text
- Identify Evidence
- Key Ideas and Details
- Craft and Structure

"Saving the World One Click at a Time" by Renée Carver

Language
- Academic Vocabulary
- Word Study: Context Clues

Reading Informational Text
- Identify Evidence
- Key Ideas and Details
- Craft and Structure

SPEAKING AND LISTENING

Present Research Findings
- Collaborate and Present

Rubric: Research Presentation
- Scoring Guide

WRITING

Writing: Argumentative Essay
- Read the Model
- Analyze the Model
- Gather Evidence
- Develop Your Argument
- Language Study: Concluding on a Strong Point
- Conventions Study: Use Phrases and Clauses
- Revise, Edit, and Publish
- Performance Task Rubric

EXTENDED READING

Informational Excerpt
from ***The Life You Can Save***
by Pete Singer

Academic Vocabulary

from *The End of Poverty* by Jeffrey D. Sachs

Rate your understanding of each word. Then read its meaning and write a sample sentence. If an example is given, write the meaning.

Word	Meaning	Example
impoverished *(adj.)* p. 287 ① ② ③ ④	very poor	
neglect *(v.)* p. 290 ① ② ③ ④		I neglected my garden, so my plants died.
instability *(n.)* p. 290 ① ② ③ ④	the state or quality of being unpredictable and likely to change suddenly	
policy *(n.)* p. 291 ① ② ③ ④	a way of doing something that has been officially chosen by a government or a business	
prosperity *(n.)* p. 291 ① ② ③ ④		Good leaders helped the nation achieve prosperity.
development *(n.)* p. 291 ① ② ③ ④		Our downtown needs more money for business development.

Rating Scale ① I don't know the word. ② I've seen it or heard it. ③ I know its meaning. ④ I know it and use it.

Word Study

Base Words and Suffixes

You can use base words and suffixes to help you determine the meanings of unfamiliar words.

The suffix ***-ment*** can have two meanings:

- the result of an action *(contentment, embarrassment, enjoyment)*
- an action or process *(development, government; improvement)*

Use base words and suffixes as clues to answer the questions below.

1. *Entertainment* means _____.
2. An *argument* is _____.
3. *Development* is _____.
4. List three types of development:

from The End of POVERTY

by Jeffrey Sachs

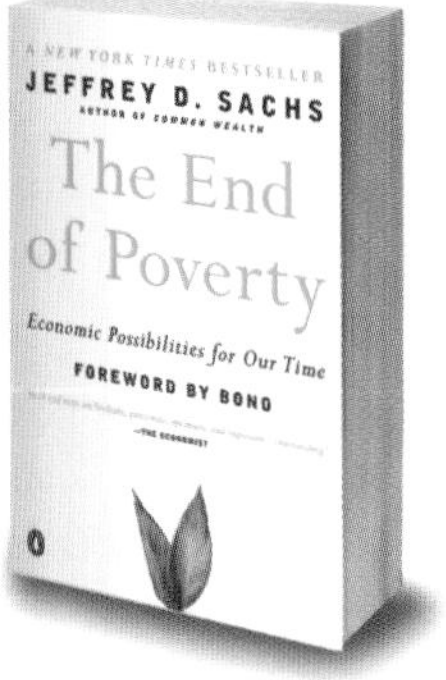

Introduction

¶1 This book is about ending poverty in our time. It is not a forecast. I am not predicting what will happen, only explaining what can happen. Currently, more than eight million people around the world die each year because they are too poor to stay alive. Our generation can choose to end that extreme poverty by the year 2025.

¶2 Every morning our newspapers could report, "More than 20,000 people <u>perished</u> yesterday of extreme poverty." The stories would put the stark numbers in context—up to 8,000 children dead of malaria, 5,000 mothers and fathers dead of tuberculosis, 7,500 young adults dead of AIDS, and thousands more dead of diarrhea, respiratory infection, and other killer diseases that prey on bodies weakened by chronic hunger. The poor die in hospital wards that lack drugs, in villages that lack <u>antimalarial bed nets</u>, in houses that lack safe drinking water. They die namelessly, without public comment. Sadly, such stories rarely get written. Most people are unaware of the daily struggles for survival, and of the vast numbers of **impoverished** people around the world who lose that struggle.

Words to Know

<u>perished</u>: *(v.)* died

<u>antimalarial bed nets</u>: *(n.)* mosquito nets designed to protect sleeping people from malaria by protecting them from mosquito bites. Malaria is spread by infected mosquitoes.

Close Reading

Writing

1. What assertion does the author make in **paragraph 1**?

Argumentative Text

An **argumentative text** attempts to persuade the reader of something by presenting facts, statistics, evidence, and reasons. Argument writing usually begins with an **assertion**, which is a statement of the claim that the author is making.

Academic Vocabulary

2. In what ways does poverty kill "impoverished people around the world"? Why does the author include statistics about poverty-related deaths?

Close Reading

Academic Vocabulary

3. What does *destabilized* mean? According to the author, what happens when societies are "destabilized by extreme poverty"?

Key Ideas and Details

4. How does the author explain the claim that giving more money to "solve the crisis of extreme poverty" would "provide for U.S. national security"?

Text Structure

5. **Paragraph 4** includes data about how much money the United States spends to help the poor. Why does the author include this information?

¶3 Since September 11, 2001, the United States has launched a war on terror, but it has **neglected** the deeper causes of global **instability**. The $450 billion that the United States will spend this year on the military will never buy peace if it continues to spend around one thirtieth of that, just $15 billion, to address the plight of the world's poorest of the poor, whose societies are destabilized by extreme poverty and thereby become havens of unrest, violence, and even global terrorism.

¶4 That $15 billion represents a tiny percentage of U.S. income, just 15 cents on every $100 of U.S. gross national product, or GNP. The share of U.S. GNP devoted to helping the poor has declined for decades, and is a tiny fraction of what the United States has repeatedly promised, and failed, to give. It is also much less than the United States should give, both to solve the crisis of extreme poverty and thereby to provide for U.S. national security. This book, then, is about making the right choices—choices that can lead to a much safer world based on a true reverence and respect for human life.

Jeffrey Sachs established "Millennium Villages" in 10 African countries, supplying each with seeds, clean water, health care, education, anti-malarial bed nets, and a communication link to the outside world.

Words to Know

plight: *(n.)* a condition or situation, especially a bad or unfortunate one

gross national product (GNP): *(n.)* the dollar value of all the products and services produced in one year by the residents of a country

¶5 I have spent the past twenty years working with heads of state, finance and health ministers, and villagers in dozens of countries in all parts of the world. I have visited and worked in more than a hundred countries with around 90 percent of the world's population. The cumulative experience of seeing the world from many vantage points has helped me to appreciate the real circumstances on our planet—the causes of poverty, the role of rich-country **policies**, and the possibilities for the future. Gaining a proper perspective on these issues has been my struggle and challenge for two decades. Nothing else in my intellectual life and political engagement has been as rewarding.

¶6 In the following pages, I will explain what I have witnessed and learned in societies as varied as Bolivia, Poland, Russia, China, India, and Kenya. You will see that all parts of the world have the chance to join an age of unprecedented **prosperity** building on global science, technology, and markets. But you will also see that certain parts of the world are caught in a downward spiral of impoverishment, hunger, and disease. It is no good to lecture the dying that they should have done better with their lot in life. Rather, it is our task to help them onto the ladder of **development**, at least to gain a foothold on the bottom rung, from which they can then proceed to climb on their own.

Words to Know

heads of state: *(n.)* leaders of countries, such as presidents and prime ministers

markets: *(n.)* an opportunity for the buying and selling of goods and services

Close Reading

Writing

6. The author mentions that he has "spent the past twenty years" visiting and working with people "in more than a hundred countries with around 90 percent of the world's population." Why does he do this?

Words and Phrases in Context

7. What is a "downward spiral"? Why does the author use this image to describe the condition of poor countries?

Words and Phrases in Context

8. What metaphor does the author use to illustrate his vision for helping poor countries? How does this metaphor illustrate a solution to the "downward spiral"?

Close Reading

Key Ideas and Details

9. What does Sachs mean when he says that "the key is not to predict what will happen, but to help shape the future"?

Text Structure

10. How does the author compare what "economics textbooks" say to what he sees in the real world? Why does he include this comparison?

Key Ideas and Details

11. According to the author, what did the economist John Maynard Keynes get "just right"? Why does the author include this information about Keynes?

¶**7** Am I an optimist? Optimism and pessimism are beside the point. The key is not to predict what will happen, but to help shape the future. This task is a collective one—for you as well as for me. Although introductory economics textbooks preach individualism and decentralized markets, our safety and prosperity depend at least as much on collective decisions to fight disease, promote good science and widespread education, provide critical infrastructure, and act in unison to help the poorest of the poor. When the preconditions of basic infrastructure (roads, power, and ports) and human capital (health and education) are in place, markets are powerful engines of development. Without those preconditions, markets can cruelly bypass large parts of the world, leaving them impoverished and suffering without respite. Collective action, through effective government provision of health, education, infrastructure, as well as foreign assistance when needed, underpins economic success.

¶**8** Eighty-five years ago the great British economist John Maynard Keynes pondered the dire circumstances of the Great Depression. From the depths of despair around him, he wrote in 1930 of the *Economic Possibilities for Our Grandchildren*. At a time of duress and suffering, he envisioned the end of poverty in Great Britain and other industrial countries in his grandchildren's day, toward the end of the twentieth century. Keynes emphasized the dramatic march of science and technology and the ability of advances in technology to underpin continued economic growth at compound interest, enough growth indeed to end the age-old "economic problem" of having enough to eat and enough income to meet other basic needs. Keynes got it just right, of course: extreme poverty no longer exists in today's rich countries, and it is disappearing in most of the world's middle-income countries.

Words to Know

decentralized: *(adj.)* individually owned and run; not controlled by the national government

Great Depression: *(n.)* a severe economic crisis in the United States and Europe that began in October 1929 and continued through the late 1930s.

¶**9** Today we can invoke the same logic to declare that extreme poverty can be ended not in the time of our grandchildren, but in our time. The wealth of the rich world, the power of today's vast storehouses of knowledge, and the declining fraction of the world that needs help to escape from poverty all make the end of poverty a realistic possibility by the year 2025. Keynes wondered how the society of his grandchildren would use its wealth and its unprecedented freedom from the age-old struggle for daily survival. This very question has become our own. Will we have the good judgment to use our wealth wisely, to heal a divided planet, to end the suffering of those still trapped by poverty, and to forge a common bond of humanity, security, and shared purpose across cultures and regions?

¶**10** This book will not answer this question. Instead, it will help to show the way toward the path of peace and prosperity, based on a detailed understanding of how the world economy has gotten to where it is today, and how our generation could mobilize our capacities in the coming twenty years to eliminate the extreme poverty that remains. I hope that by showing the contours of that promising path, we will be more likely to choose it. For now, I am grateful for the chance to share what I have seen of the world and of the economic possibilities for our time.

Words to Know

capacities: *(n.)* abilities

contours: *(n.)* shapes

Close Reading

Writing

12. What factors make "the end of poverty a realistic possibility by the year 2025"? Cite and explain what the author means by this.

Words and Phrases in Context

13. According to Sachs, what would be the benefits of healing "a divided planet"?

Text Structure

14. How does Sachs end the Introduction to his book? What does he hope his book will persuade readers to do?

Identify Evidence | Analyze Individuals, Events, and Ideas

Reread the introduction to ***The End of Poverty*** identifying examples and evidence Sachs offers to explain the effects of extreme poverty and to support the claim that rich countries can and should help end extreme poverty. How does he introduce, illustrate, and elaborate on his ideas?

- As you read, use the Evidence column to record examples from the text that present Sachs's ideas about how to end poverty.
- In the Explanation column, explain how the evidence introduces, illustrates, or elaborates an idea.

Evidence	Source	Page	Explanation
1. "Currently, more than eight million people around the world die each year because they are too poor to stay alive. Our generation can choose to end that extreme poverty by the year 2025."	Sachs	287	Sachs sets up his main claim—that poverty is a huge problem, but we could choose to end it in a fairly small amount of time.
2.			
3.			
4.			

Evidence	Source	Page	Explanation
5.			
6.			
7.			
8.			

Key Ideas and Details

Determining the Central Idea

1. Summarize the key idea of *The End of Poverty*. What is the central idea of the text? Use text evidence to support your response.

2. According to Sachs, extreme poverty causes millions of deaths each year and contributes to global instability. Summarize Sachs's argument about how poverty causes each effect below.

   Death:

   Global Instability:

3. Sachs argues that several key factors make ending poverty possible. Identify two of these factors and write a brief explanation of each.

   Factor 1:

   Factor 2:

Craft and Structure

Structure of the Argumentative Text

1. Writers of argumentative essays use data—facts, figures, and statistics to illustrate and support their claims. Review the Introduction to *The End of Poverty,* looking for numbers Sachs cites to support his argument. In the chart below, write the claims Sachs makes and list the data he uses to support those claims.

Claim	Supporting Data

Data and Statistics

Data are information or facts about something.

Statistics are numbers that illustrate or represent facts.

Authors of argumentative texts often use data and statistics to support an assertion, or claim.

Author's Purpose

2. What is Sachs's main message for the reader about poverty? Summarize his message. Provide evidence from the text to support your analysis.

Academic Vocabulary

"Saving the World One Click at a Time"

by Renée Carver

Rate your understanding of each word. Then read its meaning and write a sample sentence. If an example is given, write the meaning.

Word	Meaning	Example
charity (*n.*) p. 297 ① ② ③ ④	a group that gives money, goods, or help to people in need	
potential (*adj.*) p. 297 ① ② ③ ④	possible or likely to become something in the future	
reduce (*v.*) p. 299 ① ② ③ ④	to make something smaller in size, amount, or price	
provide (*v.*) p. 299 ① ② ③ ④		The soup kitchen will provide food to people in need.
legitimate (*adj.*) p. 300 ① ② ③ ④		Be sure the Web site is legitimate before you use the information in your research paper.

Rating Scale | ① I don't know the word. ② I've seen it or heard it. ③ I know its meaning. ④ I know it and use it.

Word Study

The sentences below are from Renée Carver's article. Read each sentence. Find the context clues to determine the meaning of the bold words. Then use a dictionary to verify the meaning.

1. Verify that the charity you choose is legitimate and well run. Some organizations might be **scams** to trick people out of their money.

2. Check that any charity to which you give an online donation is using proper security **measures** to protect your personal information.

Saving the World One Click At A Time

by Renée Carver

¶1 You decide you want to help other people, in the United States or around the world. Would you sit around waiting for a **charity** to contact you by phone or by mail? No! You would locate a charity yourself, most likely using a tool that is right at your fingertips: the Internet.

¶2 Because there are many people like you, smart charities make sure that their Web sites present detailed information about what they do, why their causes are important, and how others can support their efforts. **Potential** donors and volunteers can learn about issues and investigate programs at any time, day or night. They can download resources to set up fund-raisers, or create and sign online petitions. They can make one-click donations. They can even use social media to communicate with others about new ways to help a cause.

¶3 The Internet has made it easier for charities to reach people around the world. Many charities use the Internet to reach a target group of people for whom the Internet is a significant part of their lives—namely, young people like you! Let's take a tour of some Web sites you can use to make a difference in the world!

Words to Know

fund-raisers: *(n.)* events held to raise money for a charity or cause

petitions: *(n.)* formal requests to the government or people in charge, asking for a particular action to be taken, and signed by people who agree with the request

Close Reading

Text Structure

1. What point of view does the author use? Why does the author use this point of view?

Point of View

Point of view is the perspective from which a text is written.

In first-person point of view the author is included in the events and information that he or she relates. *(I, me, my, we, us, ours)*

In second-person point of view the author addresses someone or gives information directly to someone. *(you, yours)*

In third-person point of view the author shares events and information from another perspective. *(he, she, her, it, they, them)*

Writing

2. Summarize the information on this page. What claim does the author make at the beginning of **paragraph 3**?

FreeRice *Feeds the World*

¶4 One grain of rice doesn't seem like much. Neither do 100 grains of rice. But what about almost 39 billion grains of rice? If you need about 19,200 grains of rice to cook two meals a day for one person, then 39 billion grains of rice can feed over 2 million people. That is how many grains of rice that people playing the FreeRice vocabulary game earned within the first year the site went online.

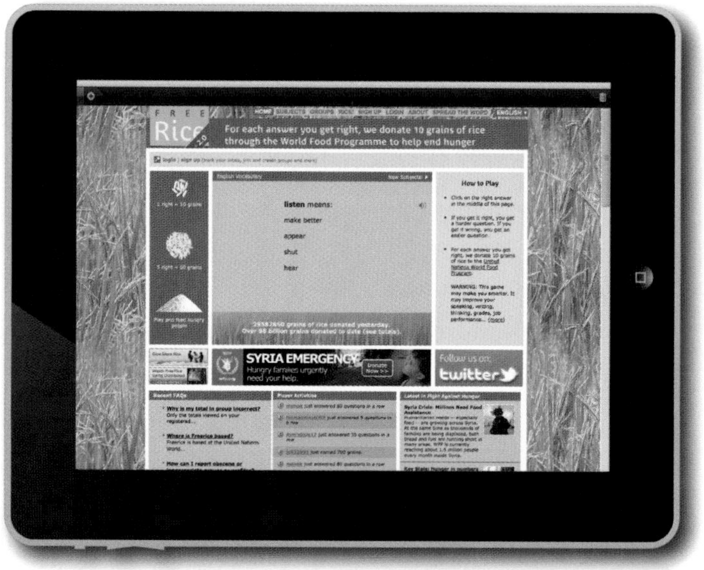

How to Play

¶5 When playing FreeRice, you define a series of words, picking each correct definition from a set of four possibilities. For every word you define correctly, sponsor organizations donate 20 grains of rice to the United Nations World Food Program. As you define more and more words correctly, the words you are given increase in difficulty. Soon you'll have mastered all sorts of new vocabulary words. You'll end up helping both yourself *and* others! You might hold a tournament with classmates to see who can donate the most rice. Some students have even motivated their parents to play. And if you don't have time to play, you can always make an online donation.

Words to Know

sponsor organizations: *(n.)* groups that give money or goods to a charity or cause on behalf of people who have completed a specific task (such as playing FreeRice)

Close Reading

Text Structure

3. How is the information on this page different from the information on **page 297**? How do the section heads help you understand this article?

Writing

4. How does the information about FreeRice support the author's claim in **paragraph 3** about charities and the Internet?

Key Ideas and Details

5. In what way does the FreeRice game allow you to help "both yourself *and* others"?

Heifer International: *Gifts that Keep on Giving*

¶6 Heifer International hopes to **reduce** poverty and hunger worldwide by **providing** people with the tools and skills they need to earn income and strengthen their own communities. Since its foundation in 1944, Heifer has given aid to over 8.5 million people in more than 125 different countries.

¶7 You can help Heifer by purchasing a gift from its Web site or asking others to purchase one for you. A Heifer gift isn't a present like a computer game or a new shirt. It might actually be a heifer—a real cow—or another type of livestock.

¶8 When you scroll through the Heifer gift catalog, you can put animals such as water buffalo, goats, ducks, rabbits, and even honeybees in your online cart. Once you pay for them, these animals will be given to families in need.

Helping Heifer

¶9 Students at Harrison Elementary in Marion, Ohio, raised $160 through a plant, bake, and lemonade sale. A class at Pinetree Community School in Canyon Country, California, raised $600 by recycling plastic bottles for a whole school year. At Berkeley Carroll's Middle and Upper School in Brooklyn, New York, students crafted and sold ceramic bowls to raise over $6,000 for Heifer.

Words to Know

livestock: *(n.)* farm animals

ceramic: *(adj.)* made of clay or similar materials

Close Reading

Academic Vocabulary

6. What does the word *provide* mean? What is the goal of *providing* people with tools and skills?

Key Ideas and Details

7. How does the internet help Heifer International connect with donors to help "families in need?"

Text Structure

8. Why does the author include anecdotes about schools that raised money for Heifer International?

Close Reading

Academic Vocabulary

9. How does the Internet open up "a whole world of charitable opportunities"?

Text Structure

10. Why does the author include the "Choosing a Charity" section in the article? Why might potential donors need such a list?

Academic Vocabulary

11. How might a charity that is not "legitimate" behave?

Words and Phrases in Context

12. How can you "make the most of your money with a matching gift program"?

Choosing a Charity

¶**10** How can you make a difference in a way that is personal to you? When you surf the Internet, a whole world of charitable opportunities opens up. Here are some steps you can follow to find and aid causes that are just right for you.

1	Decide who and what you want to help.
2	Once you've picked an issue or area of interest, try a Google search. You can also visit Network for Good's online site, which helps locate charities that serve your issue or interest.
3	Verify that the charity you choose is legitimate and well run. Some organizations might be scams to trick people out of their money. Others might waste donations instead of handling them wisely. Charity Navigator and the Better Business Bureau both have Web sites that allow you to research charities.
4	Check that any charity to which you give an online donation is using proper security measures to protect your personal information.
5	Make the most of your money. Find out if anyone you know works for a company with a matching gift program that might double or triple your donation.
6	Spread the word to friends and family members that you would like them to make donations to charities of your choice <u>in lieu</u> of presents on holidays and birthdays.
7	Keep a record of what you donate and to whom you send <u>funds</u>.

Words to Know

<u>in lieu</u>: *(adv.)* instead; in place

<u>funds</u>: *(n.)* supplies of money for a specific purpose

What Can You Do?

¶11 As you get involved with Internet charities, think about what you can do beyond donating money. How can you spread the word to others and convince them to help? It's great to make a personal difference, but why not encourage others to get involved as well? One way is to check if a charity's Web site has a blog or other area where you can share a tale of giving. Then take a moment to post about your experience with fund-raising or why this charity is important to you. Perhaps reading your words will inspire someone else to start exploring the world of Internet charities, too.

Words to Know

beyond: *(adv.)* more than; over and above

convince: *(v.)* to persuade; to talk someone into

Close Reading

Key Ideas and Details

13. How can people go "beyond donating money" to get involved with Internet charities?

Writing

14. How does **paragraph 11** help support the author's claim that the Internet "has made it easier for charities to reach people around the world—and for people around the world to support charities"?

Identify Evidence | Analyze Individuals, Events and Ideas

Reread **"Saving the World One Click at a Time,"** identifying examples and evidence the author offers to explain how the Internet has helped connect charities to larger numbers of donors and volunteers. How does she introduce, illustrate, and elaborate on her ideas?

- As you read, use the Evidence column to record examples from the text that present the author's ideas about charities and the Internet.
- In the Explanation column, explain how the evidence introduces, illustrates, or elaborates on ideas.

Evidence	Source	Page	Explanation
1. "Potential donors and volunteers can learn about issues and investigate programs at any time, day or night."	*Carver*	*297*	*The author presents one advantage that websites offer to charities seeking support, which supports the claim that the Internet has made it easier for people to find places to donate.*
2.			
3.			
4.			

Evidence	Source	Page	Explanation
5.			
6.			
7.			
8.			

Key Ideas and Details

Determining the Central Idea

1. Summarize the key idea of "Saving the World One Click at a Time." What is the central idea of the text? Use text evidence to support your response.

2. The author presents examples of how charities reach out through the Internet. List examples, and the results of their efforts, in the chart below.

Example	Result
Charity websites provide information about how they work and who they help.	Potential donors have an easy way to learn about charities they might want to contribute to.

3. Summarize the author's most important advice on how to choose a charity.

Craft and Structure

Structure of an Informational Article

1. The author claims that the Internet "has made it easier for charities to reach people around the world." Read each article section listed below. Summarize the information in each section. Then explain how the information supports the author's claim.

Article Section	Example of How It Works	How the Example Supports the Author's Argument
FreeRice		
Heifer International		
Choosing a Charity		
What Can You Do?		

Claim and Evidence

A **claim** is an arguable statement or position. An author may include examples and anecdotes as evidence to illustrate or support a claim.

Author's Purpose

2. What is the author's message for readers about charities and the Internet? Summarize her message.

3. Compare and contrast Sachs's and Carver's purposes for writing.

Sachs's Purpose	Carver's Purpose

Collaborate and Present

Research a Charity and Present Findings

Assignment: Heifer International and FreeRice both claim to help reduce hunger in the world. How successful are they? Work with a group to research one of these charities. Use multiple resources to determine how successful the charity's efforts are.

Analyze the Content

1. Consider the following questions:
   - How much money do supporters donate to the charity each year? What percentage of that money is spent to purchase food or livestock or otherwise help people in need?
   - How many people does the charity help each year? In how many countries do they live? How much money/assistance per person does the charity give?
2. Gather evidence from your research. Create a chart to organize information that supports your claim(s) about how successful the charity's efforts are.

Name Of Charity:

My Claim	Reasons	Evidence
I think this charity's efforts are . . .	I think so because . . .	

Organize Your Presentation

3. Use the items in your chart to organize talking points for your presentation.
   - Draft an outline of the information you will present to the class.
   - Prepare visual aids—such as charts, graphs, and photos—that support your talking points.

Present

4. Deliver the results of your research to the class in an oral presentation.

Seeking Clarification

- In other words, you believe that . . .
- If I understand you correctly, you feel that . . .
- So, you think that . . .

Reporting Ideas

- ____ compared . . .
- ____ concluded . . .
- ____ believes . . .

Presentation

- Use formal English.
- Face your audience.
- Stand up straight and speak with confidence.
- Avoid fidgeting.

Research Presentation Checklist

Use the checklist below to evaluate your collaboration skills, reasoning, and final presentation.
Think carefully about your work. If you know you completed an item thoroughly, give yourself a check (✓).

COLLABORATE AND PRESENT CHECKLIST		
Comprehension & Collaboration	**Evidence & Reasoning**	**Presentation of Knowledge & Ideas**
☐ Come to discussions prepared, having read and studied material. ☐ Refer to evidence when contributing to the discussion. ☐ Follow rules for discussions and lead by example. ☐ Ask and answer specific questions. ☐ Make comments that contribute to the topic under discussion and bring the discussion back on topic. ☐ Acknowledge new ideas expressed by others and, when warranted, modify my opinions. ☐ Present claims with relevant details.	☐ Explain the purpose of the presentation. ☐ Accurately describe the charity's claim. ☐ Clearly evaluate how successful the charity's efforts are. ☐ Support the evaluation with relevant and well-organized evidence. ☐ Include supporting evidence from multiple valid sources.	☐ Adapt language to a variety of contexts and tasks to demonstrate knowledge of formal English. ☐ Include multimedia components (e.g., graphics, images, music, sound) and visual displays. ☐ Use appropriate volume/tone (clear, not too fast, too slow, or too loud) and avoid using "like" or "ummm." ☐ Have strong posture, a confident stance, and make frequent eye contact. ☐ Occasionally move from one spot to another without fidgeting. ☐ Smile and act relaxed.
Number of ✓s in this category: ___	**Number of ✓s in this category: ___**	**Number of ✓s in this category: ___**
Total # of ✓s: __		

Add up the total number of checks (✓) in each category. Then use the scoring guide below to calculate your final score.

Scoring Guide			
16 to 18 ✓s	**13 to 15 ✓s**	**11 to 12 ✓s**	**10 or less ✓s**
④ Exemplary	**③ Meets Standards**	**② Needs Work**	**① Does Not Meet Standards**

Read the Model

In the essay below, the writer evaluates two authors' claims and distinguishes those that are supported by reasons, facts, and evidence.

Argumentative Essay

An argumentative essay provides a clearly stated assertion, or claim, that is supported with logical reasoning and relevant evidence.

The introduction states the titles and authors of the text that the writer will analyze.

- **Identify the claim.**

The body paragraphs provide logical reasons to support the claim.

- **Identify two reasons that support the claim.**
- **Identify examples of text citations.**

The conclusion follows from narrated events and contains the resolution.

- **Identify the conclusion**

Agreeing on a Solution to World Poverty

By Anna Dimitru

Jeffrey Sachs, author of *The End of Poverty*, and Peter Singer, author of *The Life You Can Save: Acting Now to End World Poverty*, argue that world poverty can be ended in the near future. The writers effectively call for nations and individuals to work together to achieve this goal.

In *The Life You Can Save: Acting Now to End World Poverty*, Peter Singer makes a clear case for ways individuals can help end world poverty in this century. Singer challenges readers to "think about our obligations to those trapped in extreme poverty" (Singer 320). He insists that it's not enough for wealthy people to take on this burden. According to Singer, "We can, each of us, do our part . . ." (320). He argues that 95 percent of Americans could afford to give 5 percent of their income to charity (321) by reevaluating how they spend money on items they don't really need, such as bottled water . This reading is just a preface, but it is apparent that the full text includes convincing details.

In *The End of Poverty*, Jeffrey Sachs claims, "Our generation can choose to end . . . extreme poverty by the year 2025" (Sachs 287). He supports this claim with several pieces of evidence. He argues that wealthy countries can assist struggling nations to overcome "the downward spiral of impoverishment, hunger, and disease" (289). One solution Sachs suggests is that the United States spend more on infrastructure, health, and education in developing countries (290). In a few short paragraphs, he effectively demonstrates how changes like this could improve quality of life around the world.

Both authors make logical arguments that ending poverty is an achievable goal, and both support their claims effectively. Generally, Sachs would have prosperous nations contribute more money. Singer sees a solution through individual donations. Together, the authors make a persuasive argument for ending poverty in our time.

Analyze the Model

A claim-and-evidence chart can help organize details for an argumentative essay.

Use the model and the graphic organizer to trace the authors' lines of argument. List specific claims and reasons, facts, and evidence from the texts that support each author's claims.

Introduction

Thesis:

Body Paragraph 1: *The Life You Can Save* (Singer)

Claim	Evidence
	•

Body Paragraph 2: *The End of Poverty* (Sachs)

Claim	Evidence
	•

Conclusion

Supporting Evidence

In an **argumentative essay**, the writer presents an assertion, or claim, in the thesis statement.

The writer supports his or her claim with an organizational structure that effectively and logically presents reasons and supporting evidence. The topic sentence of each body paragraph clearly states a reason for the writer's claim. The writer supports these reasons with relevant evidence.

- Evaluate whether each reason supports the thesis.

Relevant evidence includes evidence from relevant sources. This evidence can be a direct quotation or a paraphrase from the text, and should include the text title, author, if given, and page number on which the evidence appears in the source.

- Identify how the writer included evidence from ***The Life You Can Save*** in her essay.

Step 1 | Gather Evidence

Trace the authors' lines of argument regarding effective ways to fight poverty. Evaluate the specific claims, distinguishing which claims are supported by reasons, facts, and evidence, and which are not.

What You Need to Know | Examine the evidence you have collected (see pages 294 and 302) that describes and supports each author's view of ways to end poverty.

What You Need to Write | Use the note-taking guide to list details from the texts that describe and support each author's claims.

The End of Poverty

Claim:

Evidence:

Page # _______

Claim:

Evidence:

Page # _______

Claim:

Evidence:

Page # _______

"Saving the World One Click at a Time"

Claim:

Evidence:

Page # _______

Claim:

Evidence:

Page # _______

Claim:

Evidence:

Page # _______

Step 2 | Organize Ideas

What You Need to Know | Construct an argument, drawn from your evidence, about how successfully the authors support their claims of effective ways to fight poverty.

To develop your argument:

1. Identify key claims Jeffrey Sachs and Renée Carver make about how to fight hunger and poverty.
2. Use text evidence from *The End of Poverty* and "One Click at a Time" to determine whether both authors effectively support their claims.

What You Need to Write | Use a graphic organizer to list and organize relevant text evidence from the note-taking guide to form your argument.

Body Paragraph 1

Claim	Evidence

Body Paragraph 2

Claim	Evidence

Step 3 | Draft

Write a draft of your essay on the computer or on paper.

Language Study | Conclude on a Strong Point

See It | A strong conclusion to an argumentative essay should restate the main thesis or position.

- Always avoid introducing new information in a concluding paragraph, since new ideas cannot be supported with details and evidence there.
- Try not to introduce a concluding paragraph with overused phrases such as *In sum* or *In closing.*

Try It | Read the following versions of conclusions to an argumentative essay.

To summarize, we need to continue to evaluate solutions to the problem of homelessness in the United States today. Harris urges building of more inexpensive dwellings, such as Habitat for Humanity homes, so that families can take pride in owning their own homes. Blackwell argues that increased economic prospects and low mortgage rates have a good chance of helping to solve the problem. Both authors present sensible solutions to problems that plague our homeland, and both have some merit. Here's another thing: It's a good idea to bulldoze empty houses, so they don't bring down neighboring property values.

It is clear from this analysis that we need to continue to evaluate solutions to the problem of homelessness in the United States today. Harris urges building of more inexpensive dwellings, such as Habitat for Humanity homes, so that families can take pride in owning their own homes. Blackwell argues that increased economic prospects and low mortgage rates have a good chance of helping to solve the problem. Both authors present sensible solutions to problems that plague our homeland, and both have some merit.

Apply It | **Choose one of the frames below to write a conclusion for your essay that restates the key ideas and summarizes some of the supporting details.**

1. In their articles on ways to end poverty, ____________ (author 1) and ____________ (author 2) both effectively support their claims with solid evidence. ____________ (author 1) states ____________ (claim/evidence). ____________ (author 2) believes ____________ (claim/evidence). Both authors ____________ (summary statement).

2. In their articles on ways to end poverty, ____________ (author 1) effectively supports his/her claims with solid evidence, but ____________ (author 2) does not. ____________ (author 1) states ____________ (claim/evidence). ____________ (author 2) believes ____________ (claim/reason claim is not supported). ____________ summary statement.

3. In their articles on ways to end poverty, neither ____________ (author 1) nor ____________ (author 2) effectively support their claims with solid evidence. ____________ (author 1) states ____________ (claim/reason claim is not effective). ____________ (author 2) believes ____________ (claim/reason claim is not effective). Neither author ____________ summary statement.

Conventions Study | Use Phrases and Clauses Correctly

Phrases and clauses can add more information about the words they describe. To avoid confusion, phrases or clauses should be placed close to the words they modify.

- Correct: *From the classroom, the students saw some birds.*
  Incorrect: *The students saw some birds from the classroom.*
- Correct: *While running for the bus, the girl dropped her book.*
  Incorrect: *While running for the bus, her book dropped.*

Read the following excerpts from the model essay. Find the words that the underlined words modify.

> Jeffrey Sachs, author of *The End of Poverty*, and Peter Singer, author of *The Life You Can Save: Acting Now to End World Poverty*, argue that world poverty can be ended <u>in the near future</u>.
>
> He argues that 95 percent of Americans could afford to give 5 percent of their income to charity, by reevaluating how they spend money on items they don't really need, <u>such as bottled water</u>.
>
> <u>In a few short pages</u>, he effectively demonstrates how changes like this could improve the quality of life <u>around the world</u>.

Rewrite some sentences from your draft to avoid dangling or misplaced modifiers.

Step 4 | Revise and Edit

Revise your draft with a partner.

Organization and Clarity					
State the text titles and author names in the introductory statement. Effectively state the position.	Self	1	2	3	4
	Partner	1	2	3	4
Logically organize details about the authors' claims and evidence, and include a separate body paragraph for each text.	Self	1	2	3	4
	Partner	1	2	3	4
Summarize and restate the position in the conclusion.	Self	1	2	3	4
	Partner	1	2	3	4
Evidence and Reasoning					
Offer evidence from the Unit texts to indicate whether authors support their claims.	Self	1	2	3	4
	Partner	1	2	3	4
Analyze the authors' use of data, examples, and anecdotes.	Self	1	2	3	4
	Partner	1	2	3	4
Language and Conventions					
Place phrases and clauses appropriately in a sentence to avoid misplaced and dangling modifiers.	Self	1	2	3	4
	Partner	1	2	3	4
Use academic and domain-specific language to clearly state ideas.	Self	1	2	3	4
	Partner	1	2	3	4
Use correct spelling, capitalization, and punctuation throughout the essay.	Self	1	2	3	4
	Partner	1	2	3	4
Conclude on a strong note.	Self	1	2	3	4
	Partner	1	2	3	4

Scoring Guide | ① needs improvement ② average ③ good ④ excellent

Step 5 | Publish

Publish your essay either in print or digital form.

Publish

Publish your argumentative essay either in print or digital form. Use the rubric below to consider the success of your final performance task.

PERFORMANCE TASK RUBRIC

Score Point	Organization and Clarity	Evidence and Reasoning	Language and Conventions
Exemplary ④	• introductory paragraph includes a **strong thesis statement** that **makes a convincing claim** for how to end world poverty • body paragraphs are **well organized by text** and **present logical reasons and evidence** to support the claim • includes **well-chosen** text evidence, precise language, and phrases and clauses • concluding statement **restates the thesis statement** and reasons for the claim	• **accurately explains** the authors' views for ending world poverty **and convincingly evaluates and persuades of the effectiveness of the authors' claims** • includes **relevant** factual evidence from the informational texts to support each reason for ending world poverty	• demonstrates a **strong command** of the conventions of standard English grammar and usage, as well as of standard English capitalization, punctuation, and spelling • vocabulary is **appropriate** to the topic (vocabulary about ending world poverty; accurate vocabulary for supporting claims with logical reasons; effective phrases and clauses that add information about who the text is about or what is happening)
Meets Standards ③	• introductory paragraph **includes an adequate thesis statement that makes a claim** for how to end world peace • body paragraphs are **logically organized by text** and **present reasons and evidence** to support the claim • includes **some** text evidence, precise language and phrases and clauses • concluding statement **restates the thesis statement**	• **adequately explains** the authors' views for ending world poverty **and generally persuades of the effectiveness of the authors' claims** • includes **some relevant** factual evidence from the informational texts to support each reason for ending world poverty	• demonstrates **a near command** of the conventions of standard English grammar and usage, as well as of standard English capitalization, punctuation, and spelling **with some errors** • vocabulary is **appropriate** to the topic (vocabulary about ending world poverty; accurate vocabulary for supporting claims with logical reasons; effective phrases and clauses that add information about who the text is about or what is happening)

PERFORMANCE TASK RUBRIC			
Score Point	**Organization and Clarity**	**Evidence and Reasoning**	**Language and Conventions**
Needs Work ②	• introductory paragraph **includes a weak thesis statement that attempts to make a claim** about how to end world poverty • body paragraphs are **somewhat logically organized and partially present reasons and evidence** to support the claim • includes **a limited amount** of text evidence, precise language and phrases and clauses • concluding statement **attempts to restate the thesis statement**	• **partially explains** the authors' views for ending world poverty **and minimally argues the effectiveness of the authors' claims** • includes **one or two examples of relevant** factual evidence from the informational texts to support each reason for how to end world poverty	• demonstrates a **marginal command** of the conventions of English grammar and usage, as well as of standard English capitalization, punctuation, and spelling • there **are many errors; however, the text is still understandable** • includes only **one or two examples** of vocabulary that is appropriate to the topic (vocabulary about ending world poverty; accurate vocabulary for supporting claims with logical reasons; effective phrases and clauses that add information about who the text is about or what is happening)
Does Not Meet Standards ①	• introductory paragraph is **unclear** and does not include a thesis statement • body paragraphs are **not organized logically** and/or **do not present reasons and evidence** that support the claim • essay includes **little text evidence** and phrases and clauses • concluding statement is **unclear**	• response is a **partial explanation** of the authors' views for ending world poverty • includes **no factual textual evidence** from the informational texts	• demonstrates **almost no command** of the conventions of standard English grammar and usage, as well as of standard English capitalization, punctuation, and spelling • there **are many errors that disrupt** the reader's understanding of the text • **does not include** vocabulary that is appropriate to the topic (vocabulary about ending world poverty; accurate vocabulary for supporting claims with logical reasons; effective phrases and clauses that add information about who the text is about or what is happening)

Questions

Text Structure

1. Why does the author begin his text with the story of Wesley Autry? Provide reasons for your thinking.

Key Ideas and Details

2. What claim does the author make in **paragraph 2**? What facts does he present in **paragraph 3** to show that he is qualified to make this claim?

from *The Life You Can Save*

by Pete Singer

¶**1** When he saw the man fall onto the subway tracks, Wesley Autry didn't hesitate. With the lights of the oncoming train visible, Autry, a construction worker, jumped down to the tracks and pushed the man down into a drainage trench between the rails, covering him with his own body. The train passed over them, leaving a trail of grease on Autry's cap. Autry, later invited to the State of the Union Address and praised by the president for his bravery, down-played his actions: "I don't feel like I did something spectacular. I just saw someone who needed help. I did what I felt was right."

¶**2** What if I told you that you, too, can save a life, even many lives? Do you have a bottle of water or a can of soda on the table beside you as you read this book? If you are paying for something to drink when safe drinking water comes out of the tap, you have money to spend on things you don't really need. Around the world, a billion people struggle to live each day on less than you paid for that drink. Because they can't afford even the most basic health care for their families, their children may die from simple, easily treatable diseases like diarrhea. You can help them, and you don't have to risk getting hit by an oncoming train to do it.

¶**3** I have been thinking and writing for more than thirty years about how we should respond to hunger and poverty. I have presented this book's argument to thousands of students in my university classes and in lectures around the world, and to countless others in newspapers, magazines, and television programs. As a result, I've been forced to respond to a wide range of thoughtful challenges. This book represents my effort to distill what I've learned about why we give, or don't give, and what we should do about it.

¶**4** We live in a unique moment. The proportion of people unable to meet their basic physical needs is smaller today than it has been at any time in recent history, and perhaps at any time since humans first came into existence. At the same time, when we take a long-term perspective that sees beyond the fluctuations of the economic cycle, the proportion of people with far more than they need is also unprecedented.

Most important, rich and poor are now linked in ways they never were before. Moving images, in real time, of people on the edge of survival are beamed into our living rooms. Not only do we know a lot about the desperately poor, but we also have much more to offer them in terms of better health care, improved seeds and agricultural techniques, and new technologies for generating electricity. More amazing, through instant communications and open access to a wealth of information that surpasses the greatest libraries of the pre-Internet age, we can enable them to join the worldwide community—if only we can help them get far enough out of poverty to seize the opportunity.

¶**5** Economist Jeffrey Sachs has argued convincingly that extreme poverty can be virtually eliminated by the middle of this century. We are already making progress. In 1960, according to UNICEF, the United Nations International Children's Emergency Fund, 20 million children died before their fifth birthday because of poverty. In 2007, UNICEF announced that, for the first time since record keeping began, the number of deaths of young children has fallen below 10 million a year. Public health campaigns against smallpox, measles, and malaria have contributed to the drop in child mortality, as has economic progress in several countries. The drop is even more impressive because the world's population has more than doubled since 1960. Yet we can't become complacent: 9.7 million children under five still die annually; this is an immense tragedy, not to mention a moral stain on a world as rich as this one. And the combination of economic uncertainty and volatile food prices that marked 2008 could still reverse the downward trend in poverty-related deaths.

¶**6** We can liken our situation to an attempt to reach the summit of an immense mountain. For all the eons of human existence, we have been climbing up through dense cloud. We haven't known how far we have to go, nor whether it is even possible to get to the top. Now at last we have emerged from the mist and can see a route up the remaining steep slopes and onto the summit ridge. The peak still lies some distance ahead. There are sections of the route that will challenge our abilities to the utmost, but we can see that the ascent is feasible.

Questions

Key Ideas and Details

3. How does the information in **paragraph 4** support the claim the author makes at the end of **paragraph 2**?

Words and Phrases in Context

4. Use context clues to define the phrase "a moral stain" in **paragraph 5**. Why is the death of 9.7 million children annually a "moral stain on a world as rich as this one"?

Questions

Text Structure

5. Analyze the author's use of the second-person point of view on this page. What effect does he achieve by using this point of view?

Key Ideas and Details

6. The author states in **paragraph 9** that his book presents "a very demanding—some might even say impossible—standard of ethical behavior." What does he claim that people need to do in order to meet his standard of "living a morally good life"?

¶**7** We can, each of us, do our part in this epoch-making climb. In recent years there's been a good deal of coverage of some among the very rich who have taken on this challenge in a bold and public way. Warren Buffett has pledged to give $31 billion, and Bill and Melinda Gates have given $29 billion and are planning to give more. Immense as these sums are, we will see by the end of this book that they are only a small fraction of what people in rich nations could easily give, without a significant reduction in their standard of living. We won't reach our goal unless many more contribute to the effort.

¶**8** That's why this is the right time to ask yourself: What ought I be doing to help?

¶**9** I write this book with two linked but significantly different goals. The first is to challenge you to think about our obligations to those trapped in extreme poverty. The part of the book that lays out this challenge will deliberately present a very demanding—some might even say impossible—standard of ethical behavior. I'll suggest that it may not be possible to consider ourselves to be living a morally good life unless we give a great deal more than most of us would think it realistic to expect human beings to give. This may sound absurd, and yet the argument for it is remarkably simple. It goes back to that bottle of water, to the money we spend on things that aren't really necessary. If it is so easy to help people in real need through no fault of their own, and yet we fail to do so, aren't we doing something wrong? At a minimum, I hope this book will persuade you that there is something deeply askew with our widely accepted views about what it is to live a good life.

¶**10** The second goal of this book is to convince you to choose to give more of your income to help the poor. You'll be happy to know that I fully realize the need to step back from the demanding standards of a philosophical argument to ask what will really make a difference in the way we act. I'll consider the reasons, some relatively convincing, others less so, that we offer for not giving, as well as the psychological factors that get in our way. I'll acknowledge the bounds of human nature and yet provide examples of people who seem to have found a way to push those bounds further than most. And I will close with a reasonable standard that, for 95 percent of Americans, can be met by giving no more than 5 percent of their income.

¶**11** I should say up front that I believe you should be giving more than 5 percent, and that I hope you'll ultimately move in that direction. But that's not easy to hear and not easy to do. I recognize that most people aren't likely to be moved merely by philosophical argument to make drastic changes in the way they live, and, further, that one cannot make such drastic changes overnight. The ultimate purpose of this book is to reduce extreme poverty, not to make you feel guilty. So I'm going to advocate a standard that I'm confident will do a lot of good. That means suggesting a level that will get you started, and put you on a path toward challenging yourself and working toward doing more.

¶**12** For reasons that I'll explore in this book, many of us find it difficult to consider giving money to people we've never met, living in distant countries we've never visited. This obviously doesn't get any easier during periods of economic uncertainty, when many people are justifiably anxious about their own economic prospects. While I don't seek to diminish in any way the challenges that attend tough economic times, we should remember that even in the worst of times, our lives remain infinitely better than those of people living in extreme poverty. I'm hoping that you will look at the larger picture and think about what it takes to live ethically in a world in which 18 million people are dying unnecessarily each year. That's a higher annual death rate than in World War II. In the past twenty years alone, it adds up to more deaths than were caused by all the civil and international wars and government repression of the entire twentieth century, the century of Hitler and Stalin. How much would we give to prevent those horrors? Yet how little are we doing to prevent today's even larger toll, and all the misery that it involves? I believe that if you read this book to the end, and look honestly and carefully at our situation, assessing both the facts and the ethical arguments, you will agree that we must act.

Questions

Key Ideas and Details

7. What, specifically, does the author propose that the reader do to help fight extreme poverty? What reasons does he give to support his proposal?

Literature Circle Leveled Novels

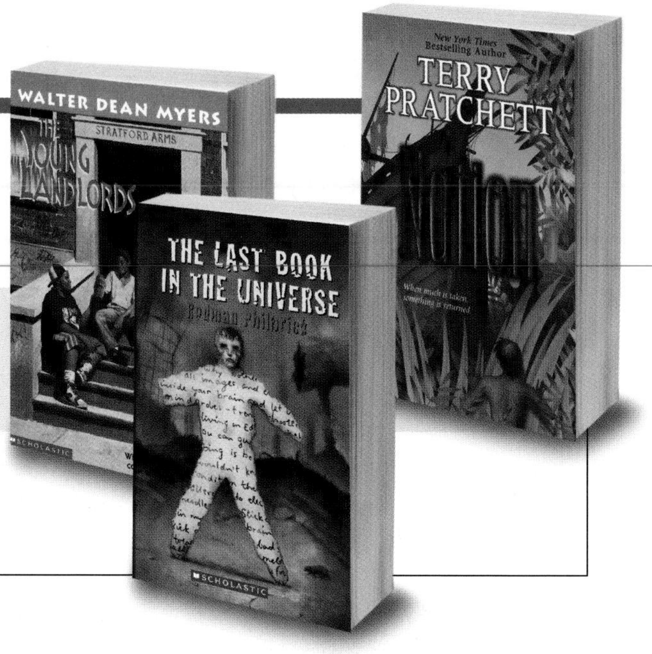

The Young Landlords *by Walter Dean Myers*
The derelict neighborhood of Stratford Arms is turned over to the 16 friends devoted to improving it. What happens when they realize there is an outrageous bunch of tenants living in the building? **Lexile**® measure: 820L

The Last Book in the Universe *by Rodman Philbrick*
In a violent post-apocalyptic world, teenager Spaz begins the heroic fight to bring human intelligence back to the planet. **Lexile**® measure: 740L

Nation *by Terry Pratchett*
A young man is the lone survivor of his island tribe due to a tidal wave in the South Pacific. He shows courage, intelligence, and compassion in overcoming his despair and lack of knowledge. **Lexile**® measure: NC790L

Fiction and Nonfiction

One Hen—How One Small Loan Made a Big Difference *by Katie Smith Milway.* Inspired by true events, this is the story of Kojo, who uses a small loan to change his community for the better. **Lexile**® measure: 810L

It's Our World, Too!: Stories of Young People Who Are Making a Difference *by Phillip M. Hoose.* Read about 14 teens who are standing up for causes they believe in. **Lexile**® measure: 840L

It's Your World—If You Don't Like It, Change It *by Mikki Halpin.* Learn how to get involved and become an activist. A variety of causes are addressed, including the environment, civil liberties, racism, and women's rights.

The Kid's Guide to Service Projects *by Barbara A. Lewis.* Students who want to make a difference but aren't sure how can find the right project or activity in this book.

The Kid's Guide to Social Action: How to Solve the Social Problems You Choose *by Barbara A. Lewis.* Students who want to make a difference but are overwhelmed with how to start will find guidance in this book.

A Leader Becomes a Leader *by J. Kevin Sheehan.* Explore the qualities and values that shape great leaders of the past and the future.

Transforming Lives $40 at a Time: Women + Microfinance *by Dana Elizabeth Whitaker.* This book profiles women whose lives have been changed by microfinance loans.

What Do You Stand For? *by Barbara A. Lewis.* The resources in this book will help young readers discover who they are and what positive traits they want to develop in their personalities.

Films and TV

Beatrice's Goat (CBS, 2005) This 60 Minutes segment examines how Heifer International made a dramatic difference in the life of Beatrice, who grew up in poverty in Uganda. (10 min.)

Erin Brockovich (Universal Studios, 2000) Based on a true story, this movie chronicles Brockovich as she brings to justice the corporation whose neglect and greed resulted in a small town's residents being riddled with illness and death. (130 min.)

Gandhi (Sony, 1982) Follow the story of Mohandas K. Gandhi as he brings the idea of nonviolent resistance to India, which leads to India's independence. (191 min.)

Life Below the Line: The World Poverty Crisis (Associated Television International, 2007) Examine the hardships faced by impoverished people around the world and learn what you can do to make a difference.

Norma Rae (20th Century Fox, 1979) Norma Rae is a textile mill worker who rallies her coworkers to fight against unfair working conditions and pay. Based on a true story. (110 min.)

Pay It Forward (Warner, 2000) Junior high school student Trevor starts a project to change the world and sets in motion a chain reaction of good deeds that reaches far and wide. (123 min.)

A Powerful Noise (Unify Films, 2009) Watch three women as they struggle with poverty and oppression and win significant victories, thereby illustrating the ability of women to make a difference in the world. (90 min.)

To Kill a Mockingbird (Universal Studios, 1962) Young Scout and Jem learn the realities of social injustice as their lawyer father, Atticus Finch, defends a black man wrongfully accused of a violent crime. (129 min.)

Websites

Design for the Other 90 Percent Explore and view photographs and written information associated with the Smithsonian exhibit.

Do Something This site gives students information on how to get involved in causes from animal welfare to poverty to human rights.

Youth Service America Explore this Web site and connect students directly with opportunities to make a difference in their community.

Magazines

E/The Environmental Magazine Learn what you can do to improve our environment. Find tips and advice for living responsibly.

National Geographic Take a look at the people around us and their involvement in the way our world is changing.

Need: The Humanitarian Magazine This online magazine addresses the need for humanitarian aid and what people around the world are doing to help.

Wildlife Conservation Travel around the world to encounter rare and endangered animals and the people who are fighting for their survival.

CREDITS

COURSE II | Table of Contents

p. 3c: © Eduardo Bertone; p. 4t: © Michael Svoboda/Getty Images, b: © James Steinberg via The iSpot; p. 5t: © Francisco Negroni, AgenciaUno/AP Images, b: © Subhash Sharma/Polaris; p. 6t: © Peter Maiden/Sygma/Corbis; 6b background: © Chones/Fotolia, bl: John Briggs/courtesy Kiva, bcl: courtesy KIVA, bc: © David Furst/ AFP/Getty Images, bcr: © Seltan Mohammad/EPA via Newscom, br: courtesy KIVA

UNIT 1 | Mapping Your Life

pp. 8–9: © Eduardo Bertone; p. 12t: © Eduardo Bertone; p. 19bl: © Eduardo Bertone; p. 27tl: Karen Lowe; pp. 28–29: Karen Lowe

UNIT 2 | Sports Report

pp. 54–55: © Michael Svoboda/Getty Images; p. 57b: © Al Pereira/New York Jets/Getty Images; p. 58br: © Dilip Vishwanat/Getty Images; p. 65tl: © Norman7/Dreamstime, tr: © Svetlana Alyuk/Thinkstock; p. 70br: © Christer Fredriksson/Getty Images; p. 71bl: © Marcos Ferro/Aurora Photos/Corbis

UNIT 3 | Your Vote! Your Rights!

pp. 96–97: © James Steinberg via The iSpot; p. 103bl: © Dean La Prairie; p. 105bl: © Dean La Prairie; p. 112br: © Matt Herron/Take Stock/The Image Works; p. 115bl: Cameron Frantz; p. 133c: Library of Congress

UNIT 4 | Nature's Fury

pp. 140–141: © Francisco Negroni, AgenciaUno/AP Images; p. 143t: © David Leindecker/Thinkstock; p. 145bl: Jim McMahon; p. 146br: Petty Officer 2nd Class Kyle Niemi/USCG; p. 149b: Mistman123/Wikipedia; p. 152br: © Karl Gobl/Zuma Press; p. 154br: © 5W Infographics; p. 161tl: © Ali O'Neal/Pacific Stock; p. 162br: © Ali O'Neal/ Pacific Stock; p. 163tl: © Ali O'Neal/Pacific Stock; p. 165b: © Warner Bros./courtesy Everett Collection

UNIT 5 | Stolen Childhoods

pp. 194–195: © Subhash Sharma/Polaris; p. 199bl: © David McLain/Aurora/Getty Images; p. 200br: © Lynn Gail/Lonely Planet Images/Getty Images; p. 208br: Jim McMahon/SODA; p. 209bl: © Subhash Sharma/Polaris; p. 210br: © Radhika Chalasani/ Redux; p. 211bl: © Visual&Written/Newscom; p. 212br: © Graeme Robertson/eyevine/ Redux; p. 233bl: Lewis Wickes Hines/Library of Congress

UNIT 6 | America Speaks

pp. 240–241: © Peter Maiden/Sygma/Corbis; p. 243b: Library of Congress; p. 244: © Dece11/Dreamstime; p. 245l: © MPI/Getty Images; p. 246r: The White House Historical Association; p. 247l: © Erika Larsen/Redux; p. 248: © Heather Pettersen; p. 249: © Heather Pettersen; p. 255t: © FafoArts/Dreamstime, b: © Pathathai Chungyam/ Thinkstock; pp. 260–261b: © il67/iStockphoto; pp. 284–285: © Chones/Fotolia

UNIT 7 | A Better World

p. 284l: courtesy KIVA, cl: © Seltan Mohammad/EPA via Newscom, ct: © David Furst/ AFP/Getty Images; rc: courtesy KIVA, br: © Marta Nascmento/REA/Redux; p. 285tl: John Briggs/courtesy Kiva, tr: courtesy KIVA, br: © Frank Huster/ZUMA Press; p. 287tl: © Agencyby/Thinkstock; p. 288br: © Thomas Mukoya/Reuters/Landov; p. 297tc: © Piksel/Thinkstock, c: Norman Kuring/NASA/NOAA/GSFC/Suomi NPP/VIIRS; p. 298r: © Ajv123ajv/Dreamstime, inset: courtesy FreeRice.org; p. 299b: © Max Kabakov/Fotolia, inset: courtesy Heifer.org; p. 301l: Jeffrey Vock, inset: courtesy Heifer.org

NOVEL STUDY COVER CREDITS

Inkheart by Cornelia Funke. Original text copyright © 2003 by Dressler Verlag. English translation copyright © 2003 by The Chicken House. Published by Scholastic Inc. All rights reserved. Cover © 2003 by Carol Lawson.

Monster by Walter Dean Myers. Text copyright © 1999 by Walter Dean Myers. Illustrations copyright © 1999 by Christopher Myers. Published by Scholastic Inc. by arrangement with HarperCollins Children's Books, a division of HarperCollins Publishers. All rights reserved.

Grateful acknowledgment is made to the following sources for permission to reprint from previously published material. The publisher has made diligent efforts to trace the ownership of all copyrighted material in this volume and believes that all necessary permissions have been secured. If any errors or omissions have inadvertently been made, proper corrections will gladly be made in future editions.

UNIT 1 | **Mapping Your Life**

"Call Me María" and "My Mother, The Rain. El Fin" from *Call Me María: A Novel in Letters, Poems, and Prose* by Judith Ortiz Cofer. Copyright © 2004 by Judith Ortiz Cofer. Reprinted by permission of Scholastic Inc.

"The Road Not Taken" by Robert Frost.

From *My Beloved World* by Sonia Sotomayor. Copyright © 2013 by Sonia Sotomayor. Reprinted by permission of Random House, Inc. All rights reserved.

UNIT 2 | **Sports Report**

"What Could Be Better Than a Touchdown?" by Kelefa Sanneh from *The New Yorker* online, October 12, 2010. Copyright © 2010 by Condé Nast Publications. Reprinted by permission of Condé Nast Publications.

From *Why We Run: A Natural History* by Bernd Heinrich. Copyright © 2001 by Bernd Heinrich. Reprinted by permission of HarperCollins Publishers.

"Confessions of a Doper" by Jonathan Vaughters from *The New York Times Upfront* magazine, November 5, 2012. Copyright © 2012 by Scholastic Inc. All rights reserved.

"Casey at the Bat" by Ernest L. Thayer.

UNIT 3 | **Your Vote! Your Rights!**

From *Twelve Angry Men* by Reginald Rose. Copyright © 1955, 1997 by Reginald Rose. Reprinted by permission of Penguin Group (USA) Inc. All rights reserved.

"Democracy" from *Selected Poems of Langston Hughes* edited by Arnold Rampersand. Copyright © 1994 by The Estate of Langston Hughes. Reprinted by permission of Alfred A. Knopf, a division of Random House, Inc.

"Democracy" from *Chicks Up Front: Poems by Sara Holbrook.* Copyright © 1998 by Sara Holbrook. Adapted and reprinted by permission of the Cleveland State University Poetry Center.

"Ain't I a Woman?" by Sojourner Truth.

"Telling Americans to Vote, or Else" by William A. Galston from *The New York Times,* November 5, 2011. Copyright © 2011 by The New York Times. Reprinted by permission of The New York Times.

UNIT 4 | **Nature's Fury**

"Super Disasters of the 21st Century" adapted from "Flooded: How One Southern City Was Destined for Disaster" by Jacqueline Adams from *Science World*, October 24, 2005 and "How Did This Happen?" by Ken Kostel from *Science World*, March 28, 2005. Copyright © 2005 by Scholastic Inc.

From *The Perfect Storm* by Sebastian Junger. Copyright © 1997 by Sebastian Junger. Reprinted by permission of W.W. Norton & Company, Inc.

"In Deference to Crisis, a New Obsession Sweeps Japan: Self-Restraint" by Ken Belson and Norimitsu Onishi from The New York Times website, March 27, 2011. Copyright © 2011 by The New York Times. Reprinted by permission of The New York Times.

"Submerged City" by Jacqueline Adams from *Science World*, January 14, 2013. Copyright © 2013 by Scholastic Inc. All rights reserved.

UNIT 5 | **Stolen Childhoods**

From *Rabbit-Proof Fence* by Doris Pilkington. Copyright © Doris Pilkington-Nugi Garamana. Reprinted by permission of University of Queensland Press.

From *Behind the Beautiful Forevers: Life, Death, and Hope in a Mumbai Undercity* by Katherine Boo. Copyright © 2012 by Katherine Boo. Reprinted by permission of Random House, Inc. All rights reserved.

From *We Were There, Too!: Young People in U.S. History* by Phillip Hoose. Copyright © 2001 by Phillip Hoose. Reprinted by permission of Melanie Droupa Books/Farrar, Straus & Giroux.

From *The Diary of Anne Frank* by Frances Goodrich & Albert Hackett. Copyright © 1955 by Frances Goodrich & Albert Hackett. Reprinted by permission of Random House, Inc. All rights reserved.

UNIT 6 | **America Speaks**

"I Hear America Singing" by Walt Whitman.

"I, Too" by Langston Hughes from *The Collected Poems of Langston Hughes*. Copyright © 1994 by The Estate of Langston Hughes. Reprinted by permission of Alfred A. Knopf, a division of Random House, Inc.

"I, Too, Sing America" by Julia Alvarez from *Writers on America: 15 Reflections.* Published by the U.S. Department of State. All rights reserved.

From *Kira-Kira* by Cynthia Kadohata. Copyright © 2004 by Cynthia Kadohata. Reprinted by permission of Atheneum Books for Young Readers, an imprint of Simon & Schuster Children's Publishing.

"One Today: A Poem for Barack Obama's Presidential Inauguration, January 21, 2013" by Richard Blanco. Copyright © 2013 by Richard Blanco. Reprinted by permission of The University of Pittsburgh Press.

UNIT 7 | **A Better World**

"Introduction" from *The End of Poverty* by Jeffrey D. Sachs. Copyright © 2005 by Jeffrey D. Sachs. Reprinted by permission of The Penguin Press, a division of Penguin Group (USA) Inc.

From *The Life You Can Save: Acting Now to End World Poverty* by Peter Singer. Copyright © 2009 by Peter Singer. Reprinted by permission of Random House, Inc. All rights reserved.